A SURVIVAL
GUIDE
TO DEBT

HOW *to* OVERCOME TOUGH TIMES
& RESTORE *Your* FINANCIAL HEALTH

MITCHELL ALLEN

GREENLEAF
BOOK GROUP PRESS

Published by Greenleaf Book Group Press
Austin, TX 78709
www.greenleafbookgroup.com

Distributed by Greenleaf Book Group LLC

For ordering information or special discounts for bulk purchases, please contact Greenleaf Book Group LLC at PO Box 91869, Austin, TX 78709, (512) 891-6100.

Design and composition by Greenleaf Book Group LLC
Cover design by Greenleaf Book Group LLC

Publisher's Cataloging-in-Publication Data (prepared by The Donohue Group, Inc.)

Allen, Mitchell (Mitchell L.), 1970-
    A survival guide to debt : how to overcome tough times and restore your financial health / Mitchell Allen. -- 1st ed.

    p. : ill. ; cm.

    Includes bibliographical references.
    ISBN: 978-1-929774-70-8

1. Finance, Personal--United States--Handbooks, manuals, etc. 2. Debt--United States--Handbooks, manuals, etc. 3. Consumer credit--United States--Handbooks, manuals, etc. 4. Bankruptcy--United States--Handbooks, manuals, etc. I. Title.

HG179 .A44 2009
332.024/02   2009928414

Part of the Tree Neutral™ program, which offsets the number of trees consumed in the production and printing of this book by taking proactive steps, such as planting trees in direct proportion to the number of trees used: www.treeneutral.com

Printed in the United States of America on acid-free paper

09 10 11 12 13 14   10 9 8 7 6 5 4 3 2 1

First Edition

CONTENTS

KNOW THE
WARNING SIGNS

Let me tell you about my friend Doug. One Monday morning when Doug arrived at his office, the phone on his desk was already ringing. The tension headache he'd been nursing off and on for most of the last six months ratcheted up a couple of notches as he reached for the phone.

"Hello?"

"Is this Doug Lewis?"

Doug grimaced. He knew he should have let the call go to his voice mail.

"Yeah, this is Doug."

"Mr. Lewis, this is Consolidated Collections. I'm calling about the past due balance on your loan."

Doug closed his eyes and slumped into his chair. He tried to listen to the agent on the other end of the call, but the words were pretty much the same as the ones he'd been hearing several times a week from two or three other collectors. He thought about the stack of unopened letters on his desk at home, the ones with "Urgent" printed in large red letters across the envelopes. He wished they were junk mail, but they weren't.

Everything had been okay until Carol lost her job. Neither of them had fully realized how dependent they were on her income. But ever since, it seemed they had been getting further and further behind, even with the unemployment payments she had begun collecting. They just hadn't been able to adjust their lifestyle to their lower income level.

"If we don't receive a minimum payment of $2,000 in our offices by 5:00 p.m. next Monday, Mr. Lewis, I'm afraid we will have no choice but to begin repossession proceedings."

Doug's attention snapped back to the call. "Excuse me? How much money did you say? And by when?"

"By 5:00 p.m. next Monday, Mr. Lewis. We need a minimum payment of $2,000, or we will begin repossession."

Doug rubbed his forehead; they might as well be asking for a million. The headache was starting to pound. He mumbled something and hung up the phone. He looked at his watch; it was ten minutes past eight. The week was just beginning . . .

Maybe this story reminds you of someone—maybe that someone is you. My guess is that if you picked up a book titled *A Survival Guide to Debt*, it's probably because you or someone close to you is in financial trouble. If so, keep reading, because, believe it or not, there is hope.

TOUGH TIMES

Let's face it: times are tough. During the calendar year ended December 31, 2008, more than one million individuals filed for bankruptcy protection in the United States according to the U.S. federal court system (www.uscourts.gov). That figure represents an increase of 31 percent from the previous year and doesn't include corporate bankruptcy filings. As if that weren't bad enough, individual filings were up by more than 34 percent for the first quarter of 2009 compared with the same period in 2008.

And that's not all. According to the U.S. Federal Reserve, U.S. credit card debt is close to a trillion dollars as of October 2008. Total U.S. consumer debt, excluding mortgages, was $2.5 trillion at the end of 2007, the Fed reports. Some are predicting that the problems faced by consumers falling behind on their credit cards will be the next crisis faced by a financial industry still reeling from the implosion of the subprime mortgage market. Speaking of mortgages, 851,000 homes were repossessed by lenders between August 2007 and October 2008 according to CNN.com. As I write this, many economists are predicting even more layoffs and business closures before the current business downturn begins to improve.

Clearly, these are difficult days. But the fact is, even in a favorable business environment, circumstances can arise in any individual's life that can create difficult financial strains. The big four—unexpected expenses and bad financial habits, job loss, grave illness, and divorce or death of a principal wage earner—can strike at any time, even in a booming economy. In a recession, of course, these negative events are magnified, and the time required to recover from them can be even longer.

All the above statistics paint a pretty bleak picture. If you're struggling with a difficult financial situation, the last thing you need is more bad news. But I want to let you know that the reason I wrote this book is to give you hope and to help you establish a plan to make things better.

I've worked with hundreds of people to help them regain control of their lives and finances, and I can tell you with complete confidence that there are ways for you not only to recover from the devastating financial and emotional effects of hard times but also to learn how to thrive. In this book you will learn what you need to know to make informed decisions about your situation, whether you are heavily in debt, facing repossession or foreclosure, or even considering bankruptcy.

In fact, what you mainly need, like all those I've worked with through the years, is correct information. When you're in deep financial trouble, your greatest enemies are fear and the feeling of helplessness. But the principal antidote to fear and helplessness is knowledge. When you know your options, and when you know the benefits and disadvantages of those options, you can begin to move forward with confidence.

You've probably heard the old Chinese adage: "The journey of a thousand miles begins with a single step." Right now it may seem to you that you're facing a journey of more like ten thousand miles—all of it uphill. But I'm going to show you how to take not only the first step of that journey but also the last one, the one that brings you all the way back to financial security.

I offer personal finance training courses that have been taken by tens of thousands of people from all parts of the country, and I've heard every reason you can imagine for why people find themselves in financial trouble. My experience indicates that the reasons people find themselves struggling in debt-survival mode is usually complicated and involves more than one factor. In fact, most of the people I work with have had some sort of double whammy from the big four: a spouse had a cut in pay or lost a job due to downsizing *and* a teenage child had a car accident that resulted in $10,000 or more of medical bills, for example.

A survey my organization conducted over two months in 2008 emphasizes the complexity of the causes of financial problems. As reflected in the list I gave on the previous page, those we surveyed about why they were taking our courses gave the following reasons for their money problems:

- Unexpected expenses (77 percent)
- Unemployment or business loss (70 percent)
- Unnecessary spending (50 percent)
- Illness or injury (38 percent)
- Divorce, separation, or death of a loved one (29 percent)
- Addictions (including gambling) and other reasons (7 percent)

As you can see, these percentages add up to more than 100 percent. The reason? As I mentioned, many people cite more than one factor contributing to their financial problems. It makes sense when you think about it. Money stress—sometimes caused by job loss or problems with a business—often leads to marital problems or can cause a person to develop dependency on drugs or alcohol. In fact, many divorce lawyers say that money trouble is the number one reason given by their clients for ending a marriage.

Or it can work the other way around: a person's drug dependencies or marital difficulties can cause work problems, which can lead to unemployment and financial crisis. No matter how you look at it, money problems are complex and often involve multiple factors.

Let's take a more detailed look at the causes cited most often by people in financial trouble.

- Poor financial decisions or bad spending habits afflict a surprising number of people. "Bad luck" also fits into this category: making a large real estate investment just before a price bubble bursts; going to work for an Internet company just before the dot-coms took their dive, or having two family vehicles die in one month. Also, addictions (including gambling) can quickly erode years of savings and even more quickly result in unemployment.

- Job loss or other reduction of income, especially in a weak economy when new or extra work is difficult to find, quickly creates shortfalls in ability to maintain cash flow and make payments on time.
- Serious medical problems, even when covered by insurance, can drain savings and income and lead to large debt balances. At the same time, poor health compromises earning ability.
- Divorce or death of a wage-earning spouse often reduces available household income by at least 50 percent, but usually only reduces expenses by around 20 percent or so. Furthermore, these events—especially divorce—can force someone into the workforce without adequate preparation or skills

Through the years, as I've worked with families in financial distress, it has become increasingly clear to me that what is needed is a good source of basic information about the various alternatives you have when trying to deal with overwhelming financial circumstances. That's the reason I decided to write this book: to give you a place to find the solid, basic facts you need, and also to direct you to other resources for more information and assistance. There are steps you can take to protect yourself from the seizure or loss of assets and to get started on the road back to financial security. In this book I will help you discover those steps and learn the best way to apply them to your particular situation.

HOW YOU GOT WHERE YOU ARE

The economy is always a source of concern for a majority of the population. As I write this in early 2009, however, the economy is arguably in the worst shape it has been in since the Great Depression of the 1930s. The stock market has lost almost half its value since its last peak in 2007 (from just over 14,000 in October 2007 to about 7,500 in November 2008: 6,500 points, or 46 percent). Financial institutions that were once believed beyond even the thought of danger have been taken over by federal authorities or have received emergency infusions of public funds to prevent failures of catastrophic proportions. Some of America's largest and oldest corporations are begging Congress for emergency loans, warning of imminent insolvency if they don't get the funds. Unemployment recently hit a sixteen-year high, and corporations continue to announce layoffs in the face of what most economists believe will be the worst recession in decades. In fact, the Associated Press reported recently that businesses laid off more than a half million workers in November 2008, the most layoffs in a single month in thirty-four years.

But even if you haven't lost your job or faced the failure of a business, you aren't immune to financial crisis. As I've already said, three of the other big four—divorce, death of a wage-earning spouse, severe medical problems—can happen without regard for business cycles or the health of the broader economy.

FINANCIAL GPS

Principal causes of financial difficulty are

- Unexpected expenses or poor financial decisions
- Job loss or other reduction of income
- Grave illness
- Divorce or death of a wage earner

Other factors can contribute to financial troubles. Poor choices (such as excessive or impulsive spending), failed investments, addictions, or working for an employer that becomes insolvent (the "Enron" scenario) can put a serious strain on your ability to maintain your obligations in a timely manner.

The unpleasant fact is that any number of factors—some of which you can control and some of which, though you can minimize their impacts, you still can't completely control—can help create a scenario that can land you in the middle of serious money problems. Ask any small contractor who loses a key client to competition or unexpected government regulation; ask someone who worked for the same corporation for twenty years and watched helplessly as top executives ran the company—and the value of the stock in her pension—into the ground, eliminating a comfortable retirement income and forcing her to try to find work to pay for basic expenses.

DANGER SIGNALS

Let's assume that, for whatever reason, you or someone close to you is having more and more trouble making those monthly payments. Are you paying current bills with credit cards or unsecured loans and lines of credit? Watch out; this process is likely to magnify the dimensions of your problem. Even as you pay a bill, you're digging yourself into a deeper hole. As a banker once told a friend of mine, "You can't borrow your way out of debt."

Do you have a stack of unopened mail from your credit card companies? This is often one of the early signs of debt growing beyond your ability to maintain it. The trouble is, ignoring the problem isn't the solution. In fact, it usually makes the problem even worse.

Perhaps creditors are starting to call about your past-due balances. Creditor calls can be almost crippling in their effects on your self-confidence, productivity, and general emotional health. It can reach the point where you spend more time dreading the ringing of the telephone than engaged in useful work. Not only that, but creditor calls at work can be embarrassing—or worse. Some employers take a very dim view of employees who are falling behind on their obligations, believing it reflects poorly on the company. Getting harassed by your creditors can make you feel helpless. If you don't know how to deal correctly with creditor calls, the resulting spiral of consequences can make bad situations even worse. Later in the book, I'll give you some important advice about how you can reduce or eliminate creditor calls as you work out how to repay your debt.

Maybe it's gone beyond discomfort and dread of the telephone. Maybe you've been notified that your bank is about to initiate legal repossession of your car. Or perhaps you're facing foreclosure on your mortgage, as more than a million Americans did in 2008. These two events are what most people in debt trouble fear the most. Losing your home to the bank because of nonpayment or losing a vehicle you need to get to and from work can cause desperation to turn quickly into despair.

FinanciaL GPS

Warning signs of debt trouble include

- Paying current bills with credit cards or unsecured loans
- Unopened mail from creditors
- Creditor calls
- Notices of repossession or foreclosure

THERE IS HOPE

Sometimes financial trouble is like "the elephant in the room": it's crowding out everything else in your life, but it's the last thing you want to talk about. You don't even want to admit that it exists. But you need to remember the old saying that the way to eat an elephant is "one bite at a time." Once you take that first bite, the rest gets easier.

No matter how bad things are for you right now, don't lose heart. I will say this in various ways throughout this book: *you* are not your debt! Whether you got into financial trouble because of poor decisions and bad financial management, or you were thrust into it because of circumstances beyond your control, your worth as a person is not measured by your net worth, your past-due balances, or your lack of sufficient income. Once you know the various courses of action available to you, you'll be more able to focus on a plan for your future rather than simply worrying about things you seem helpless to do anything about. And that is a great feeling.

HOW TO USE THIS BOOK

A Survival Guide to Debt is divided into three parts. In part 1, "When the Wolf Is Scratching at the Door," we'll look at the problem of too much debt and what happens when you start to get behind. Then we'll explore all the ways you can work to improve your situation—on your own or with help. Sometimes, by simply making a couple of changes in spending habits or taking some proactive steps with creditors, people are able to get themselves back on an even keel and resume control of their finances. You may not be in as much trouble as you think, and in the part 1 chapters, you can learn what to do to keep from getting in beyond the point of being able to help yourself.

But sometimes people need a bit more help in order to get their financial affairs in good order. Fortunately, we live in a civilized society where people are no longer incarcerated simply because of debt. The U.S. bankruptcy code was written to provide a compassionate, though strict, system for allowing individuals in difficult circumstances to discharge their debts. However, you have to know a bit about the way bankruptcy works and the forms of relief it makes available to you before you can make a smart decision. In part 2, "In Case of Emergency, Break Glass," we'll cover the various aspects of bankruptcy: what it can do for you, what it can't do for you, its benefits, and its consequences. The goal of part 2 is not to make you a legal expert in bankruptcy or even to offer legal advice. In fact, I will emphasize over and over that I am not a lawyer and that I believe bankruptcy matters should be discussed with a qualified attorney. Still, the part 2 chapters will give you "the lay of the land" and help you make an informed decision if you believe that your interests and assets would be best protected by filing bankruptcy.

Part 3, "Blocking, Tackling, and Digging Ditches," is, in many ways, the most important section of the book. Here, we'll discuss what you need to do to ensure that you never again find yourself in the situation that caused you to fall into financial trouble. Whether you are ultimately able to handle your situation by making lifestyle changes and communicating effectively with your creditors, or whether you require the protection of the courts in a bankruptcy proceeding to begin your financial "do-over," you must establish the habits and disciplines that will help you stay out of trouble and begin to lay the foundation for a solid financial future. As a football fan, I like to refer to this process as the "blocking and tackling" of personal finance; these are the basic offensive and defensive skills that you'll need to develop in order to gain long-term control and peace of mind. It has been said that insanity can be defined as "doing the same thing over and over again in the same way and expecting a different result." Part 3 will help you avoid financial insanity and begin to rebuild your life, even if you are emerging from bankruptcy.

The point of this book is not to explain to you how deep a hole you're in; you already know that. Instead, I hope to offer you a ladder to climb up and out of that hole and a map to use to avoid future financial pitfalls. By reading this book, you are beginning a journey that can take you to a much better place than you may be in at the present time. If you will absorb and follow the advice I present, I promise you that the future can be brighter than the past has been.

As you can see from the statistics I presented at the beginning of this section, millions of Americans are facing grave financial difficulties. Your situation, though it is of intense concern to you, is probably not unique. You are not alone, but you alone are responsible for making decisions and taking steps to address your particular situation.

This book will show you how.

PART ONE

WHEN THE WOLF IS AT THE DOOR

"Is robbing Peter to pay Paul like using your Mastercard to pay Visa?"

Chapter 1

FACING THE PROBLEM

GUIDEPOSTS

In this chapter, you'll learn

- How to act immediately to temporarily stop creditors from taking certain actions, such as foreclosure, repossession, and calls

- How to take stock of your current financial situation—cash flow, net worth, assets, liabilities—so that you can take smart first steps to get out of the woods

- How to analyze and classify your debts—secured, unsecured, or something in between—to determine a path for resolving them

When you're sick and you go to the doctor's office, the first thing he or she asks (when the doctor finally gets to you) is usually something like, "So, what seems to be the problem?" That's when you get to describe your symptoms so the doctor can start figuring out what medicines to prescribe and what other treatments to recommend.

Debt trouble is a lot like being sick. The problem is, many people can't or won't admit to themselves that they have this particular illness until they're already in the financial equivalent of critical condition. What could have been handled in the early stages with a few simple preventative measures now requires an emergency room visit, followed by admission to the financial ICU.

Eventually, of course, one way or another, debt trouble will reach the point where it can no longer be ignored. As I mentioned in the introduction, if you're reading this book right now, it's probably because you are facing money problems you don't know how to handle. You're in financial stress: getting increasingly stern warnings from creditors in the mail; receiving creditor calls; maybe facing the loss of your car, your home, your business, or other assets.

If you've finally concluded that you're in real trouble, congratulations! I really mean that. As anyone who has ever been through a recovery process knows, the first step in solving a problem is admitting to yourself that you have a problem. The one advantage of debt trouble is that it won't allow you to ignore or deny it forever. Your creditors will, without fail, remind you repeatedly that there is a situation developing that must be addressed and, eventually, action will be taken—either by you or by them. This book is going to show you how to go from being a passive, avoidant victim of debt to being a proactive, confident debt survivor. And the first step comes in realizing that you are responsible for taking action to improve your situation. Maybe you need to start opening that mail from creditors instead of stacking it on the corner of your desk and wishing it would go away. Maybe you

The first step in solving a problem is admitting to yourself that you have a problem.

need to learn how to respond to creditor calls instead of just dreading them. Maybe you need to know how to work with creditors who are initiating repossession or foreclosure instead of helplessly watching it happen. Whatever stage you are in and whatever your situation, *now* is the time to take action. And I'm going to show you how.

STOP THE BLEEDING

Returning to our medical analogy, emergency room physicians use a process called "triage" that involves assessing all situations in the emergency room to decide which is the most critical need to address first. If you have a fever and the guy next to you has blood squirting from an artery, they're going to take care of him first. If you have multiple symptoms ranging in severity, they're going to treat the most life-threatening symptoms first and leave the others alone until you're stable enough that they can get to them. Right now, you need financial triage. If you're bleeding to death financially, the first thing you need to do is apply a tourniquet so that you can buy enough time to address the underlying issues that got you into trouble in the first place. We'll start with the most severe conditions and work our way down from there.

Delaying Foreclosure

For most of us, losing our home to the bank is probably the thing we fear most, and with good reason. Our homes are usually the single largest and most valuable asset we have. Not only does a house provide financial benefits, it also affords shelter, both physical and emotional. If you've reached the point where your mortgagor is threatening or has initiated foreclosure proceedings, that's the first thing you must address.

As I will state several more times throughout this book, communication is your most useful tool as you work your way out of debt. Now is the time to begin using it. Call your mortgage lender and tell them about your circumstances. Have you lost a job or had your hours drastically reduced? Has a serious illness cut into your income or generated medical bills that have caused you to fall behind? Has a divorce and its attendant court-ordered alimony or child support payments impaired your ability to stay current? Tell your lender. Believe me, the lender *does not want* to foreclose on your home; foreclosure is expensive and time-consuming. If you are honest and forthcoming in your explanation, your lender will almost always work with you on a reasonable plan to help you get current.

The important thing to remember is that your lender wants to hear from you. A lender's favorite form of communication is a full payment received on time, but if that is impossible for you, by all means, communicate this in some fashion. A call from you explaining your circumstances and asking for additional time to work things out is vastly preferable, from your lender's perspective, than no communication at all.

An important word of caution: don't allow your panic over possible foreclosure stampede you into responding to one of the many scams that promise to halt foreclosure. These fraudulent schemes use phrases such as "We can save your home," "Stop foreclosure now!" and "We guarantee to save your home." Some will even offer a money-back guarantee. The problem is, by the time you realize they aren't going to do what they promised, your money—and, sometimes, what is left of your equity—has vanished, along with the guarantee.

The Federal Trade Commission has more information on avoiding scams and also what you can legitimately do to delay foreclosure. Their online report, "Mortgage Payments Sending You Reeling? Here's What to Do," is especially helpful. Log onto their website at www.ftc.gov and type "mortgage reeling" into the search box. Another good publication by the FTC is "Foreclosure Rescue Scams: Another Potential Stress for Homeowners in Distress." To locate it on the FTC website, you can just key "foreclosure scam" into the search box.

For more information on avoiding and delaying foreclosure, see the chapter 4 sections titled "The Foreclosure Process: An Overview" and "RESPA and Foreclosure."

Bankruptcy proceedings can also stop or stall foreclosure. I'll discuss this option in detail in part 2.

Stalling Repossession

Following closely behind our homes in importance are our automobiles. Usually, car payments are second only to house payments in our chart of monthly expenses. That's not surprising because for most Americans, the car provides transportation to and from our places of employment and also gets us or our kids to school, to church, to stores, and to friends' houses. It's difficult for me to imagine what my life would be like if I didn't have my vehicle constantly available to take me where I need to go. I'm sure your life is much the same.

If your debt troubles have become severe enough that your lender is taking steps to repossess your car, there are some things you can do to give yourself a little more time as you form a plan for getting out of debt. Here again, communication is at the top of the list.

Although repossession of a vehicle is easier for a lender than foreclosure on a mortgage, it is still a costly process that the lender would much rather avoid if it thinks there is a reasonable alternative. Call your lender and explain your situation. If you can send them even a partial payment, let them know that. If you've fallen on hard times, give them specific information, especially if you think you'll be in a better position in the future. As I will emphasize again later, if you agree to send a payment or even something as simple as calling back in three days to give them an update, *follow through*. Consistent, honest communication from you may not keep your car safe from the tow truck indefinitely, but it can certainly buy you a bit of time as you begin working on your personal financial recovery plan. And right now, a little time and breathing space is your greatest need.

Again, filing for bankruptcy protection can stop or stall the repossession process, as I discuss in detail in part 2.

Deal with Creditor Calls and Mail

Creditor calls are no joke, especially if those creditors are contacting you during working hours. Fortunately, recent laws governing debt collection have greatly improved debtors' ability to protect themselves from harassing or threatening calls from creditors. Later in the book, I'll discuss these laws and the main protections they offer, but for right now, let's talk about how you can get your creditors to stop calling you at work because, let's face it, if you're fortunate enough to be gainfully employed, the last things you need are the distraction of dunning calls and the potential embarrassment and/ or disfavor with your employer they can cause. If you lose your job because of creditor calls, that's only going to make matters worse.

Request That Creditors Cease Contacting You at Work. Asking creditors to stop calling you during working hours sounds ridiculously simple—and it is—but many people just don't realize that they have this right. The next time a creditor calls you at your place of employment, simply say something like this: "I must ask you to stop calling me at this number during working hours. I am not trying to avoid this debt, but you are potentially jeopardizing my employment. Please do not call me at this number from the hours of [give your working hours] again."

Be courteous but firm, recognizing that the law clearly states that the creditor may not contact the consumer at work if the creditor knows that the consumer's employer prohibits it. If the calls continue, document the fact in writing; it may give you grounds for filing a formal complaint with the FTC. Trust me: your creditors do not want to fall afoul of this or any other regulatory body.

As a matter of fact, the law states that creditors may not communicate with consumers "at any time or place which is unusual or known to be inconvenient to the consumer" (www.ftc.gov). Times within the hours of 8:00 a.m. to 9:00 p.m. are presumed to be convenient unless you can prove otherwise. If you work a twelve hour shift during this time frame, these hours may not be convenient for you. However, you should exercise caution in pushing too hard on this point; creditors who feel they have no other recourse to communicate with a debtor may file a lawsuit, which provides specific means for communication between the parties.

Write a Cease-and-desist Letter. Another way to get creditors to stop contacting you is to send them a letter. Again, this sounds like an obvious course of action, but many people are so intimidated by their situation that they never think of simply sending a written demand to cease contact. I've included an example of a typical cease-and-desist letter on the opposite page.

Here again, the laws governing debt collection provide that creditors who are in receipt of a properly worded cease-and-desist letter must stop contacting you except for the specific instances allowed by the law: (1) to inform you that they have ceased efforts to collect the debt; (2) to inform you that they may invoke "specified remedies" (which sometimes means

SAMPLE CEASE-AND-DESIST LETTER

Your Name
Your Address
City, State, ZIP
(Sent via CERTIFIED RETURN MAIL with RETURN RECEIPT)

Date:

XYZ Collection Agency/Law Firm
1234 Main Street, #100 Any town, USA 10021

Re: File #00000 - ABC Bank - #444556688900 - For: $5,555.55

Dear Debt Collector /Debt Collector Attorney:

This will serve as your legal notice under provisions of federal law, the Fair Debt Collection Practices Act (FDCPA), to cease all communication with me in regard to the debt referenced above. If you fail to heed this notice, I will file a formal complaint against you with the Federal Trade Commission who is responsible for enforcement, the States Attorney General office and/or the American Collectors Association or local State Bar Association.

I/We have decided that we do not desire to work with a collection agency under any circumstances. I/We will contact the original creditor to resolve this matter directly, as circumstances warrant.

You are also notified that should any adverse information be placed against my/our credit reports as a result of this notice appropriate actions will be taken. Give this very important matter the attention it deserves.

Sincerely,
Your Name

a lawsuit); or (3) to inform you that they intend to invoke "a specified remedy" (www.ftc.gov/os/statutes/fdcpa/commentary.htm#805; accessed 12/6/2008).

What this means to you is that you should probably tread carefully in the area of sending a cease-and-desist letter. Why? Because for some creditors, receiving a letter from you forbidding them to contact you any more—even though it is your legal right to send such a letter—may cause the creditor to conclude that it's in their best interest to utilize their legal right to bring a suit for collection of the debt. As you can probably figure out, this is a situation you want to avoid if at all possible.

While I'm on the topic of mail, if you're one of the many debtors who have tried to avoid looking at those demand letters you've been getting, let me urge you to start opening and reading your mail. No matter what course of action you eventually decide to pursue on your way to regaining financial health, you have to know where you are before you can figure out where you need to go. One of the most important tools you have at your disposal in this task is communication—not only with your creditors but also with family members and other involved parties. Right now, though, I want to emphasize the importance of maintaining lines of communication with your creditors.

FINANCIAL GPS

Communication, communication, communication!
The very first step you have to take when creditors come calling is to communicate with them consistently, clearly, and professionally.

This is especially important if you decide to work directly with your creditors to satisfy the debt, an alternative I'll discuss more fully a bit later. Creditors are much more willing to give the benefit of the doubt to consumers who are honest, forthcoming, and respectful in their communications, whether by phone or by mail. Collection agents spend the majority of their time trying in vain to establish contact with debtors. By returning their calls and answering their written communications, you immediately place yourself on a different—and better—list than debtors who are uncommunicative or who otherwise give the appearance of trying to avoid making good on their obligations.

Now, that doesn't mean you should agree to all their demands. A collector's job is to convince you to send money; if you could have done that, you wouldn't be behind in the first place, right? However, there are things you can do and say that will encourage your creditor to be more patient with you as you work on a plan for repayment. Chief among these are honest acknowledgment of your responsibility for the debt, maintaining a respectful tone, and following through on anything you agree to do, including subsequent communications. I know that the last thing you may want to do is send a follow-up letter to a creditor or take a phone call from a collector, but sometimes, a bit of time spent in communication with the creditor can pave the way to an easier path out of debt. It can also sometimes help keep you out of a lawsuit.

SURVIVAL TIP:
HOW TO REDUCE CREDITOR CALLS

1. Request that creditors cease contacting you at work or during working hours.

2. Acknowledge responsibility for the debt.

3. Inform your creditors of any plans you have for addressing your debt.

4. Inform your creditors if you are facing legitimate financial hardship because of illness, divorce, or other major life events.

5. Request additional time to work on your debt.

6. Follow through on any promises you make, or communicate with your creditors to adjust their expectations if necessary.

TAKE STOCK OF YOUR CIRCUMSTANCES

Now that you've got the bleeding stopped temporarily, it's time to survey your situation so you can form a plan of action.

Do you remember the scene in the movie *The Princess Bride* where the hero and his two friends, a giant and a swordsman, are about to storm a castle guarded by dozens of armed soldiers? The hero asks his two allies, "What are our assets?" A bit later, he chides them for failing to mention that they have a cloak with certain special properties. "You might have listed that among our assets," he says, sarcastically.

You're in a similar predicament: You're about to go into a situation where the odds seem stacked against you; because of that, it's extremely important for you to know exactly what your resources are—your assets, your liabilities, your sources of income, and your essential expenses.

At this point, some of you may be feeling a vague sense of discomfort because you suspect that I'm about to ask you to develop or review a budget.

Before you start flipping pages, looking for an easier place to start, listen to this important advice: not knowing your available resources or having an accurate picture of your liabilities may be what got you into money trouble in the first place. You're in a tight spot; don't make it worse by continuing the same behaviors that got you there.

Look at it this way: If you had tickets to the Super Bowl or an NBA playoff game, but you didn't know how to get to the stadium or arena, would you just take off driving and hope you found it? My guess is that you'd either call somebody and get precise directions, or you'd get on your computer and go to an Internet mapping site to find out exactly what you needed to do to get where you needed to be.

This trip you're about to take with your finances may be the most important journey you've ever made. Don't risk blowing it by not knowing where you are and what you have to work with. I'm going to offer you some simple worksheets and other resources that will make the process as painless and easy as possible. You don't have to be a CPA or an economics whiz to know the necessary facts to get started toward financial health. All you need to know is how to add and subtract, and all you have to do is invest the time required to gather some basic information. So let's get started.

Monthly Cash Flow Statement

For most of us, the month is our basic unit of financial time. We get paid once a month, and our bills come due once a month. Therefore, the logical place to start assessing our situation is to find out what we've got coming in and going out each month. For that, we need a monthly cash flow statement, which shows income minus expenses.

Income. Find a copy, either paper or online, of your most recent paycheck. If you are not self-employed, getting the basic information for your income is a little easier. Write down your monthly net pay, the amount you actually deposit in your account on payday after all deductions. Note, however, that if you have payments being payroll-deducted for things like car payments, personal loans, or other payments on obligations, add these amounts back into your monthly net pay; we'll deduct those amounts later, when we look at your monthly expenses.

You don't have to be a CPA or an economics whiz to know the necessary facts to get started toward financial health.

If you are self-employed or if you really want to do a complete analysis of your income, start by writing down your gross pay—the amount of your income before any deductions. Then subtract the deductions listed on your pay stub: Social Security, pension, payroll taxes, Medicare, and insurance are the most common ones. If you're self-employed, you should be deducting each month for the estimated income tax payments you're supposed to be sending in each quarter. After you've totaled all the deductions, subtract that amount from your gross pay; the result is your monthly net income.

Whichever method you use to derive your monthly net income, write the amount in the space provided on the worksheet.

If your spouse works, follow the procedure described above to list the spouse's income. You can simply combine both incomes into a single amount on the same line.

Monthly Cash Flow Statement

INCOME

Monthly gross income	$ _____
Payroll taxes	$ _____
Social Security	$ _____
Medicare	$ _____
Insurance	$ _____
Union dues	$ _____
Retirement	$ _____
Other	$ _____
Monthly deductions	$ _____
Monthly net income (gross pay minus deductions)	$ _____
Other income	$ _____
Other income	$ _____
Other income	$ _____
Other income	$ _____
Total other income	$ _____
Total monthly income	$ _____

Next, list any other sources of monthly income. Do you receive rentals? Have you got a freelance job that brings in extra income? Are you receiving a pension or other retirement benefits? Do you receive alimony or child support payments? Calculate the total and add it to your monthly income. If your extra income is from freelance work, don't forget to allow for the estimated quarterly tax payment because this is probably classified as self-employment income.

Expenses. Get out your checkbook or look at your record of online payments. For expenses that vary from month to month, such as utility payments or clothing, you may need to review the last several months and get an average amount for budget purposes.

Monthly Cash Flow Statement

EXPENSES

Rent or mortgage	$ _____
Electricity	$ _____
Gas	$ _____
Telephone (cellular and/or landline)	$ _____
Cable	$ _____
Internet	$ _____
Water	$ _____
Food	$ _____
Clothing	$ _____
Medical	$ _____
Car payments	$ _____
Car maintenance	$ _____
Gas	$ _____
Other commuting costs (train, bus, etc.)	$ _____
Recreation/entertainment	$ _____
Charitable contributions	$ _____
Life insurance	$ _____
Medical insurance	$ _____
Auto insurance	$ _____
Home insurance	$ _____
Renter's insurance	$ _____
Other insurance	$ _____
Alimony	$ _____
Child support	$ _____
Total monthly expenses	$ [ ]
Bottom line (subtract expenses from income)	$ [ ]

List amounts for the categories shown: rent or mortgage; utilities, including electricity/gas, telephone (cellular and/or landline), cable/Internet fees, and water; food; clothing; medical; transportation, including car payments, if any, gasoline, maintenance, or other commuting costs such as taxis, trains, buses, or other mass transit; recreation/entertainment; and charitable contributions. Next, enter amounts for life, medical, auto, home, renter's, or other insurance payments you make each month. In a separate category, enter alimony or child support payments you are required to make. Write down any payments you're making on other debt (credit cards, merchant charge accounts, other installment payments). Finally, list any other taxes or fees you are required to pay (if some of them are paid other than monthly, divide the annual amount by 12 and enter the result).

Bottom Line. Subtract your total monthly expenses from your total monthly income to find your net income. If income is equal to or more than expenses—congratulations! Maybe your situation isn't as bad as you thought. But be cautious! Just because you're in the black on paper doesn't mean that's what is happening in reality. If you carefully track your expenses, you might find that you are right on the edge every month, mostly because of small expenditures like daily coffee runs and eating lunch out.

If you come up with a negative net income, it may be that you simply need to take a closer look at impulsive or unplanned spending. A little later, we'll discuss the importance of distinguishing between needs and wants. Clearly, categories such as food, shelter, clothing, and necessary transportation are needs. Things like entertainment and recreation indicate wants. When you're in difficult financial times, it's essential to know the difference between needs and wants and act accordingly.

FinanciaL GPS

Your cash flow statement compares your monthly income to your monthly expenses. If you've got more income than expenses, you're in a good position to work directly with your creditors to resolve your debts.

If your monthly expenses are more than your income, you've got to ask yourself some hard questions. For example, look at your housing costs; if your mortgage is absorbing more than 29 percent of your monthly income, then according to the Federal Housing Administration, you may be "house poor," a fairly common situation for many people who find themselves in financial trouble. Let's say your monthly income from all sources totals $3,000; your total expense for housing, including all loan payments, escrow, taxes, and insurance, should be no more than $870. If your housing is costing more than that each month, you need to take a serious look at what you're paying versus what you can afford. It may be that you got into your present home when your income was greater, but your circumstances have changed. It may also be that your original mortgage fell within acceptable guidelines, but you've since taken second liens to pay off other debt, and now that payment, added to your original home loan, is putting you over the line. Whatever the reason, you are probably paying more than you can afford for your home. Whereas providing shelter for yourself and your family is definitely a basic need, you may actually be satisfying a want—and at this point, you may not be able to continue to indulge in that choice.

Another area that can be a budget-buster is transportation. If you're making payments on two car loans—not uncommon for double-income families—how long do you think you can continue that scenario? Should you consider selling a car—assuming you can sell it for enough to satisfy your outstanding loan balance—and figure out how to manage with a single vehicle? Can you begin using public transportation to save on gas or to enable you to do without one of your cars? Here again, though transportation is a basic need, you may be making choices that transfer it into the "want" category.

Later in the book, we'll take a more comprehensive look at ways to get better at living within your means. For now, it's important that you have a realistic picture of where you are. Not only is this information important for you to have, but if you decide to work directly with your creditors, the information you've just gathered will be essential. For example, in order to qualify for many creditors' hardship repayment plans (which we'll discuss in detail later), you must first provide the creditor with such basic information as that collected for the monthly cash flow statement.

Personal Net Worth Statement (Balance Sheet)

Now that you've begun to get a handle on your monthly cash flow, it's time to take a look at a broader picture of your financial health: your net worth.

Personal Net Worth Statement

ASSETS

Checking account	$ _____
Savings account	$ _____
Cash on hand	$ _____
Life insurance policy cash surrender/loan value	$ _____
Total cash/cash equivalent holdings	$ ⬜

Real and Personal Property

Property #1	$ _____
Property #2	$ _____
Property #3	$ _____
Automobile #1	$ _____
Automobile #2	$ _____
Automobile #3	$ _____
Personal property	$ _____
Personal property	$ _____
Personal property	$ _____
Total real and personal property	$ ⬜

Retirement, Pension, and Investment Plans

Stocks	$ _____
IRAs	$ _____
401k plans	$ _____
Certificates of deposit	$ _____
Mutual funds	$ _____
Total retirement, pension, and investment plans	$ ⬜
Total Assets	$ ⬜

Simply put, this will allow you to look at your complete financial makeup and determine if your assets (what you own) exceed your liabilities (what you owe), or vice versa.

To get the answers needed for this section, you'll need your most recent statements from your home, student loan, and vehicle lenders, if any, as well as all your most recent credit card and bank statements. If you have retirement accounts, brokerage or investment accounts, or other valuable assets that

Personal Net Worth Statement

LIABILITIES

Home Debt

Home loan	$ _____
Second lien	$ _____
Home-improvement loan	$ _____
Total home debt	$ [　　　]
Automobile loan	$ _____
Student loan	$ _____
Credit card	$ _____
Personal loan	$ _____
Any other debt	$ _____
Total liabilities	$ [　　　]
Bottom line (subtract liabilities from assets)	$ [　　　]

you own free and clear, you'll need those statements and information as well. Finally, if you own cash value life insurance, find out the loan and/or cash surrender value of your policies (you may have to call your agent to do this, but frequently you can obtain this information online).

Assets. First, list amounts held in all your checking and savings accounts, as well as any significant amounts of cash you have on hand. Next, write down the cash surrender or loan value of your life insurance policies. These items, totaled together, are your holdings in cash and cash equivalents.

Next, list the value of any real estate you own, either as rental income property or your primary residence. Unless you've owned the property for ten years or more, you may want to simply show this as the amount you originally paid, unless you are certain there have been recent dramatic changes—either positive or negative—in the value of property in your area. Next, list the value of any vehicles you own. Again, you can probably just write down what you paid for the car, but if you want to look at your vehicle's resale value (or if you've had the car more than three years or so), you can go online to sites like the Kelley Blue Book (www.kbb.com) or others to get an idea of what your car might be worth on the market. The final entry in this section is the value of any personal property, such as jewelry, art, collectibles, or other valuable personal property you may have. Estimates are fine, but if you happen to have actual appraisals available, use those figures. Total all these categories together; this is the value of your real and personal property. Unless you have some items of real value, the value of your personal property is likely quite low, at least for this exercise.

Finally, you need to know the value of your retirement, pension, and investment plans, if any. Enter the most recent total value of all these from your latest statements. This could include things like stocks, IRAs, 401k plans through your employer, certificates of deposit, and mutual funds. Total these up and enter the result as "retirement, pension, and investment plans." The grand total of all these categories on the personal net worth statement is the amount of your total assets.

Liabilities. Now, take another look at your most recent mortgage statement. It will show the current amount still owed on your home loan. If you have a second lien or a home improvement loan, add the outstanding loan balance to your primary mortgage. This total is your home debt.

On your last car loan statement, find the amount still owed and enter it on the appropriate line on the worksheet. Do the same for any student loans, credit cards, personal loans, or other debt you have. If you presently owe back taxes, either state or federal, enter that amount. Total up all your debt; this amount constitutes your total liabilities.

Bottom Line. Hopefully, your assets are worth more than your liabilities and you have a positive net worth. However, if you're like many Americans with adjustable-rate mortgages, the amount still owed on your home is more than its current value. More than likely, your vehicles—especially if you purchased them recently—would not sell for enough to liquidate the debt standing against them. If you have lots of credit card debt, it can easily cancel out the value of assets you may have. In other words, many Americans are "upside down": they owe more to the bank, the car lender, and the credit card companies than they could realize by selling everything they have lock, stock, and barrel.

If you're in the latter situation, don't despair. Later, I'm going to give you information on how to deal with your negative net worth and form a plan to put your finances on a better footing for the future.

TAKE A LOOK AT THE LANDSCAPE

Now that you've completed a quick cash flow analysis and personal net worth statement, it's time to step back out of the trees and try to see the forest. The makeup of your assets and liabilities will become very important as you begin to formulate a plan for resolving your financial problems, and now that you have these two important financial blueprints in hand, you're in a position to start making some decisions about how to proceed.

It's time for a little more math. From your cash flow statement, total the amount of all necessary expenses: mortgage or rent, food, clothing, court-ordered child support or alimony payments, and necessary transportation. Subtract this amount from your monthly income. The result is the amount of money available to put toward satisfying your debts.

Now, from your personal balance sheet (net worth statement), total up the amounts of your debts by the following categories:

- Secured debt. This includes debts like your mortgage, a second lien, car loans, or other loans backed by property. Include student loans and back taxes, if any, in this category as well, because taxing authorities can place liens on your property in order to collect amounts due them.

- Unsecured debt. This category includes amounts owed to credit card companies (including gasoline and merchant cards) and personal loans from banks or credit unions (sometimes called "signature loans"). Medical bills also fall in this category.

How much of your debt is secured, and how much is unsecured? The answer to this question will be very important in making your plan for becoming debt-free because you must deal with these two debt types very differently.

Now that you have a basic breakdown of the makeup of your debt, let's discuss the various types of debt and their implications for your situation.

Secured Debt

For individuals, this is the equivalent of corporate "senior debt": it represents the most critical obligations—those that must be satisfied before all others. At the top of the list is your mortgage. Because it is collateralized by your home, if you fail to meet this obligation, the mortgage lender has the legal right to take back possession of your house, forcing you to live somewhere else. Mortgage debt is generally considered one of the most secure loans, since people will usually give up almost everything else they have in order to keep their homes.

Secured debt represents the most critical obligations— those that must be satisfied before all others.

Fortunately for homeowners, strict laws govern foreclosure on home loans, and the process by which a bank may repossess a home for nonpayment of a mortgage obligation is carefully regulated by the states. Currently, no state allows a foreclosure in less than one month, and some states mandate a minimum time period of as much as seven months for foreclosure. Laws vary, of course, and are subject to change, so these are general guidelines only.

A second lien against your home (often called a "home equity loan"), whether taken to finance a home improvement or to secure cash to pay off other, higher-interest debt, also represents a secured loan, though it ranks below your primary mortgage in priority. The second-lien holder, like the primary mortgagor, has a legal interest in your home that can be satisfied once the primary mortgage holder is taken care of. Many people, in response to the active marketing programs by banks, have taken second liens against their homes, not fully realizing that they are giving someone else in addition to their original mortgage lender the right to take possession of their residence in the event of inability to pay.

Your car loan, if you have one, is also a secured loan because it is collateralized by your vehicle. If you get far enough behind in your payments, the bank or other lender can and will repossess your vehicle. You will typically receive a written warning—though many states don't require this of lenders—and, sometimes, a follow-up call. One or both of these notices may advise you of a grace period that the lender may extend, during which you have the opportunity to bring your account current and avoid repossession.

Depending on the terms of the loan and the laws governing repossession in your state, the lender may be entitled to repossess the car at any time of the day or night and may use any means to do so, as long as the repossessing agent does not commit a "breach of the peace" by using force, or threats of force, or by breaking into a locked building. Once the car has been repossessed, typically the only way you can get it back is by making all past-due payments and also paying fees and costs incurred for the repossession—and these can be quite hefty. If you don't pay all the fees and back payments by a certain time period, the car will be sold at auction.

Not Secured, but Almost

Obligations such as student loans and back taxes are not technically secured obligations, but because they are issued by or owed to agencies of government with the authority to levy and collect taxes, you can almost place them in the same priority as secured loans. The IRS, for example, has the authority to garnish your wages—to collect a portion of each paycheck before it even hits your desk—in order to satisfy unpaid taxes. They can place liens on your property, repossess your vehicle, and require you to sell assets in order to pay obligations owed them.

Student loans, which are usually backed by federal guarantees, are another form of debt that, although not strictly secured in the legal sense, would be close to the last type of debt on which you'd want to default. Even bankruptcy cannot usually relieve you of the responsibility for student loans.

Court-ordered child support and alimony payments, though not really a form of debt at all, are another obligation that should be near the top of your "must-pay" category. In most states, failure to pay child support or alimony makes you subject to prosecution, garnishment of wages, property liens, and other unpleasant consequences, including jail time.

Unsecured Debt

The leading form of unsecured personal debt in the United States is credit card debt. Remember all those "pre-qualified" and "zero-interest" offers you got in the mail? That's because the banks that issue credit cards decided they could make more money by doing minimal underwriting—determining how qualified potential borrowers were—and at the same time issuing thousands of cards, hoping that most of the people who got them would use them and keep them current. Unfortunately, as you know, things don't always work out as planned, either for the banks or the consumer.

If you make a late payment or miss a payment, most credit card agreements give the issuer the right to raise your interest rate from that temptingly low introductory rate up to rates sometimes in excess of 25 percent! If you loaned money to someone and charged that kind of interest, you could go to jail. But then, you're not a credit card company.

So, you can see how once you start to get behind on credit card payments, things can snowball. Once the company starts adding on late fees and all that extra interest, your debt can begin to grow faster than mildew in a junior high locker room.

In order to collect on debt that has fallen behind, the credit card companies have collection departments whose sole job is to call people who have late payments or who have stopped making payments and try to convince them to send in money. Eventually, if the debt isn't brought current, the bank's accounting rules require them to charge off the debt. But that doesn't mean they've completely abandoned efforts to get you to pay. Often, credit card companies will assign charged-off accounts to independent collection companies who, for a fee (sometimes as much as 50 percent of the amount collected), will continue calling you and may even bring a lawsuit against you to force payment of the debt.

Because credit card debt is unsecured, the lender has no contractual recourse to any of your property in order to satisfy the debt. However, if the company sues you and is successful in obtaining a legal judgment against you, the terms of the judgment can entitle the creditor to certain of your assets in satisfaction of the debt. Some states exempt certain types of assets, or assets up to a certain value, from the claims of unsecured creditors. Laws vary significantly by state, so this is an area where you should consult with a qualified attorney to determine exactly what an unsecured creditor can and cannot take if the creditor wins a court judgment against you.

There are a number of steps you can take with credit card companies to work things out before they reach the lawsuit stage, and in the next chapter I'll discuss several of these options. For now, you should know that unsecured debt, though it comes with legally enforceable remedies for nonpayment, should not be prioritized ahead of secured debt, in most cases. In other words, credit card debt should not be ignored, but neither should it become more important to you than taking care of your mortgage and other secured debt. The same is true for other forms of unsecured debt, such as personal loans from banks or credit unions, medical bills, merchant credit cards, and gasoline credit cards.

SURVIVAL TIP:
PRIORITIZE YOUR DEBTS

1. Secured debts that could result in the loss of your home or vehicle should be priority number one.

2. Debts that aren't secured but are "must pay," such as child support, taxes, and student loans, should be priority number two.

3. Unsecured debts that are likely to appear on your credit report, such as credit cards, should be priority number three.

4. Unsecured debts that are less likely to go to collection, such as bills from doctors, should be priority number four.

YOUR SITUATION, YOUR STRATEGY

As you can probably tell by now, the type of debt making up your liabilities also makes a big difference in how you approach getting out of financial trouble. There are things that a mortgage holder can do to satisfy a debt that a credit card lender cannot. There are things that a student loan lender can do that a signature loan lender cannot. Likewise, there are steps you, as a debtor, can take with certain types of debt that are impossible with others. As you begin to put together your plan for getting out of debt and back on an even keel, you need to know a bit about the characteristics of the types of debt you have.

How much of your debt is tied up in your mortgage, your second lien, or a home improvement loan? Do you owe back taxes? Are you liable for student loans or making child support or alimony payments? Or are your financial troubles mostly caused by delinquent—and growing—credit card balances? Using your cash flow statement and personal balance sheet, you now have the ability to answer these questions. As we proceed to the next parts of our discussion, these answers will become important pieces of the picture we will assemble: your plan for a debt-free, financially secure future.

STEPS IN THE RIGHT DIRECTION

1. Communicate with your creditors.

2. Take immediate action to temporarily forestall foreclosure or repossession or to stop creditor calls while you figure out your next steps.

3. Create a cash flow statement that identifies all of your income and expenses.

4. Create a net worth statement (a personal balance sheet) that identifies all of your assets and liabilities.

5. Analyze and classify your debts as secured, must pay, and unsecured and then prioritize them accordingly.

Chapter 2

DEALING WITH FINANCIAL TROUBLE ON YOUR OWN

GUIDEPOSTS

In this chapter, you'll learn

- How to maximize your income

- How to minimize your expenses

- How to work with creditors, using proven strategies

After a review of your situation, maybe you've concluded that your best course of action is to handle everything yourself. That's a perfectly good decision, especially if you're not facing imminent legal action. If you've been notified that a lender is beginning repossession of your home, or if one of your credit card companies or a collector has had an attorney send you a letter notifying you of a pending suit, you would be well advised to speak to an attorney. I'll discuss these scenarios in more detail in a later chapter, but for now, let's assume that things haven't progressed that far, and you still have the option of settling your debts yourself, without hiring an attorney, a credit counseling company, or a debt settlement company.

Now is the time when you'll begin to really use some of the information we assembled in chapter 1. One of the first things a creditor will ask you, for example, is how much money you think you can put toward your debt on a regular basis. With your cash flow statement in hand, you should be in a position to answer that question accurately and honestly. Other creditors, prior to offering special terms for satisfying the debt, will want to know what your assets and liabilities are. Now that you've compiled your personal balance sheet, you can give them the information they need to decide how they can best work with you.

Before we get into specific strategies to use with different types of creditors, however, let's talk about some things you can do to put yourself in a better position to successfully complete any repayment plan you enter into. The first thing you can do to help yourself comes from basic accounting: look for ways to maximize income and minimize expenses. To borrow a sports metaphor, I call it, "Better Offense, Better Defense."

BETTER OFFENSE, BETTER DEFENSE

The basic strategy here is to make more and spend less, thus freeing up as much cash as possible to go toward satisfying your creditors and getting out of debt in the shortest time possible.

You may be thinking, "If I could just make more money, I wouldn't be in this mess in the first place." That's possibly true, but there may be some ways of generating extra income that you haven't considered.

Better Offense: Take a Part-time Job for More Income

A simple alternative that may be open to you is to ask for more hours at your present job or to work some overtime, if it's available. By law, most companies must pay at a higher rate for overtime, and that additional cash can help you satisfy your creditors that much quicker.

If you're doing a great job for your employer, do you have the opportunity for a raise, either as part of an annual review process or some other advancement provision of your employer? Now is the time to find out; you can't afford to be shy. In fact, don't be embarrassed to tell your employer that you need to pay off some debt; chances are, your boss can relate, on some level. You can even use my phrase: "I'm trying to put in a better offense by earning more money to apply toward my debt and have a better defense by cutting expenses." As I will emphasize throughout the book, honest and open communication is your best tool as you work on bringing your debt under control. This certainly applies to your present job and your supervisor or employer. Especially if you are a valued employee, your boss will probably want to do whatever possible to help you out.

Could you possibly take a part-time job? With the mid-2009 increase to $7.25 per hour, even a minimum-wage position at ten hours per week could generate as much as $290 per month (before taxes). Even though that doesn't sound like a lot of money, having that much extra each month dedicated to paying down a balance with a creditor could mean the difference between moving forward and staying where you are. Not only that, but creditors generally look more favorably on consumers who can document that they are doing all they can to take care of their obligations. And remember, there's no requirement that you must take a minimum-wage job. You may have skills and experiences that qualify you for a much better rate of pay. Make it a habit to scan your local newspaper's "help wanted" ads. Take a

Creditors look more favorably on consumers who can document that they are doing all they can.

look at a few online job boards, such as CraigsList.org or HelpWanted. com. Your state's employment or workforce commission probably has an online job search page as well. You may find an opportunity from one of these resources that will help you get back on your feet.

Another idea is starting a home-based business or performing freelance or consulting work. Especially now, with the ability to work online, there are legitimate opportunities to do work for decent pay to bring in some extra money. Although you should certainly exercise the normal level of caution about "get-rich-quick" schemes—on the Internet or anywhere else—the chance to earn some extra income to go toward your debt is certainly out there if you're willing to look for it.

If there are two adults of working age in your household but you presently live on a single income, it may be time for the unemployed adult to seriously consider entering the workforce. The second income can really help, as long as you don't increase your spending level so as to absorb all the extra money before it can go toward debt. You should plan on some increase in expenses, of course—more spent on transportation, for starters, and possibly child care costs if there are still children under school age in the home—but if you can control these additional costs within acceptable limits, you should give this alternative careful consideration, at least as a temporary measure.

Better Offense: Turn Your Junk into Cash

Have you got some stuff you could sell? With the nearly universal presence of the Internet, sites like eBay and Craigslist have become more popular than ever with people who want to reach the largest possible number of potential buyers. Take an inventory of your garage and attic: that set of barbells and weight bench that you haven't used in three years could possibly raise the money to help bring a credit card account current. What about that crepe maker you bought on sale last winter, the one that's still in the box? Somebody, somewhere is looking for it and is willing to pay cash to own it—cash that you can use to help make ends meet this month.

Now that we've looked at some ways of increasing income ("Better Offense"), let's consider some ideas for reducing expenses ("Better Defense").

Better Defense: Too Much House?

Let's start with a biggie: downsizing your home. Because being "house poor" gets so many people into financial distress, you should at least consider the possibility that you may be living in more house than you can afford. Especially if you've lived in your home long enough to accumulate any equity at all, it may be worth at least talking with a local real estate professional about the possibility of selling your home and buying a smaller one—or renting, temporarily. The money you'll save on monthly payments can go toward paying off debt, and if you happen to sell in a favorable market, you could even clear a lump sum beyond what you need to secure new housing. That money can also be used to pay down what you owe.

Getting Real about Assets. While we're on the topic of home ownership and equity, let me make another point. Many people have an inaccurate idea of what constitutes an asset. If you can't sell it for more than you owe on it, or if the amount of money you're required to spend each month on utilities and upkeep are draining you beyond your ability to cope, it's not an asset—it's a liability. At least it's that way right now, and in your present situation, you may not be able to afford the time to turn things around.

This is especially true of automobiles because they typically devalue dramatically as soon as you drive them off the dealer's lot. Unless the debt against it is paid off, a vehicle should usually be viewed not as an asset but as a necessary liability, at best.

This can also be true of a house. Many consumers, desperate to get into a "dream home," take on adjustable rate mortgages in order get their payments low enough to qualify for financing. When interest rates adjust—and they almost always do it at the most inconvenient time—the increased cost of borrowing usually means an increase in the monthly payment. Some homeowners in this situation find themselves facing not only dramatically higher monthly payments but also a loss in the value of their homes due to falling real estate values. In other words, they can't qualify for refinancing on more favorable terms. In fact, they can't even sell the home for enough to pay off the amount they originally borrowed. For people in this situation, their home isn't an asset; it's a liability—a leaden drag on their net worth.

Owning a home is often described as the American dream. I don't think that's quite accurate. Owning a home *free and clear* is the American dream; taking possession of a house by means of financing you can't afford can quickly turn into a nightmare.

FINANCIAL GPS

If you can't sell it for more than you owe on it, it's not an asset.

Better Defense: Selling or Downsizing an Extra Car

Let's look at some more ideas to improve your defense by decreasing your expenses. If you have two vehicles, would it be possible for you to get by with only one—even temporarily? Selling the "extra" car might seem like an inconvenience, but if you can figure workable alternate solutions for your transportation needs, it's one way to free up some monthly cash flow that can be used to pay off debt. This presumes, of course, that you can sell the car for enough to liquidate anything you still owe on it.

Maybe it's unrealistic for you to attempt the one-car-family lifestyle. If you've got a luxury vehicle in your driveway (just to be clear: I'm including cars made by Lexus, Cadillac, BMW, Porsche, Jaguar, Mercedes-Benz, Hummer, and even some of the tricked-out SUVs by domestic manufacturers in this class), could you sell it and buy something more economical? Taking a $700 monthly payment on your Escalade down to a $300 monthly payment on a low-mileage, dependable Camry, for example, could make a huge positive difference in your cash flow, even before you factor in what you'll save each month on gasoline and the cost of maintaining insurance coverage. Even better, you might clear enough to pay cash for your replacement vehicle.

I include this last idea for one simple reason: I have counseled, time and again, with people in severe financial straits who were still trying to hold on to the BMW *and* the Escalade *and* the Harley. Why? Because too many of us confuse the *trappings* of wealth for actual wealth. Having those cars in the garage makes us feel better about ourselves.

Just because you can temporarily afford to make payments on all those beautiful vehicles doesn't mean owning them is in your best long-term financial interest. Nevertheless, when people come in to see me for financial counseling, they tell me over and over, "I want to keep all the cars." The simple fact is, if you're in debt trouble, you can no longer afford to spend time, energy, and, above all, money maintaining the appearance of prosperity. You've got to get brutally honest with yourself about "needs" versus "wants." And that brings us to our next idea for improving your financial defense.

Too many of us confuse the *trappings* of wealth for actual wealth.

Better Defense: Right-Sizing Your Lifestyle

Look for ways to economize in your lifestyle. Does the idea of coupon-clipping appeal to you? Can you find ways to save on necessary household supplies, either by buying in larger quantities less frequently or by reducing consumption? Consider thrift and resale stores for clothing purchases. Some shoppers have raised this almost to an art form; they know exactly when the local Goodwill gets in the latest barely worn designer clothes from the local college students, and they swoop in to scoop up the bargains. If you need to replace a necessary appliance, turn to the classifieds or garage sales instead of the local do-it-yourselfer superstore.

If you've been in the habit of going to the movies a few times per month, consider renting movies instead or, better still, investigate the movies you can borrow free of charge at your local public library. Eating out at restaurants gets expensive pretty quickly, especially for families with two or three children. Think about limiting your nights out to one or two per month, and also try to find places where the food is good but not too pricey. In your vacation planning, instead of focusing on theme parks and expensive hotel stays, take a look at public parks or beaches. Consider taking several nearby weekend getaways rather than a week- or two-week-long "grand tour."

Here's an important point: most of these cost-saving measures involve carefully analyzing needs versus wants. If your family is anything like mine, purchases can, at any given time, quickly grow to absorb 120 percent of the available funds. But when we exercise careful discretion and are honest with ourselves, our wants are almost always much greater than our needs. If you are in financial trouble, one of the reasons may be a difficulty in distinguishing between the two. You must learn to discipline yourself to take care of the needs first and defer the wants until there is money available to satisfy them. In a later chapter, we'll discuss this more thoroughly, but for now, remember to ask yourself—and answer honestly—"Do I need it, or do I just want it?" If the answer is the latter, you should probably pass it up.

SURVIVAL TIP:

QUICK WAYS TO REDUCE MONTHLY EXPENSES

- Stop going to movies; rent or, even better, check out movies from your public library.
- Start brown-bagging it at work instead of eating lunch out.
- Buy clothing at thrift stores and resale shops instead of going to the mall.
- Start walking or riding a bike for errands close to home, instead of driving. You'll not only save money, you'll get in better shape!

Now that you've reviewed your offense by looking at ways to maximize your income and tightened up your defense by carefully scrutinizing and trimming your expenses, it's time to figure out how to take the cash flow you've freed up and put it to use in the smartest way possible. Let's discuss how to get the maximum benefit from your newly allocated financial resources: to get started climbing out of the hole of debt.

WORKING WITH CREDITORS—THE SMART WAY

Perhaps the most important change many debtors need to make on the way to financial health is to stop being afraid of their creditors. If you've spent the last few months afraid to pick up the telephone because it might be a collector calling, this advice may sound a bit scary. However, if you're that intimidated by them, it probably means you haven't been communicating with them. And that is the first thing you must change if you want to work with your creditors to get out of debt. Just as the three most important rules of real estate investing are location, location, location, the three most important keys to success in working with your creditors are communication, communication, communication.

As I mentioned in chapter 1, most collection agents spend the majority of their time dialing phone numbers that no one answers. But if you're going to work things out with them, you have to talk to them—it's that simple. Not only that, but the fact that you're actually speaking to them with respect and honesty automatically encourages them to place you in a different category from the dozens of accounts they're working where they can't get anyone to respond to their calls.

The first thing your creditors need to hear you say is that you acknowledge the debt and that you're not trying to avoid it. At that point, you can begin making your case for any form of consideration or assistance they can offer you. You need to explain to them why you *can't* pay so that they won't continue to think that you're one of those who just *don't want* to pay.

FINANCIAL GPS

The "Better Offense/Better Defense" Strategy in the case of divorce or death

Better Offense: Make sure you're squeezing every bit of income you can from your situation by working extra or selling unnecessary items to raise cash.

Better Defense: Scrutinize your monthly expenses for ways to reduce them. Be brutally honest about "needs" vs. "wants" and downsize wherever possible.

This is where you will need to have done your financial homework, as we discussed in chapter 1. Using your cash flow statement, you can discuss your income and expenses with your creditor. If you've recently suffered a setback due to one of the big four circumstances that can create considerable financial strain—unexpected expenses and bad financial habits, job loss, grave illness, and divorce or death of a principal wage earner—or for some other reason, share this information with your creditor. If you expect additional income or a lump sum payment at some point in the future, mention this as well. Your creditor may be willing to be somewhat more patient with your delinquency if there is a legitimate possibility that you will be in a better position to make payments in the not-too-distant future.

SURVIVAL TIP:
WHAT YOUR CREDITORS WANT TO HEAR

- Acknowledge the debt and your responsibility for it.
- Explain why you can't pay; be as specific as possible.
- Perform any follow-up actions as agreed.

The main point here is that you must be honest and forthcoming with your creditors if you expect them to come to your assistance. If you promise to call back in a week with additional information—do it. If you tell them that you can send a partial payment by the tenth of the month—mail it on time. Each time that you fulfill an expectation, you give them another reason to continue working with you on settling your debt.

Hardship Plans and Other Special Considerations

It may surprise you to learn that many credit card companies are able to offer special hardship terms to debtors who can demonstrate genuine need. Often, these terms include reductions in interest rates, waiver of late fees and other charges, and even forgiveness of some portion of the amount you owe. Some creditors offer arrangements called "60/60" plans that allow the creditor to satisfy the obligation by paying 60 percent of the balance owed over a sixty-month period. But before you can be offered any favorable options your creditor may have available, you must convince the creditor of both your need and your sincerity about following through on your end of the deal. And in order to convince the creditor of your need and your sincerity, you must—here comes that word again—communicate honestly and effectively.

Talking with your creditor about a hardship plan is perhaps the single most important self-help technique for consumer debt relief—and one that most consumers are afraid to use. Why? Because no one likes to think about speaking with a bill collector. However, if you can overcome this fear, you can make immediate, significant progress toward getting out of debt, and you can do it at a much smaller cost than if you enroll in a debt management plan with a credit counseling agency or employ the services of a debt negotiator (more on these options in the next chapter).

Start by contacting your creditor (or waiting until the next time they call you). Have your financial planning documents in front of you: your monthly cash flow statement and your personal net worth statement (balance sheet), prepared according to the instructions in chapter 1. Jot down the name and phone number of the person you speak with and try to always talk with the same individual, if possible. Also, write down and keep any case numbers, file numbers, or other identifying information the creditor gives concerning your case. This will facilitate better communication, both between you and the creditor and within the creditor's organization. Keep everything organized, including the dates of all spoken communications.

Explain your situation to your creditor; be as specific as possible, including pertinent information from your financial documents. Be very clear that you intend to pay back what you owe but are having difficulties currently because of whatever factors—unemployment, divorce, reduced income, illness—are negatively impacting your ability to make payments. Remember that you are trying to lay out in very clear terms the reasons you cannot make payments.

Tell the creditor, "I am trying to avoid bankruptcy." Believe me, this simple, truthful statement will catch their attention, because they know that if you do file bankruptcy, as an unsecured creditor they will be at the end of the line for receiving any money on your debts to them. Credit card companies do not want you to file bankruptcy, and most will work with you in any way possible to help you avoid it.

At this point, depending on how far past due your payments are, the creditor may offer some sort of special plan that includes a reduced payoff amount, longer payout terms, reduced interest rates, or some combination. If they don't, ask them, "Do you have any sort of hardship repayment plan available?" Don't be too quick to use "insider" terminology such as the "60/60" plan. Instead, you might consider phrasing your request something like this: "Do you have any kind of plan where I could pay back at least part of the balance over a longer term?

SURVIVAL TIP:
TALKING WITH CREDITORS ABOUT HARDSHIP PLANS

1. Contact your credit card company and fully explain your situation.

2. Be very clear that you intend to pay them back but are currently having financial difficulties stemming from [specifics of your situation].

3. Tell them, "I am trying to avoid bankruptcy."

4. The creditor may offer some sort of special plan. If they don't, ask them, "Do you have any sort of hardship repayment plan available?" or, "Do you have any kind of plan where I could pay back at least part of the balance over a longer term?"

5. Be persistent. Agree to call back in a specified time, and don't be afraid to repeat the phrase, "I'm trying to avoid bankruptcy."

Be persistent. If they don't offer terms on the first call, don't give up. Tell them you will continue to monitor your situation and agree to call back at a later time. Follow up, and don't be afraid to repeat the phrase, "I am trying to avoid bankruptcy," as long as this is the truth.

Understand that even if your creditor agrees to some sort of reduced payoff such as a 60/60 plan, your credit history will still be negatively impacted because the debt was not paid back 100 percent, according to the terms of the contract. However, for reasons that I will explain later, this may not be the main thing you need to worry about at this stage.

If student loans are a part of your financial difficulties, you may be eligible to defer your payments for a period of time. Depending on the specific type of loan you have and when you obtained it, you may qualify for temporary deferment of payments because of unemployment or financial hardship (studentaid.ed.gov). You need to remember, however, that with certain types of student loans, interest continues to accrue during the deferment period (with others, interest does not accrue during the defer-

SURVIVAL TIP:

OPTIONS FOR DEALING WITH STUDENT LOAN PAYMENT PROBLEMS

1. Temporary forbearance

2. Reduced or deferred payments

3. Hardship provisions

4. Extended repayment

5. Income-sensitive repayment

For more information on these and other options, contact your education loan provider or visit the following:

- Student Loan Marketing Association ("Sallie Mae"; www.salliemae.com)

- U.S. Department of Education (www.ed.gov)

ment; you must check the provisions of your specific loan contract to be certain). Also, a change in your financial circumstances can affect your eligibility. Finally, deferment, as the name implies, isn't permanent. It doesn't make your debt go away, it only delays the payments for a specified time— usually no more than three years, if you continue to qualify.

Financial Hardship and Mortgages

The mantra about communication applies to mortgage loans as well. If you're behind on your house payments, it's almost always better if you take the initiative to talk to your lender about it before they start calling you. Once again, it may surprise you to learn that mortgage lenders are not eager to foreclose on your home. Foreclosures are time-consuming and expensive; they exist as a last resort for lenders who have run out of other options to rehabilitate a nonperforming asset. Many banks—almost all of the larger ones—have a "workout department"—some of them call it a "loss mitigation department"—that exists for the sole purpose of figuring out ways for people who have fallen behind on their mortgages to get caught up and resume making regular payments. Among the tools mortgage lenders have at their disposal are

- Temporary forbearance—a period of time during which reduced or no payments are made
- Reinstatement—often used in combination with forbearance, in which a borrower is allowed to pay the delinquent amount in a lump sum at a future date
- Repayment—a period of time during which the borrower is allowed to pay portions of the past-due amount along with regular payments, gradually becoming current
- Loan modification—actually rewriting the loan contract and changing its terms to make it easier for the borrower to get and remain current (e.g., extending the term of the loan to reduce payments, moving missed payments to the end of the loan, and changing an adjustable-rate mortgage to a fixed rate).

In order for your lender to work with you in any of these ways, you must demonstrate an authentic financial hardship; you must convince the lender that you want to pay, but can't. In the same vein as our discussion about working with credit card companies, you need to provide your lender with enough hard financial data to allow the lender to make an informed decision. This is a situation where your monthly cash flow statement and personal balance sheet—as developed in chapter 1—will come in handy.

To find out what your mortgage lender is willing to do to help you in your current situation, get in touch with them and tell them the specific reasons for your difficulties. Give them facts and figures, along with any anticipated changes in your situation that could have a positive or negative impact. Keep **Mortgage lenders are not eager to foreclose on your home.**  track of all dates, names, phone numbers, and identifying information for your case, and follow up as agreed. The lender may opt to send out a packet to you, explaining your various options, as listed earlier.

You might consider writing a letter to your mortgage lender requesting consideration of hardship provisions for your mortgage. I've included a sample hardship request letter on the following page.

Other Measures to Consider

Another benefit of developing your personal balance sheet is that it forces you to look at all your assets and liabilities. In the process, you may actually discover or remember an asset that you could dispose of to raise much-needed cash. You may even be able to use these assets as collateral for a loan at a favorable interest rate. You can use the proceeds of the loan to pay off higher-interest loans, which will usually reduce the amount of monthly payments by a combination of lower interest and a longer time allowed for repayment. Home equity loans, or second liens, are an example of this strategy.

SAMPLE HARDSHIP REQUEST LETTER

Your Name
Your Address
City, State, ZIP

Dear Sir /Madam:

Please review my loan, [your loan number], and consider if I could qualify for any hardship or workout provisions you can offer. I am having difficulty making my scheduled monthly payments because of financial problems stemming from [divorce, unemployment, reduced income, illness, etc.]. These issues first arose on or around [date]. I [do/do not] anticipate that my situation will improve in the foreseeable future. [If you anticipate improvement:] I expect to be able to [increase/resume regular payment] by [date] because of [reason for improvement]. Currently, my monthly income is [amount] and my monthly expenses are [amount].

I am willing to provide any financial records that you may request in order to verify my situation. I am asking for [a reduction in my interest rate/a decreased monthly payment/temporary forbearance, etc.] so that I can take care of my obligations and avoid filing for bankruptcy protection.

I appreciate your careful consideration of this request.

I/We, [your and co-borrower's names] state that the information provided above is true and correct to the best of my/our knowledge.

[Your signature and date] / [Co-borrower's signature and date]

The Upside and Downside of Home Equity Loans. Home equity loans can be a source of low-interest funds to get rid of debts like credit cards that are often at punitive interest rates. Also, because they are secured by the equity in your home, the period of time to pay back the loan is longer, usually resulting in a lower monthly obligation. Additionally, some individuals may be able to deduct the interest paid on home equity loans on their income taxes—though you should consult with your tax adviser to verify the deductibility of any loan interest. For these reasons—along with aggressive marketing by banks—many homeowners have utilized second liens to pay off credit card debt.

However, you need to be careful here. As mentioned in the introduction, you can't borrow your way out of debt. What's more, we noted in chapter 1 that by converting home equity into more debt—even at a favorable interest rate and repayment term—you are exchanging an asset for an additional liability. It's not so bad if you're using the second lien to make improvements to the home that can increase its value—maybe by enough to offset the increased debt, thus preserving your asset/liability ratio. But when you use home equity to pay off unsecured debt, you are reducing the value of your asset and getting nothing in return. You still have the debt; you've merely converted it from unsecured to secured.

Home equity loans can work for the right candidates. For example, if you have a lot of equity in your house, you have stable income, and you're current on all your bills—including credit cards—but you want to get rid of high-interest debt, maybe a home equity loan makes sense. Depending on your tax bracket and income, you may even be able to deduct the interest, which you can't do with credit card payments. Let's say your average credit card interest rate is 15 percent and you can qualify for a home equity loan at 7 percent: the math could work pretty well in your favor, especially on a monthly cash flow basis. But you should still talk to your tax or financial adviser before committing.

FInancIaL GPS

Consult your tax adviser about the deductibility of a home equity loan.

As we'll discuss a bit later, a body of laws—generally referred to under the heading of "homestead exemptions"—protect your ownership and occupancy of your primary dwelling. When you give a lender a second lien on your home, however, it can imperil one of the most durable and essential assets you have. Don't do it lightly.

Borrowing from Family and Friends: Getting Past the Embarrassment. Many of us would rather have a root canal than ask family members and friends for money. Often, we'd prefer to discuss our sex lives with someone else than talk about our finances—even when things are going well. Especially in our American, self-sufficient, pull-yourself-up-by-your-own-bootstraps culture, asking for money from family when you're supposed to be independent and out on your own carries with it the image of failure. It can make you feel like a complete loser.

But remember: you are not your debt. You are also not defined by the temporary predicament you're in. Your main task at this point is to figure out how to get out of the predicament and back to living your life without being afraid of the telephone and the mail. I don't mean you should ask loved ones to jeopardize their retirement or even next summer's vacation. But if you have family and friends with the financial means to help you solve your problem, this is an avenue you should explore. Get past your embarrassment and simply have an honest conversation with them about your situation. Ask them if they can help—a little or a lot. If they can't, they'll tell you, and that's that. You will at least have the satisfaction of knowing that you've explored every possibility.

As a matter of fact, some creditors will ask you if a loan from family or friends is a possibility for you. If you've already secured funds this way or have inquired and determined that family and friends aren't in a position to help you, you can honestly answer the question when your creditor asks.

Of course, you should consider more than just the financial implications when approaching family members and friends to loan you money. There are emotional and relational aspects you should think about as well. A friend of mine once shared this maxim he heard in a college finance class: "Before you ask for money from friends, consider which you need more." There is some truth in this. Money disputes cause more family/friend rifts than almost anything else.

It's also true, however, that financial problems are the number one cause for divorce, as I said in the introduction. If money trouble is putting a strain on your marriage, you may need to decide which you'd rather risk: embarrassment with your relatives or divorce. When you think of it that way, they may be more sympathetic to your plight than you'd expect. They may even be willing to present the help as an outright gift, with no expectation of repayment.

If you do decide to try to secure a loan from family or friends, it may help to carefully calculate when and how quickly you'll be able to repay the loan, once your situation has improved. Here again, honest communication may enable you to avoid both embarrassment and an estranged relationship. If you clearly communicate a realistic scenario and then follow through on your representations, there's no reason why your temporary difficulties should cause long-term damage to your family connections or your friendships.

Debt Payoff Plans: Making the Most of Your Cash. Just for a moment, let's assume that you are able to raise a sizable amount of cash to make a dent in your debt, either from a home equity loan or by borrowing from family or friends. In a perfect world, it would be enough to completely pay off all your problem debt. In that case, the only thing you have left to figure out is how to pay back the home equity loan or the people from whom you borrowed.

However, as we all realize, we don't live in a perfect world. Suppose, then, that the amount you're able to raise is enough to get a good start on your debt, but not enough to completely eliminate it. What's the best way to get the biggest bang for your debt payoff buck?

There are a couple of main schools of thought on the best strategy to use for paying off debt. I'll sketch them both for you, then give you the reason why I favor one over the other.

Snowball Payoff Plan. The idea here is to begin eliminating debts completely as soon as possible by paying off those with the smallest balances. As soon as one debt is paid off, you add the amount you've been paying on that obligation to the next one in line, and so on. The advantage often claimed for the "snowball" method is that you develop momentum and motivation by quickly seeing the number of your creditors dwindle while seeing the amounts you're paying against your debt steadily increasing.

Highest-Interest-First Payoff Plan. With this strategy, you prioritize your debt for payoff by the rate of interest being charged by the creditor. Whichever debt has the highest interest rate gets the most attention and the most money each month until it is paid off. Then, you add that payment amount to the debt with the next-highest interest rate, and so on.

Hybrid Payoff Plan. Some personal finance writers advocate a third method that is a sort of hybrid of the two above. With this method, you calculate which of your debts has the lowest ratio of monthly minimum payment to debt balance and focus your energies there. Often, this method works out very similarly to the snowball strategy.

My preference is for the interest-rate method. The reason is that, in most scenarios, it will result in both the shortest payoff period and the smallest amount of money needed to finish off the debt. Having said that, the principal advantage the snowball method has is that it usually results in a smaller monthly amount needed to stay on track. However, if you've got the discipline to stick with it, you should focus your payoff resources, starting with the money you raise by any of the above methods, on targeting those higher-interest-rate debts first.

If you find yourself in the position of having some cash to pay off debt and wondering about the best way to get started, I encourage you to research the various payoff strategies to decide which one is likely to work the best for your situation. You can do an Internet search for phrases like "debt payoff strategy" or "credit card payoff plan" and find any number of sources that will advocate one or another debt payoff strategy; from there, it's up to you to pick the one that makes the most sense for you. Once you get started and see some success, it will become addictive to pay off your debts, and that will lead to even faster success!

ARE YOU "JUDGMENT-PROOF"?

Certain debtors may not need to take action to protect themselves from creditor demands. Those who have very few assets and whose sources of income are protected from the claims of creditors may be in a condition sometimes called "judgment-proof." In other words, they have nothing that a creditor could take, even if the creditor could win a judgment against them in court.

Determining whether or not you are judgment proof can be complicated, and taking the wrong path can lead you to greater financial difficulties. I highly recommend that you speak with an attorney to determine if this is the case.

Mrs. Johnson's Story

Evelyn Johnson, an elderly woman collecting Social Security and a minor veteran's pension from her deceased husband, was very worried. She had run up a $2,000 credit card balance while Christmas shopping for her grandchildren; she simply got carried away and lost track of how much she was charging. When the bill came, she knew there was no way she would be able to make even the minimum payment from her meager income. Having nowhere else to turn, she called her nephew, an attorney, and asked what she should do.

Mrs. Johnson's nephew knew that she rented a small apartment in a housing community for seniors. She kept only small balances in her checking account. The balance owed to the credit card company was the only real debt she had; her other monthly obligations were utility payments, her rent, groceries, and her church contribution.

"Aunt Evelyn, I don't think you need to do anything," her nephew said, after reviewing her situation. "Your Social Security and pension are protected from creditors by law. You don't own a house, so they can't come after that. You really don't have anything they can take. My advice to you is just to ignore the notices when they start sending them. When your pension and Social Security checks come in the mail, cash them instead of putting them in your checking account, just to be on the safe side. And if you start to get phone calls from them, tell them to call me; I'll be your representative. If they keep calling you, they'll be violating collection laws, and we can make them stop."

Mrs. Johnson stared at her nephew. "You mean . . . I don't have to pay them?"

"You can't pay them, Aunt Evelyn," he said. "And they don't have any way to make you. It would cost them more to file a suit against you than they could get from you if they won. I'll write a letter telling them that you can't pay and asking them to stop calling you. I'll let them know that you'll pay what you can, when you can. But for now, I think you're judgment-proof."

Admittedly, for most wage earners with even modest property holdings, this scenario isn't representative. Still, it is worth knowing that certain types of income are generally exempt from the claims of creditors. These usually include Social Security benefits, veteran's benefits, disability payments, worker's compensation, public assistance, child support, and alimony. Under certain circumstances and in some states, Mrs. Johnson might even be able to exempt her house, if she had one, from a creditor's lien. Certain other types of assets can be exempted from claims of creditors, depending on the laws in your state.

However, "judgment-proof" is not always a permanent condition. Let's say that one day Mrs. Johnson received a small inheritance from a long-lost, deceased relative. If her creditors found out about it, they might decide it was worthwhile to sue her for the balance she owed them. If the court determined that Mrs. Johnson had sufficient nonexempt assets to satisfy the debt, she could be ordered to use them to pay her past-due balance.

I have stressed the importance of honesty from the beginning, so I probably don't need to add this next part, but I'm going to anyway. If, as you read this section, you wondered about the possibility of making yourself "judgment-proof" by "gifting" assets to a friend until your creditors give up on getting anything from you—think again. Transfers that are undertaken for no reason other than avoiding the payment of debt are considered fraudulent by most courts, and if you end up in a lawsuit, you will likely be ordered to pay the debt anyway.

In any case, before you take it upon yourself to decide that you're judgment-proof, you need to have a long, careful conversation with an attorney—even if he's not your nephew. Especially if you believe your financial situation may improve in the future, think long and hard before you assume you have nothing your creditors can take to satisfy your debts.

BUT IF YOU CAN'T DO IT ON YOUR OWN...

Some of you may have read this far and are already feeling better about your situation. You've identified a strategy or two that could work for you, you've got your personal financial information organized, and you're ready to make that first call to your creditor and start working on a plan to get out of trouble and back on a positive financial footing. That's great.

But others reading this book may still be worried. Maybe you're seriously past due on several credit cards, and you don't think you can keep that many creditors at bay long enough to work things out. Or maybe you've already been notified that legal action—a lawsuit, foreclosure, or repossession—is imminent. You feel like you're running out of time and things have gotten past the point that you can handle it on your own.

In that case, it's time for you to turn to the next chapter, where we'll discuss some alternatives for getting professional help with your financial situation. There are several different types of assistance you should consider. Let's take a look.

STEPS IN THE RIGHT DIRECTION

1   Maximize your income: get more hours at work, take on an outside job, sell stuff you don't need.

2. Minimize your expenses: if you have too much house, sell it; sell a vehicle, if possible; downsize your lifestyle.

3. Talk with your lenders: Can you obtain hardship considerations? Would your mortgage holder consider forbearance or other special restructuring?

4. Consider a home equity loan (but be careful!).

5. Consider borrowing from family or friends.

6. Come up with a debt payoff plan.

Chapter 3

GETTING HELP

GUIDEPOSTS

In this chapter, you'll learn

- How to select a credit counseling agency
- Whether you should consider a debt consolidation loan
- The pros and cons of hiring a debt settlement company

You've probably seen the ads on TV: "We can cut your credit card debt in half . . ." "Get your life back; call this toll-free number . . ." and "XYZ Debt Consultants made the harassing calls stop . . ." In the last few years, right along with banks' aggressive marketing of credit and the resulting mushrooming of consumer debt, we have seen a dramatic growth in the numbers of companies advertising themselves as debt consultants, debt negotiators, and other titles signaling that they offer debt relief alternatives to people who find themselves in over their heads. As with any growth industry, the debt settlement and debt negotiation business has its share of the good, the bad, and the ugly. Once you decide this is the route you want to pursue, you still need to be careful and exercise discernment. In other words, you shouldn't call the first toll-free number that appears on your television screen and sign on the dotted line based on a quick sales presentation. A good debt settlement, credit counseling, or debt negotiation firm can definitely help you work with creditors to improve your financial situation. But, as with any scenario involving large sums of money and desperate individuals, there are plenty of unscrupulous operators out there who are perfectly willing to take your money and not give you the help they've advertised. That's the last thing you need. So how do you tell the difference between the quality firms and the sleaze vendors? Keep reading.

CREDIT COUNSELING: THE TRADITIONAL FAVORITE

Credit counseling had its beginnings in the United States during the early 1950s, the period of the postwar economic boom. With the dramatic increase in lending that powered a dramatic expansion in home construction and other consumer lending, creditors and lawmakers recognized a need for an organization that could advocate for the credit granting industry and also work with consumers who needed assistance. The National Foundation for Credit Counseling (NFCC) was created in 1951, and the first local credit counseling franchises began operating in the early 1960s, providing financial education and credit counseling to consumers.

In addition to the NFCC, the principal industry organization for consumer credit counseling firms is the Association of Independent Consumer Credit Counseling Agencies (AICCCA), founded in 1993. At the very least, any credit counseling or debt management organization you consider working with should be a member of one of these trade groups.

Because the credit counseling industry was essentially the idea of lenders, and those lenders still provide the primary financial support for credit counseling firms (more on this later), it should come as no surprise that the principal objective of most credit counseling firms is to enroll you in a debt management plan (DMP) that will eventually result in full repayment of your debt.

So what's the advantage to the consumer? For starters, when you enroll in an approved DMP with an accredited credit counseling agency, the collection calls will stop. The agency will contact your lenders to inform them that you are enrolled in a DMP and are in the process of satisfying your debt. As long as you fulfill the terms of your DMP, including making timely payments for the typical five-year term, the collection calls will be halted.

Next, once you enroll in credit counseling and begin making timely payments on your DMP, your past-due accounts will often be "re-aged." This means that the lender agrees to remove late payment notations from your credit record and, as long as you remain in good standing with your DMP, you'll end the process with a cleaner credit report. Note that re-aging the account does not remove negative entries that originated from the period prior to enrollment in the DMP, but it does give consumers the ability to get a fresh start and begin rebuilding a good credit record. The fact of your credit counseling will be on your report (a negative), but it will also show your successful completion of the DMP (a positive).

Finally, because all your debt is usually consolidated into a single payment under the terms of your DMP, you gain the simplicity of a single monthly payment, rather than multiple payments to different creditors. Not only that, but the payment is often less than the sum of your former payments. One reason for this is that the credit counseling company essentially works for the banks issuing the credit, so lenders will accept lower payments from consumers who are enrolled in a DMP. The other reason is that credit counseling agencies are usually able to get your interest rates reduced, allowing not only more money to go toward the debt's principal balance, but also decreased payments overall.

You may be wondering, "What's the downside? I get a lower monthly payment and lower interest rates, the collection calls stop, and I rebuild my credit record. What's not to like?" Not only that, but since most credit counseling organizations are set up as nonprofits, it seems as if there should be very little risk or worry for consumers, as long as they maintain their DMPs in a timely manner. While this is true, there are some details you should be aware of before working with such an organization.

First of all, credit counseling firms receive consumers' payments on their DMPs and forward those funds to the issuing lenders—less a portion called the "fair-share payment," which stays with the credit counseling agency. In other words, the lenders, in essence, are paying the credit counseling firms a fee to collect and distribute payments from consumers. Formerly, fair-share payments were around 15 percent of the amount collected, but in recent years, payments have reportedly fallen into a 4 to 10 percent range.

Next, credit counseling firms can collect up-front fees from consumers. Whereas agencies affiliated with the NFCC—usually designated as "Consumer Credit Counseling Services," or "CCCSs"—typically charge a nominal setup fee of around $10, some agencies can charge significantly more.

Finally, nonprofit credit counselors may solicit voluntary donations from consumers who are enrolled in DMPs. These contributions are reportedly to be used to defray costs associated with setting up and administering DMPs and providing credit and financial counseling, according to the terms of the organization's nonprofit charter. However, some consumers have reported difficulty in extricating themselves from these so-called voluntary programs.

A number of state and federal entities have begun investigating the practices of some nonprofit credit counseling agencies. Some have had their nonprofit status revoked. Among the complaints filed by consumers against these firms are high up-front fees, nonrefundable or compulsory donations, failure to deliver promised financial counseling services, and failure to provide implied benefits. In fact, some consumers have actually completed their DMPs, only to discover that their credit score was lower than when they started! Before working with an organization, be sure to do your research and verify its reputation.

Finding a Reliable Credit Counseling Company

There are many good organizations that deliver the services and benefits they advertise. One way you can help yourself narrow the field down to some of the companies that are more worthy of your trust is by working only with agencies accredited by and affiliated with one of the principal credit counseling industry trade groups: the NFCC or the AICCCA. Take some time to browse each organization's website to learn a bit more about it and to get a list of accredited and/or licensed credit counselors in your area. Go to www.ASurvivalGuidetoDebt.com for a list of reputable organizations.

SURVIVAL TIP:
LEARN ABOUT LICENSED CREDIT COUNSELORS

Visit the websites of these principal credit counseling trade groups to learn about and get a list of accredited and/or licensed credit counselors in your area:

• www.ASurvivalGuidetoDebt.com

• National Foundation for Credit Counseling (NFCC): www.nfcc.org

• Association of Independent Consumer Credit Counseling Agencies (AICCCA): www.aiccca.org

Code of Ethics

In order to maintain good standing with its trade organization, a credit counseling firm must typically subscribe to and comply with a code of ethics or conduct in its dealings with consumers. Additionally, many states regulate or license credit counseling firms operating within their borders. Before you sign up with any credit counseling firm, it's a good idea to ask if they have a written copy of their code of conduct or a web page from which it can be easily downloaded. Find out about your state's licensing or regulatory requirements for consumer credit counseling (some states do not regulate or require a license for credit counselors).

Don't Forget the Counseling!

Many consumers are so focused on getting out from under debt that they may forget one of the principal reasons credit counseling was developed: to provide sound financial planning and education for consumers to enable them to make better decisions in the future. Don't be in such a hurry to ask about DMPs and halting creditor calls that you forget to learn about the credit and financial counseling services the firm offers.

Keep in mind that the whole idea of working through a credit counselor is to position yourself to make better financial decisions in the future. Otherwise, you're wasting one of the best potential long-term benefits of the program. When you ask about the counseling services, pay close attention to the answer; if the representative seems at all disinterested or too eager to get you signed up for a DMP, take a step back. Reputable credit counselors place as much emphasis on providing consumer education as they do on collecting your money and forwarding it to creditors.

Check Their Reputation

You wouldn't go to a restaurant that had a reputation for bad food or lousy service, would you? The same principle applies to choosing a credit counseling firm. One way you can get an idea of the company's reputation is by checking with your local Better Business Bureau. For one thing, any firm you deal with should ideally be a BBB member. Also, any complaints filed against the firm will be a matter of record with the BBB. Your state attorney general's office and local or state consumer protection agencies are also good places to check for information about negative experiences consumers may have had with your prospective credit counselor. The National Association of Attorneys General has a website (www.naag.org) that you can use to get in touch with your state attorney general's office.

If you do surface complaints against a provider you're considering, don't be afraid or embarrassed to ask about them. After all, you're potentially placing a significant amount of trust in them with very important financial matters; they shouldn't mind satisfying your need to know about their dependability. Besides, asking about the situation gives them the benefit of the doubt; it signals that you understand there are two sides to most stories. By listening to their side, you demonstrate the same sort of fairness you'd expect from them in their dealings with you.

What About the Fees?

Everybody knows there's no such thing as a free lunch. Still, you have a right to know, before signing up for anything, how much you will pay for the services the credit counselor is providing. How much of your monthly payment into the DMP will go toward satisfying your debts, and how much will go to the credit counselor? Are there setup fees? If so, how much are they? Are there any other fees, contributions, or payments expected of you as a part of the program? How are program fees calculated? Remember, this is your money, and you have a right to know the answers to these questions. Ask for a printed schedule of fees and the services they pay for.

Some Additional Cautions

Just because you enroll in a DMP with an accredited or licensed credit counselor, you can't shift all further responsibility for your situation onto your credit counseling firm. First of all, if you do decide to enroll in a DMP, it should be because you and your credit counselor have carefully examined your situation and determined that a DMP really is the best way for you to get your debt settled. DMPs are not the only alternative, however, and if you get into one, you need to be satisfied, on the basis of sound analysis of your situation, that a DMP is the best way for you to go.

SURVIVAL TIP:
LEARN ABOUT CONSUMER
CREDIT ISSUES

The U.S. Federal Trade Commission has a series of free publications on consumer credit issues, including "Fiscal Fitness: Choosing a Credit Counselor," and "Knee Deep in Debt." Both are available on the FTC website (www.ftc. gov/credit) or by calling 1-800-FTC-HELP (382-4357).

Most DMPs are set up on a five-year term. This has advantages and disadvantages: The main advantage, from the perspective of most consumers, is that the five-year term allows for smaller monthly payments, allowing a bit more breathing room in the month's cash flow. The principal disadvantage is that such a long payout often proves difficult for many consumers to complete. If they are unable to maintain the payment schedule until completion of the DMP, they often find themselves right back in the same situation they entered credit counseling to escape. As a matter of fact, according to some estimates, up to 80 percent of those who enroll in DMPs with credit counseling firms are unable to complete their plans.

Another thing to keep in mind is that credit counseling firms, as noted previously, get most of their money from the banks that issue credit cards and other forms of consumer debt. If you are in credit counseling, you will, in most cases, pay back 100 percent of the debt that is enrolled in your DMP. For consumers struggling with a heavy load of both secured and unsecured debt, this can prove difficult or impossible. There are other options that do not require 100 percent payback; as noted in chapter 2, for example, some credit card companies will offer a partial payback as a settlement option in cases of demonstrable financial hardship. This is one reason you should not automatically assume that a DMP is the best way to settle your debt.

Keeping Your Counselor Honest

If you do enroll in a DMP with an accredited or licensed credit counselor, you should commit not only to making your monthly payments on time and in full but also to closely examining your monthly statements to be certain that your payments are being applied to your debt and that agreed-upon communication between your credit counselor and your creditors is taking place. Some consumers have complained that because of the timing of payments from the credit counselor to the creditors, they continued to accumulate late payments or other negative credit notes on their credit histories, even though they paid into the DMP on time each month. This is where your personal responsibility for your situation comes into play. Don't defer responsibility to your credit counselor, even if the company has an excellent reputation. Those statements are provided to you for a reason—read them!

Some credit card companies offer a partial payback as a settlement option in cases of demonstrable financial hardship.

Here's another important note: be sure your credit counselor provides you with proof that your creditors have accepted your DMP. It seems obvious, but unless a creditor agrees that your performance of the terms of the DMP is an acceptable way for you to satisfy your obligations, your payments into the DMP will not make any positive difference on your credit report.

SURVIVAL TIP:
ASK A PROSPECTIVE
CREDIT COUNSELOR

- What services do you offer?
- Are you licensed to offer your services in my state?
- Do you offer free information?
- Will I have a formal written agreement or contract with you?
- What are the qualifications and training of your counselors? Are they accredited or certified?
- Have other consumers been satisfied with your services?
- What are your fees? Are there monthly or setup fees?
- How are your employees paid? Are they paid more if I sign up for certain programs or services?
- How will you ensure the privacy of any confidential information I give you?

(Source: www.ftc.gov.)

As previously mentioned, credit counseling and DMPs are not the only alternative for settling your debts. They do provide a way that has worked for many consumers to rehabilitate their credit and get back on track financially, but for some of the reasons shown earlier, they are not necessarily the best option for all situations. Let's look at some other options to manage your debt.

DEBT CONSOLIDATION LOANS: SHOULD YOU, OR SHOULDN'T YOU?

We've already briefly mentioned this topic in chapters 1 and 2. You may recall that many debt consolidation loans work by taking out a loan secured by your home equity or other assets, then using the proceeds to pay off high-interest loans—usually unsecured debt, like credit cards. Because the consolidation loan is secured debt, you generally get more favorable repayment terms, like lower interest rates and longer repayment schedules. This means that you can replace higher monthly payments with lower ones, giving you a way to work out your debt with a little less strain on your monthly budget. Not only that, but instead of making multiple payments to several creditors, you're making a single payment each month to gradually reduce your debt. Sounds great, right?

But remember, another way of looking at these types of debt consolidation loans is by recognizing that they are a way of converting unsecured debt into debt secured by assets that may be among your most important— like your home. Owing money to credit card companies is bad, but losing the equity in your home can sometimes be even worse. Before you get serious about using your equity to secure a debt consolidation loan, you've got to do the math. You must carefully analyze the anticipated monthly payment's effect on your short-term and long-term budget, and you must, above all, be convinced of your ability to maintain the payments and *not run up additional unsecured debt* until the loan is paid off. Otherwise, you've just exchanged the frustration of dealing with an unsecured creditor for the very real possibility of losing your home.

A Real-World Example

Let's take a look at a debt consolidation scenario using figures from the credit card statements of a friend of mine. Hank's situation is not too different from many folks who are looking for a way to save on their debt. He has four credit cards with a total balance of $48,300, and a personal loan from his credit union with a balance of $8,000. The figure on the next page shows how Hank's unsecured debts and payments break down.

Hank's Unsecured Debts

Source of Debt	Balance Owed	Interest Rate	Monthly Payment
Credit Card 1	$11,000	12%	$290
Credit Card 2	$11,600	7.99%	$208
Credit Card 3	$14,700	6.99%	$280
Credit Card 4	$11,000	14.99%	$216
Personal Loan	$8,000	6.99%	$200
TOTAL	$56,300		$1,194

Hank, fortunately, has enough equity in his home to cover the amount of his unsecured debt. He wants to save some money on his monthly payments, so he talks to his friendly neighborhood banker. The banker looks at Hank's situation and his credit report and agrees to make Hank a debt consolidation loan at the annual rate of 10 percent, with his home equity as collateral. Hank signs on the dotted line and uses the loan proceeds to pay off all the credit cards and the personal loan. His monthly payment on the $56,300 loan is $800, a monthly savings of almost $400.

Is Hank happy? Well, it depends. On the one hand, he's got an extra $394 per month to use for things other than making payments on his debt. On the other hand, according to the amortization schedule in his new loan contract, he has 107 payments (8 years and 11 months) until he's finished with the debt. If he missed payments to his credit card companies, they could call him, add late fees, and increase his interest rates. If he got far enough behind, they could sue him. But if he misses payments on his new loan, he could lose his house.

Let's say Hank is a good boy: he makes his payments on time and keeps the credit cards put away for the nine years until the debt is paid off. He will have paid an extra $12,000 or so in interest during the extended life of the secured debt consolidation loan, but it's also possible that his CPA will tell him he can deduct the interest on the loan as mortgage interest because the loan, combined with his primary mortgage, doesn't exceed the amount of his home equity. (NOTE: the deductibility of second-lien interest is subject to a number of variables, including your tax bracket and the actual value of your equity; consult a tax professional before including it as a deductible expense on your tax return.) So, if he factors in his tax savings versus the additional interest he will pay, he might come out okay at the end.

But what if Hank succumbs to the temptation to use those credit cards that now have a zero balance? He would then be paying on the consolidation loan *and* making payments on new, unsecured debt. He would well be on his way to putting himself even deeper in the hole than he was at the beginning—and he no longer has much, if any, equity in his home.

FINANCIAL GPS

"You can't borrow your way out of debt."

By the way, I prepared this example using a free online debt consolidation loan calculator I found by doing an Internet search on the term *debt consolidation calculator*. Spending some time with a similar tool and a carefully prepared monthly budget can help you decide if a debt consolidation loan is a good idea in your particular situation.

DEBT SETTLEMENT AND DEBT NEGOTIATION: HEROES, VILLAINS, AND HOW TO TELL THE DIFFERENCE

The rapid increase in consumer debt during the past decade has spawned a new player on the consumer debt relief stage: debt settlement and debt negotiation firms. Although there are legitimate debt settlement firms that have helped consumers in trouble, there are many horror stories on the Internet and elsewhere of people who have spent large amounts of money with fly-by-night operators who promised to make their debt problems go away, only to find themselves facing legal action with no professional assistance in sight. Let me make this point very clearly: Debt settlement is a legal way for you to satisfy your creditors and perhaps significantly reduce the amount you must pay back, but it is not easy, quick, or inexpensive. Any person or company who represents otherwise should be viewed with extreme caution.

How Debt Settlement Works—In Theory

The main principle behind debt settlement and debt negotiation is summed up by the old adage "Half a loaf is better than none." Your unsecured creditors know that if your financial situation gets bad enough, you could file bankruptcy (more on this later), and they would very likely end up with nothing. Accordingly—once you are far enough behind that they are convinced you'll have trouble paying back 100 percent of what you owe—they are sometimes willing to accept less than the full amount and still declare the account settled. This, in fact, is the idea behind the hardship plans discussed in chapter 2.

Debt settlement is a legal way for you to satisfy creditors and perhaps reduce the amount you pay back.

Note that I refer specifically to unsecured creditors—primarily, credit card companies and holders of personal loans that are not collateralized. Secured debt is a different ball game, as I'll discuss more fully a bit later, and the consequences of nonpayment are much different.

Let's say you've fallen on tough times because of one of the big four: unexpected expenses and bad financial habits, job loss, grave illness, and divorce or death of a principal wage earner. You're having trouble keeping up with things like your house and car payments, and you've gotten farther and farther behind on your credit cards. In a debt settlement, you convince your creditor to accept a part of the balance—50 percent, let's say—as full payment. You agree to pay this amount in a lump sum at a specific point in the future. Your creditor puts its agreement with the terms in writing, you send the money at the appropriate time, and the account is considered as "settled" by your creditor. Your credit report reflects a settled account with a zero balance due, though the late or missed payments will still show, in most cases. The creditor gets some, if not all, of what you originally owed. Everybody walks away with something. This, in principle, is what constitutes a debt settlement.

If your debt problems are primarily caused by your delinquency with a single creditor, you might be well advised to work directly with your creditor rather than talking to a debt settlement firm. Sometimes, credit card companies will even offer to reduce your interest rate during the repayment period covered by the hardship plan. If you're successful in negotiating a hardship repayment plan that allows you to pay back less than the full debt, you will have accomplished for yourself the same thing that a debt settlement company would charge you serious money to do.

However, if you have several creditors you need to settle with, things get more complicated. In this situation, if you decide to pursue debt settlement, you may actually need someone experienced in working with creditors who can run interference for you. This is where a dependable, professional debt settlement firm can be helpful. The operative words here are *dependable* and *professional*.

Finding the Princes, Avoiding the Toads

Unfortunately, the debt settlement business is in its formative years, and the process of separating the wheat from the chaff is still ongoing. Here again, though, as with the previous discussion about finding a good credit counselor, there are some things you can do to increase your chances of avoiding the sharks and the shysters who only want to collect a fee.

Though the debt settlement industry is still in a bit of an awkward phase, responsible professionals within the trade have recognized the need for associations that can develop and provide standards, codes of ethical and professional behavior, guidelines for consumer protection, and public advocacy for both consumers in need of debt settlement and the industry seeking to provide the service. The principal trade groups for the debt settlement industry are the Association of Settlement Companies (TASC) and U.S. Organizations for Bankruptcy Alternatives (USOBA). Each of these groups provides codes of ethics and professional standards for companies or individuals affiliated with or accredited by them. Also, the International Association of Professional Debt Arbitrators (IAPDA) is a professional organization that provides education, certification, and training for persons providing debt management services. Go to www.ASurvivalGuidetoDebt.com for a list of reputable settlement organizations.

SURVIVAL TIP:
VISIT THE WEBSITES OF MAJOR DEBT SETTLEMENT TRADE AND TRAINING GROUPS

- The Association of Settlement Companies (TASC): www.tascsite.org
- U.S. Organizations for Bankruptcy Alternatives (USOBA): www.usoba.org
- International Association of Professional Debt Arbitrators (IAPDA), which provides training, certification, and education for individuals in the industry: www.iapda.org
- Or go to www.ASurvivalGuidetoDebt.com

Even though certification or accreditation by a trade group is no guarantee that you're working with an up-front, honest firm, it's definitely better than nothing. At the very least, you have some sort of umbrella organization, in addition to the Better Business Bureau or the Federal Trade Commission, to complain to in the event of problems.

As with credit counseling firms, you need to ask lots of questions and request lots of written confirmation from any debt settlement firm you are considering employing to help you negotiate with your creditors. Following are some of the most important questions you can ask:

- How much will I pay you, and what happens to the money I send you each month?

- Can you provide documentation of settlements you've successfully negotiated for other people in my situation?

- When will you communicate with creditors on my behalf?

Let's take a look at these questions and why they are especially important with regard to working with a debt settlement company.

How Much Will I Pay You, and What Happens to the Money I Send You Each Month? Unlike credit counseling firms, debt settlement companies make no pretense or claim of being nonprofit; their services are provided on a fee basis, and the fee is paid by the consumer. The reason it is so important to understand the debt settlement company's fee structure is that, also unlike credit counseling firms, debt settlement firms are not geared toward 100 percent repayment, nor are they funded by banks or consumers' payments into a DMP. Instead, the money you send to a debt settlement firm goes into a trust account with the goal of accumulating funds that can be used for a payoff. In other words, you are no longer sending any money to your creditor; instead, you are building up a cash reserve that will be used at some point in the future to make a lump sum payment of a portion of your balance that the creditor will accept as final settlement for the account. Halting all payments to the creditors is central to the debt settlement model. The reasoning goes that as long as you are paying money in any amount to the creditor, they have little incentive, in most cases, to consider a partial payment as a settlement. Remember the basic tenet of debt settlement, from the lender's perspective: "Half a loaf is better than none." If the lender has any reason to expect the full loaf, it won't settle for half.

The money you send to the trust account is your payoff fund; therefore, it's very important for you to understand how the debt settlement company treats it. The reason you should insist on a debt settlement company that works with a trust account, by the way, is that you don't want the debt settlement company itself holding or controlling your assets. However, even debt settlement companies that use a trustee still charge fees for their services, and they typically collect their fees before disbursing any funds to your creditors. Usually, these charges will include a setup fee for the trust account and an administrative or service fee for the debt settlement company. It is very important that you know the amounts of these fees and how and when they are deducted from the money you send. The problem is that, by their own admission, debt settlement companies have multiple methods for calculating, allocating, and collecting fees. Still, any reputable company should be willing to clearly communicate its method, including printed documentation.

Can You Provide Documentation of Settlements You've Successfully Negotiated for Other People in My Situation? The reason for asking this should be obvious: track records are important. No company can or should hand out clients' confidential financial information to the public, of course, but debt settlement firms base their appeals on their ability to settle debts for significant savings over what consumers could negotiate on their own. A reliable company should be able and willing to provide proof of its successes on behalf of other customers.

Not only that, but it's important for you to verify that the company you are considering will be doing the actual settlement negotiations rather than outsourcing them to a third party; its name, and not a third party's, should appear on the settlement documents. This is important because in order to receive the client support you will want during the negotiation and settlement process, you need to be dealing directly with the entity that is doing the actual work on your behalf.

When Will You Communicate with Creditors on My Behalf? This question gets at one of the stickiest points in the debt settlement process. Most debt settlement companies will not actually get directly involved in working with your creditors until you have enough or almost enough money in your trust account for them to make an offer of settlement. Not only that, but they will not represent you in any legal actions surrounding your debt. Their mission is very specific: to negotiate with your creditors and attempt to get them to agree to a payoff amount less than the full balance owed.

This means that during the time you are building up your payoff fund—a period that can easily be a year or more—you are the only one who will be communicating with your creditors about your debt, and you will probably continue to get calls from collectors (although, if you read chapter 1, you at least know how to get them to stop calling you at work). Is it possible that a creditor might get tired of waiting and file a lawsuit against you? Yes. Will your debt settlement company represent you in that lawsuit? No.

On a more positive note, most competent debt settlement firms have developed working relationships with many of the larger lenders, and they know more than most consumers about how forbearing each lender is likely to be. The reliable debt settlement companies also have a good working knowledge of the laws surrounding credit and collection practices, and they can

Hiring a debt settlement firm does not relieve you of the legal responsibility for your debt.

offer informed advice to consumers about how best to work with lenders to avoid legal action.

But make no mistake: hiring a debt settlement firm does not relieve you of the legal responsibility for your debt. Any debt settlement firm that makes easy claims about quick settlements, deep discounts on payoff amounts, or problem-free negotiations with creditors should be viewed with skepticism.

Now do you see why those late-night TV ads can be so dangerous?

Debt Settlement and Your Credit Rating

A final point about debt settlement: it is not intended nor does it function as a way to salvage your credit rating. Once you take the step of halting payments to your creditors, you begin accumulating negative notations on your credit report. Even if you are successful in settling your accounts by making discounted payoffs, these negative reports will still be in your credit history. For reasons that I will discuss more fully in a later section, your credit rating may not be the most important consideration at this point in your financial life, but for those consumers who are willing to do almost anything to preserve as high a credit score as possible, debt settlement may not be the way to go.

Another thing that many consumers don't realize is that debt settlement can actually create taxable "income." When a credit card company forgives some portion of the debt you originally owed them, they may actually send you a 1099, showing the amount as income paid to you. You would need to report this on your tax return and possibly pay taxes on it. You may want to consult with your tax adviser on the potential tax consequences of any debt settlement before you agree to it.

FINANCIAL GPS

If your credit card company agrees to a settlement that is less than 100 percent repayment, they can send you a 1099, and you may be required to pay income tax on the difference between the full amount and the payoff.

As I mentioned at the beginning of the section, the debt settlement business has been around a relatively short time, as compared to credit counseling companies that are members of the NFCC or the AICCCA. There is very little regulation covering debt settlement firms, and their fee structures and rates are anything but uniform. Not only that, but there are a number of less-than-up-front firms that are more interested in collecting fees than in helping you work constructively with your creditors.

However, there are good, professional debt settlement firms out there that are doing their best for their clients. If you find one of these companies, they can often help you settle your accounts with creditors for less than the full amount you owe. If that's an advantage you need, then ask lots of questions, try to get referrals from other people they've helped, and read the agreement you have with them carefully before you sign. Now that you know some of the questions to ask, you can at least go into the relationship with your eyes wide open.

You may recall that in the beginning of the section explaining how debt settlement works, I made the statement that I was referring specifically to unsecured debt like credit cards and uncollateralized personal loans. Then

I said, "Secured debt is a different ball game, and the consequences of non-payment are much different."

Now it's time to look at some of those consequences, along with the laws that govern the relationship between creditors and debtors. If you're in debt trouble, it's more important than ever for you to know what was in some of that fine print on your credit card agreements and mortgage contracts. It's also vital for you to know both your rights as a consumer and a debtor and your lenders' rights as holders of secured or unsecured debt. To start learning, turn to the next chapter.

STEPS IN THE RIGHT DIRECTION

1. If you've tried to resolve your debt problems on your own but have been unsuccessful, consider working with a credit counseling firm or debt settlement company.

2. Find a reputable credit counseling organization by going to www.ASurvivalGuidetoDebt.com or the NFCC or AICCCA websites.

3. Find a reputable debt settlement company by going to www. ASurvivalGuidetoDebt.com or the TASC, USOBA, or IAPDA websites.

4. Ask your credit counselor or debt settlement company lots of questions to make sure you feel comfortable with the organization and the person you are working with.

5. Be honest with the organization you work with so that they can help you develop a beneficial, workable plan.

6. Consider applying for a debt consolidation loan. Only obtain this type of loan if you feel very confident that you'll be able to pay it back; otherwise, you could lose the collateral (your house or vehicle) in your attempt to pay off unsecured debts.

Chapter 4

YOUR RIGHTS, THEIR RIGHTS

GUIDEPOSTS

In this chapter, you'll learn

- How different types of debt impact your financial situation

- The principal laws that protect you in your dealings with bill collectors, credit card–company billing practices, and with your credit rating, its calculation, and uses by third parties

- What rights you have as a homeowner under your state's homestead laws

- The basics of foreclosure and repossession

Before you begin reading this chapter, it might be a good idea for you to get out the personal balance sheet that you developed in chapter 1. As we discuss the various types of debt, you may want to review your own situation and see how the principles we discuss will apply in your situation, and also what amount of your indebtedness they cover. Whether your debt is secured or unsecured makes a huge difference in the alternatives available to your creditor and also to the priority you should give the debt as you work out your repayment and recovery plan. For your own protection, you need to know what is permissible for creditors to do in their attempts to collect a debt, and what is not. You also need to have a general idea of the protections afforded to you by law as a debtor, especially as those protections relate to your most important assets.

THE TWO BASIC TYPES OF DEBT

As discussed in chapter 1, almost all consumer debt can be classified as either secured or unsecured. A secured debt is one that is backed by collateral—a home or other real estate, or a vehicle, for example. Unsecured debt is backed only by the consumer's creditworthiness and promise to pay. This is the category that almost all consumer debt other than mortgages or vehicle loans falls into. It includes credit cards, most personal loans, medical bills, and many—but not all—store charge cards.

Let's start by looking at the main types of secured debt held by most consumers, and what the issuers of that debt can do in the event of nonpayment.

Secured Debt

It bears repeating: your secured debt should almost always be your first priority when you allocate your cash flow. If you have to cut back or delay a payment, you should make every attempt to do it somewhere other than on your secured debt because this type of debt typically is backed by your most important possessions.

Primary Mortgage Loans. For most of us, this is the most important debt we have, because it represents our home—most often, our single most significant asset. Your mortgage loan is collateralized by your house, so the lender has the right to take back the property securing the loan if you stop making payments. They can foreclose on the mortgage, have you evicted, and sell your house to someone else. In spite of the fact that your mortgage contract is the final, binding document for *your particular mortgage,* in broad terms, most mortgage loans are very similar because they're governed by law; the main principle that underlies all mortgage loans is that the lender is advancing you, the borrower, the money to purchase a piece of property, and you, the borrower, agree to pay back the money according to the terms, amounts, and due dates set forth in the mortgage contract. If you fail in this responsibility, the lender can take back the property. It's just that simple.

However, because a secure home is such a fundamental need, many laws control the timing and process by which a lender can foreclose on a mortgage and take possession of a primary residence. In most states, many of these laws are categorized as homestead laws, or homestead exemption laws. Most of these laws are in the form of statutes or actually form portions of the constitutions of the states in which they apply.

Three basic protections are afforded by most homestead laws:

1. They prevent the forced sale of a home to meet certain creditor demands.

2. They provide protections for the spouse of a deceased homeowner.

3. They provide certain exemptions from property taxes.

Some states automatically extend homestead protection to any primary residence. In others, homeowners must apply for and receive the exemption. Usually, homestead exemptions are limited to a single property, even if other properties are owned outside the geographical jurisdiction of the law. In some states, a homestead can include a certain area of land, such as a farm or ranch. Homestead laws were typically enacted during America's agrarian past; consequently, a certain number of draft animals and other livestock can also be included in the protection afforded to the homestead. For example, in Texas, where I live, up to 200 acres can be included in the exemption for a family's rural homestead, along with two horses and a saddle and bridle for each, twelve head of cattle, sixty head of "other types of livestock," and 120 fowl. Quite a menagerie!

The important thing to remember about homestead laws is that they only protect your home and certain personal assets from being seized by creditors *other than* your primary or secondary mortgage lender. Furthermore, they cannot protect you from debts for property or income taxes, and they will not protect property that is seized to satisfy court-ordered child support or alimony payments.

Because each state's homestead laws and the amounts of property exempted by them differ so widely, you should definitely find out as much as you can about your state's laws before basing any decisions on the rights granted by the homestead laws. The website of your state attorney general's office is probably a good place to begin your research. You might also want to speak with an attorney who specializes in the laws of your state that govern real estate and home ownership.

The Foreclosure Process: An Overview. By using the process of foreclosure, a mortgage lender can take possession of a primary residence from a homeowner who is in default. As with homestead laws, foreclosure processes vary by state and can take as little as one month or as long as seven months to complete. However, there are some general principles that are consistent, and a basic knowledge of these is important if you are getting behind on your house payments.

A lender can legally begin foreclosure proceedings when the first payment is missed, but that usually doesn't happen because, as I said earlier, lenders really don't want to foreclose on properties. Foreclosures often cost lenders between 20 and 60 percent of the face value of the mortgage loan, and they will resort to the process only when they believe they have no other means to protect their investment. Typically, then, the first missed payment will generate a friendly reminder, at most, with a request for the payment plus a late fee. The next missed payment will often prompt a more sternly worded warning and perhaps one or two phone calls, and by the time your mortgage is three months behind, the lender will usually issue official notice that it intends to begin foreclosure proceedings.

There are two main types of foreclosure proceedings: judicial (through the courts and overseen by a judge) and nonjudicial, or by a process known as "power of sale," which is granted in the loan contract and does not go through the court. In states that allow foreclosure through power of sale, the borrower agrees in the mortgage contract (or "deed of trust," as it is usually called in such states) that the lender has the right to sell the property to correct any deficiency in payment of the loan. Nonjudicial, or power-of-sale, foreclosure favors the lender because it occurs on a faster time line than judicial foreclosure.

SURVIVAL TIP:
RESEARCH HOW TO AVOID FORECLOSURE

For information and resources for avoiding foreclosure in your state, go to the U.S. Department of Housing and Urban Development website: www.hud.gov/local/index.cfm.

In most states, the first step in nonjudicial foreclosure is the lender's filing of a Notice of Deficiency with the court of the county in which the property is located. A copy of the Notice of Deficiency is mailed to the homeowner's last known address, putting the homeowner on notice that he or she has a certain amount of time to correct the deficiency by bringing the loan current. This time period varies by state, but three months is somewhat typical.

If the deficiency is not corrected within the time period specified in the Notice of Deficiency, a date will be set for the sale of the property. Notice of the pending sale and its date is posted at the county courthouse and also on the property. In some states, the notice of sale must also appear in local newspapers a certain number of times—once weekly for three consecutive weeks, for example.

During all of these proceedings, the homeowner has the right to reinstate the mortgage by bringing the loan current; this right usually expires five days before the sale date. If the mortgage is not reinstated, on the date of sale the property will be auctioned on the steps of the county courthouse to the highest bidder with enough cash to complete the purchase. The winning bidder will receive the deed to the property and will immediately assume ownership. If there is no successful bidder, ownership of the property reverts to the foreclosing mortgage holder.

As I have already emphasized several times, communication with your lender is essential if you want to keep your home. It's better for you to begin talking with your mortgage holder before your loan is seriously in default, but even if you are already two or even three months behind, honest communication about your circumstances, resources, and intentions can not only delay your lender's decision to pursue foreclosure but also encourage the lender to work with you on a solution that can keep you in your house and help you get your loan back in good standing. In chapter 2 we discussed some of the tools available to lenders in working with homeowners in trouble: temporary forbearance, reinstatement, repayment, and loan modification. In order to have these options, however, you must convince your lender that you really want to work cooperatively to get back on track. To do that, you must communicate.

RESPA and Foreclosure. Though it is primarily concerned with the front end of the mortgage loan process—fair disclosure in lending and settlement of a new loan—the Real Estate Settlement Procedures Act (RESPA) affords significant protections to consumers that can also have implications for the foreclosure process, especially in cases where the lender has cut corners or been less than forthcoming in soliciting or closing the loan. If you have any reason to believe that your mortgage lender failed to disclose certain charges or fees related to your home loan, or unfairly required you to purchase certain services or products as a condition of granting your loan, you may be entitled to damages under the provisions of RESPA. Additionally, if your lender fails to make required disbursements from your escrow account for expenses like property taxes, insurance, or other related costs, you may have grounds to file a complaint based on RESPA.

This law also requires your lender to send you information annually about your escrow account and how it is calculated and disbursed. If your lender has not provided such information, you may have the basis for a complaint. Finally, RESPA rules require that if your lender sells your loan to another mortgage provider, you must be notified in writing at least fifteen days before the effective date of the loan transfer. Some homeowners have sent payments to an original mortgagor, not realizing their loan has been sold. Because the new owner of the loan either never received the payment or received it late, the loan was technically in default. If the homeowner can prove that no notification was received from the selling lender in the approved time frame, a RESPA complaint may be filed.

The first step in pursuing a RESPA complaint against a lender is sending a "qualified written request" (QWR) to the lender, stating your complaint and including any supporting documentation. A sample QWR can be found at the U.S. Department of Housing and Urban Development's website: www.hud.gov. Type "RESPA" into the search field and browse the results. You can also call HUD toll-free at 800-669-9777.

Once you have sent your QWR to the lender, it has twenty days to provide written acknowledgment of receipt and an additional sixty days to correct any errors that negatively impacted your account. During this time, the lender must also provide you with written clarification of the dispute and its resolution. Importantly, during this period of time, the lender may not provide information to any consumer-reporting agency about any overdue payment related to the dispute or the period during which it occurs.

If you believe you have the basis for filing a complaint against your lender under RESPA, it can buy you some additional time to work on your debt. Additionally, RESPA violations can provide the basis for negotiation of more favorable loan terms, or, at the very least, a bit of additional time to get caught up on your payments.

FINANCIAL GPS

Filing a complaint under RESPA can buy you time so you can focus on paying off your debt.

Secondary Mortgage Loans. Everything we just discussed about primary mortgage loans also applies to secondary mortgage loans, often called "second liens" or "home equity loans." Frequently used to finance home improvements, college, or debt consolidation, a secondary mortgage loan, like the primary, gives the lender the equity in your home as collateral for the loan. If you fail to make payments, the secondary mortgage holder has a claim against your house, though this claim is subordinated to the holder of the primary mortgage loan. Usually, before granting a secondary mortgage loan, the lender will require a current appraisal of the home's market value. This, compared with the amount you still owe on your primary mortgage, tells the prospective lender if the amount of equity you've accumulated in your home is enough to satisfy the new debt if the house must be sold to satisfy the obligation.

If a secondary loan is in default, most of the time the primary loan is in the same condition. The secondary lender knows it is in line behind the primary mortgage in terms of receiving money from any sale or auction proceeds in the event of foreclosure. And, just in case you're wondering, even if the primary loan is in good standing, the second lien holder can still initiate foreclosure if the secondary loan is in arrears. The property can still be auctioned off. The primary mortgage holder still gets paid first, and the second lien holder gets what's left.

This brings up another possibility facing homeowners in foreclosure: a deficiency judgment. This can occur if the proceeds from auctioning the home to the highest bidder are not enough to satisfy the indebtedness on the home. Let's say you have a home with a current market value of $100,000. Your primary mortgage balance is $70,000, giving you $30,000 in equity. You fall on difficult financial times, so you take a second lien of $20,000 to pay some bills. Things don't improve, and you get behind on your secondary mortgage. The second lien holder initiates foreclosure, and because you don't have the cash flow to bring your loan current, the house is auctioned off to the highest bidder, who pays $80,000 for the property. The primary mortgage holder gets the first $70,000, the amount you still owe on that loan. The secondary lien holder gets the remaining $10,000, but that still leaves a balance on the loan of $10,000. The second lien holder can file a suit against you for the deficiency, and if the court agrees, you will have a judgment entered against you that obligates you to pay the secondary lender the $10,000 shortfall. Not a pretty picture.

This is why homeowners should think and plan very carefully before handing anyone the hard-earned equity in their homes as collateral for any sort of loan. Remember that the homestead laws don't protect you from the claims of a creditor who holds your home or your equity in it as collateral. Unless you have absolutely no other choice, don't give another lender the ability to take your house away for nonpayment.

Vehicle Loans. A car payment is the most common other type of secured debt held by most consumers. For most of us, easy access to transportation is crucial not only to our jobs but also to our entire lifestyle.

Unfortunately for those of us making car payments, it is much easier and quicker for a lender to repossess a car or truck than it is for a mortgage holder to foreclose on a home. Though all the states have laws governing the timing and methods that may be used in repossessing a vehicle, generally, vehicle loan contracts give the lender the right to take back the car at any time the loan falls into arrears. Technically, if you are late on a single car payment, your lender may be able to come get your car.

Technically, if you are late on a single car payment, your lender may be able to come get your car.

By the way, in many states, this is also true if you fail to maintain adequate insurance on the vehicle to protect the loan value. Skipping car insurance payments can have the same consequences as missing loan payments.

As a practical matter, most reputable vehicle lenders don't want to take away your car any more than you want to lose it. A car, unlike a home, is a rapidly depreciating asset; as soon as you drive it off the dealer's lot, it's worth much less than you just paid for it. For that reason, vehicle lenders much prefer that you keep your car and make the payments on the loan as scheduled. They get full value for the car—plus a generous amount of interest—and you have ready transportation to work, school, the grocery store, or the soccer field.

Once you get behind on your payments, it's a different story. In most cases, the first late payment will generate an automatic notice from the lender, and possibly the assessment of a late fee. If you don't get caught up, most loan contracts give the lender the right to repossess the vehicle without notice at any time of the day or night and also to come onto your property to do so.

As discussed in chapter 1, most states prohibit any "breach of the peace" in the process of the repossession. This usually means that the lender may not use force, threats of force, or even enter your closed garage without your permission. If a breach of peace occurs, it can entitle you to file a complaint against the lender, who may be required to pay you damages or a penalty, especially if any harm is done to you or your property. A breach of peace may also give you a legal defense if the lender attempts to have a deficiency judgment entered against you.

SURVIVAL TIP:
RESEARCH VEHICLE REPOSSESSION

For an excellent summary of vehicle repossession and consumer rights, see the Federal Trade Commission website: www.ftc.gov/bcp/edu/pubs/consumer/autos/aut14.shtm.

If the lender or its assignee—a third party the lender may hire to repossess the vehicle—does seize your vehicle, any personal property inside the vehicle is still legally yours. Many states also require the lender to use "reasonable care" to prevent anyone from removing your personal property from the car. Usually, they must notify you about how you can retrieve your property. If you believe personal property was removed from the vehicle or disposed of without your permission, you may have grounds for legal action against the lender; you should speak with an attorney.

Once repossession has occurred, the lender may decide if it wants to keep the vehicle as payment for the debt or to sell it. The sale may be either a private transaction or a public auction. In some states the lender is required to notify you of the date of the sale or auction so that you can choose to attend and participate in the bidding.

You may also have the right to "redeem," or buy back, the car by paying the amount you are in arrears, any costs associated with the repossession, and, often, the remaining balance of the car loan. Some states also give you the right to reinstate your loan by making up the missed payments plus any repossession expenses. Naturally, you will then need to make future payments on time and in full in order to keep your reinstated loan in good standing.

If the car is sold or auctioned, most states require that the transaction be conducted in a "commercially reasonable manner." This doesn't mean that the lender must sell the car for full market value, but a price that is far enough below market value may be evidence that the sale was not "commercially reasonable" and can give you grounds for a damages claim against the creditor or a defense against a deficiency judgment.

As with foreclosure, your first move, once you start getting behind on car payments or think you may be in that position in the near future, is to communicate with your lender. Even though they can move on repossession much quicker and with less notice than home lenders, they usually would prefer not to. If a different time of the month would be easier for you to make your payments, tell your lender; often, due dates can be changed to accommodate your needs. If your lender does agree to a change in the loan contract, whether it is payment due dates, temporarily accepting partial payments, or even temporary forbearance, get it in writing. Any changes to the loan contract can become important to prove later, and verbal agreements are difficult to substantiate.

The Bottom Line on Secured Debt

Now you're in a better position to see why your secured debt needs to be prioritized ahead of your unsecured debt: if you don't make payments on secured debt, the lender can take away your collateral. Because of this basic fact, secured lenders are less likely than unsecured lenders to agree to measures like debt settlement that result in less than full repayment (though they may agree to discounted payoffs in certain circumstances). Why? Because their final recourse is always seizing the collateral and selling it to recover the balanced owed on the loan. This is why it's so important to understand the makeup of your debt before you decide which methods should be used to eliminate or satisfy it. If most of your problem debt is unsecured, you may have a range of options at your disposal, including everything from credit counseling to a hardship plan or debt settlement. But if your troubles are coming mostly from secured debt, your options are more limited, especially if you want to avoid bankruptcy.

Unsecured Debt

At roughly a trillion dollars and growing, credit card debt makes up almost 40 percent of all consumer credit in the United States, according to a Federal Reserve report issued December 5, 2008, and roughly 7 percent of total household debt, including mortgages. It grew from nearly $800 billion in 2003 to $976 billion in late 2008. Even though credit card debt shrank slightly during the second half of 2008, it still remains a huge portion of overall household debt.

Also included in the category of unsecured debt are things like department store charge cards, unsecured personal loans, unpaid medical bills, student loans, and overdue taxes (though these last two are more serious than most unsecured debt, as discussed in chapter 1). Court-ordered payments such as child support and alimony, though they are not secured by collateral, are also high-priority obligations that carry serious and almost unavoidable consequences for nonpayment.

You already know that your unsecured creditors can call you, send you demand letters, and, potentially, sue you for not keeping your accounts current. If an unsecured creditor brings a lawsuit against you and is successful in obtaining a judgment in its favor, it may be granted the right to attach liens to your personal property or even your home to enforce payment of the debt. Although such liens are subordinate to loans actually secured by the property, they can remain in force for years and have implications if you ever decide to sell or otherwise dispose of the property.

Let's take a look at some of the laws surrounding consumer debt, including three major consumer protection acts for the credit industry: the Fair Credit Reporting Act, the Fair Debt Collection Practices Act, and the Fair Credit Billing Act.

The Fair Credit Reporting Act: Your Right to Know

Your credit rating is based on almost everything that is knowable about your financial history: how much money you have in banks and credit unions; whom you owe money to and how much; how prompt you have been in making your payments; and where you work and how much you earn. All this information is collected by lenders and prospective lenders from the entries you make on loan applications, records of credit card transactions, and monthly payment information. The data are forwarded by your creditors to one or more of the three main credit bureaus in the United States: TransUnion, Experian, and Equifax.

Your credit rating is based on almost everything that is knowable about your financial history.

These companies maintain huge databases of information on consumers. They evaluate the sum total of your transactions and assign a credit score—both a "report card" on how well you meet your present obligations and a prediction of how well you'll meet them in the future. A credit score is expressed in a range of numbers called a FICO credit score (see the tables on pages 96–97). "FICO" stands for "Fair Isaac Corporation," the company that developed the first credit scoring system in the 1950s, still the most widely used means of evaluating creditworthiness. FICO credit scores can range all the way from 300 (the worst) to a "perfect" score of 850; a score of 700 or higher usually indicates good credit, and a score of 600 or less generally makes loan officers look for a way to end the meeting.

What's the practical difference your credit score makes, in dollars and cents? According to FICO's most recent figures, updated as of May 22, 2009 (www.myfico.com), a borrower with a FICO score higher than 760 can probably expect to pay an annual percentage rate of 4.501 percent on a thirty-year fixed-rate mortgage loan, based on national averages for a $300,000 loan, which yields a monthly principal/interest payment of about $1,520. The same individual can probably expect to pay $480 per month on a $50,000, fifteen-year home equity loan at 8.086 percent (see the top table on page 97). When it's time to buy a new car, this consumer can probably count on borrowing $25,000 for thirty-six months at a rate of 5.941 percent, yielding a monthly payment of $763 (see the bottom table on page 97).

By contrast, a borrower with a score in the range of 620–639 is probably looking at an annual percentage rate of 6.090 percent for the same thirty-year, $300,000 fixed-rate mortgage loan, making her payment $1,816. If she needs a $50,000, fifteen-year home equity loan, she's looking at a monthly payment of $616 to maintain her loan at the 12.411 percent rate she can expect. Her car payments are going to be more expensive, too: $826 on her thirty-six-month obligation to pay off her $25,000 loan at 11.619 percent. As you can easily see, a good FICO score translates into dollars saved when it's time to borrow money. Why? Because lenders compensate themselves for the higher risk of loaning to people with poor credit histories by charging premium interest rates.

30-Year Fixed-rate Mortgage ($300,000)		
FICO Score	APR	Monthly Payment
760–850	4.501%	$1,520
700–759	4.723%	$1,560
680–699	4.900%	$1,592
660–679	5.114%	$1,631
640–659	5.544%	$1,712
620–639	6.090%	$1,816

(Source of this and the two tables on page 97: www.myFICO.com, accessed May 22, 2009. APR based on national averages.)

15-Year Home Equity Loan ($50,000)		
FICO Score	APR	Monthly Payment
740–850	8.086%	$480
720–739	8.386%	$489
700–719	8.886%	$504
670–699	9.661%	$527
640–669	11.161%	$573
620–639	12.411%	$613

36-Month Auto Loan ($25,000)		
FICO Score	APR	Monthly Payment
720–850	5.941%	$760
690–719	7.403%	$777
660–689	8.882%	$794
620–659	11.619%	$826
590–619	15.385%	$871
500–589	16.208%	$881

Because your credit score and the information it is based on are so important, Congress passed the Fair Credit Reporting Act (FCRA) in 1970 to, in its own words, "ensure that consumer reporting agencies exercise their grave responsibilities with fairness, impartiality, and a respect for the consumer's right to privacy" (www.ftc.gov). Several important rights are guaranteed to consumers under the terms of the FCRA:

- The right to know what is on your credit report
- The right to be informed if someone uses information in your credit report as a basis for adverse actions or decisions

- The right to receive your credit score
- The right to dispute incomplete or inaccurate information and have it removed from your credit report
- The right to have your credit information revealed only to parties with a valid need to see it
- The right to control access to your credit information
- The right to seek damages for violation of any of your rights under the FCRA

Knowing and verifying the accuracy of your credit report information is especially important because a certain percentage of all credit reports contain some inaccurate or incomplete information. In 2004, the Public Interest Research Group, a consumer watchdog organization, published a study asserting that 79 percent of all consumer reports surveyed contained some type of error. The federal government's General Accounting Office disputed this finding, and the Consumer Data Industry Association, the trade group for credit bureaus and other consumer credit reporting organizations, testified that less than 2 percent of credit reports had data deleted because they were in error. Wherever the real number is located in this range, it can be safely said that credit reports have been known to contain errors.

Although mistakes on your credit report may not be at the top of your list of concerns while you're in debt trouble, they can be very important when you reach the stage where you are beginning to rebuild and reestablish your credit. The FCRA currently guarantees you the right to receive a free credit report once each year from each of the major credit reporting agencies; you should take advantage of this right to review your report and be certain that it fairly reflects your actual history. If you do believe that your report contains erroneous entries, you must circle the entries, attach documentation that supports your claims, and send everything, along with a letter that explains your request (see a sample on the facing page, taken from www.ftc.gov/bcp/edu/pubs/consumer/credit/cre21.shtm), to the credit reporting agency. They must investigate your claims within thirty days, unless they believe your claims are frivolous.

SAMPLE CREDIT REPORT DISPUTE LETTER

Your Name
Your Address
City, State, ZIP

Date

Complaint Department
Name of Company
1234 Main Street, #100
Any town, USA 10021

Dear Sir or Madam:
I am writing to dispute the following information in my file.
I have circled the items I dispute on the attached copy of the
report I received.

This item (identify item(s) disputed by name of source, such
as creditors or tax court, and identify type of item, such as credit
account, judgment, etc.) is (inaccurate or incomplete) because
(describe what is inaccurate or incomplete and why). I am
requesting that the item be removed (or request another specific
change) to correct the information.

Enclosed are copies of (use this sentence if applicable and
describe any enclosed documentation, such as payment records
and court documents) supporting my position. Please reinvesti-
gate this (these) matter(s) and (delete or correct) the disputed
item(s) as soon as possible.

Sincerely,
Your Name

Enclosures: (List what you are enclosing.)

This brings up an important warning: beware of the organizations that advertise aggressively on the Internet and other media their ability to improve your credit scores or help you repair your credit. Most of them operate by barraging the credit reporting organizations with complaints about supposed errors on your credit report, many of which may have no basis in fact. It should be obvious that you can't get a legitimate negative entry off your credit history just by complaining about it. However, the agencies must, by law, investigate any potentially legitimate complaint, so there is always a chance that by virtue of sheer numbers, these so-called credit repair experts might get lucky once in a while. The problem is, they often charge outrageous fees to perform activities you could do for yourself free of charge, and the benefit you receive may not be worth what you pay to get it.

Another reason it's important for you to periodically monitor your credit report is to prevent or limit the damage from identity theft. In these days of easy Internet access and clever hackers, it's always possible that someone has obtained some of your information and used it for dishonest purposes. By identifying such activity and challenging it, you can keep identity thieves from wrecking your credit history.

The Fair Debt Collection Practices Act: Keeping the Debt Collectors Honest

Congress passed the Fair Debt Collection Practices Act (FDCPA) in 1978 to regulate the debt collection industry and to eliminate abusive practices that collectors might employ against consumers when attempting to collect debts. The FDCPA will not erase your debt, but it does nevertheless set strict limits on what creditors or third-party collectors may do or say in their attempts to convince you to send money.

The principal protections afforded consumers by the FDCPA are

- That creditors and collectors must treat you fairly and respectfully
- That you may limit the times and ways in which you may be contacted about your debts
- That you must be informed about the debt and the fact that it is legitimately owed by you

- That creditors and collectors may not use harassing, abusive, or threatening means or false representations to collect debts
- That you may seek damages against any creditor or collector who violates your rights as guaranteed by the provisions of the FDCPA

SURVIVAL TIP:
LEARN ABOUT THE FAIR DEBT COLLECTION PRACTICES ACT

For a simplified summary of the provisions of the FDCPA, go to the Federal Trade Commission's website: www.ftc. gov/bcp/edu/pubs/consumer/credit/cre18.shtm.

Remember in chapter 1, where we discussed your right to ask creditors to cease calling you at work? That right comes from this act. Furthermore, if any representative of a creditor or collections agency uses threats—such as stating that your employer will be contacted about your debt, that your wages will be garnished, or that your name will be published on a list of "bad debts"—you may have grounds for a formal complaint and perhaps even a claim for damages. As a matter of fact, in November 2008, the Federal Trade Commission filed charges against a collection firm for this very practice. They won a judgment and the firm was required to pay $2.25 million to settle the charges. Among the violations committed were harassment of debtors, threats to disclose debts to third parties, and making misleading statements in their attempts to collect debts. The FTC is serious about enforcing consumer rights under the FDCPA.

Financial GPS

Practices Prohibited by the FDCPA include the following:

- Contacting you at work after you notify the collector that your employer prohibits it
- Using harassment, threats, or abusive language
- Giving information about your debt to a third party
- Making unauthorized withdrawals from your bank account
- Falsely representing themselves as attorneys
- Depositing or threatening to deposit a postdated check or other banking instrument prior to the date on the instrument

We've all heard the horror stories about debt collectors who bully and harass, who call five or ten times per day, or who otherwise seem bent on not only collecting the debt but also driving their victims over the edge of sanity. The FDCPA protects you from these characters, and you need to know your rights and assert them if necessary.

Having said all that, it's only fair to balance the discussion by mentioning the fact that the vast majority of debt collectors, whether they work for your credit card company or a third-party collection agency, are professionals who are trying to do a difficult job in a firm, yet caring manner. Chances are, if you speak to them honestly and respectfully, they'll do the same to you. Remember that simply by the act of taking the call and giving honest answers to their questions you are presenting yourself in a more favorable light than those who avoid calls, lie, make unfounded accusations, and generally behave in a way that they wouldn't tolerate others acting toward them.

Get in the habit of taking notes on any conversations you have with a collector. Keep a pencil and paper near your phone and jot down names, phone numbers, key dates, or other information about the call. This could come in handy later, especially if you're unfortunate enough to be contacted by one of those collection thugs the FDCPA was designed to protect you from.

The Fair Credit Billing Act: Know What You Owe

Many consumers don't really look closely at their credit card statements, other than to check the payment due date and amount. However, just as with the information on your credit report, you should get in the habit of reviewing your monthly statements to verify that the charges making up your balance are, in fact, charges you've incurred or authorized. Here again, mistakes do happen. If you're in debt trouble, the last thing you need is to be charged and paying interest on a transaction you didn't even make.

The Fair Credit Billing Act (FCBA) is an amendment to the Truth in Lending Act that provides specific rights and procedures for customers who believe they are being incorrectly charged by a credit card company or other revolving credit agreement, such as a department store charge card. As with the Fair Credit Reporting Act and the Fair Debt Collections Practices Act, the U.S. Federal Trade Commission is the governmental body responsible for enforcing the provisions of the Fair Credit Billing Act. Their website—at www.ftc.gov/bcp/edu/pubs/consumer/credit/cre16. shtm—gives a summary of the FCBA.

Here are the types of charges covered by the act, according to the FTC website:

- Unauthorized charges (your liability is limited to $50)
- Charges listing the wrong date or amount
- Charges for goods or services you didn't accept or that weren't delivered as agreed
- Mathematical billing errors
- Failure to post payments and other credits, such as returns
- Failure to send bills to your current address (the creditor must receive your change of address in writing at least twenty days before the billing period ends)

- Charges for which you request an explanation or written proof of purchase along with a claimed error or request for clarification

The FCBA is very clear about what you must do to assert your rights under the act if any of the above charges apply to you. You must send a written notice to the "Billing Inquiries" address on your statement—usually not the same address to which you send payments—that explains what you believe the error is (see a sample complaint letter on the facing page taken from www.ftc.gov/bcp/edu/pubs/consumer/credit/cre16.shtm). Make sure your letter includes your account number, name, and address. It must be received by your creditor within sixty days of your receipt of the statement showing the error. Usually, it's best to send such communications via certified mail with a return receipt requested, so that you can prove when the creditor received it.

The creditor has thirty days to send you written acknowledgment of your complaint, and it must resolve the complaint within two billing cycles (but no more than ninety days) after receiving your communication.

While the charge is in dispute, you may withhold payment on the item in question. The creditor may not take any collection action on this amount or item, but it will probably count against your credit limit on the account. Your credit rating or credit report may not be affected in any way by the disputed item or amount during this time. The creditor may report the matter to a credit bureau, but it must also report that you are disputing the item or amount.

If you are correct in your claim, your creditor must send you a written explanation of the corrections and adjustments that will be made to your account. If any late fees or finance charges have accrued because of the item, your creditor must remove them. If, however, your claim is determined to be invalid, you must receive prompt written notice of how much you owe and why. You may also owe finance charges that have accrued while the matter was being investigated.

By this point in the book, you know everything you need to know to either work directly with your creditors to resolve your debt or to decide what type of assistance to seek from a credit counselor, a debt consolidation loan, or a debt settlement firm. You should have a decent working knowledge of the laws that protect you as a consumer and a debtor, and

SAMPLE BILLING DISPUTE LETTER

Your Name
Your Address
City, State, ZIP
Your Account Number

Date:

Billing Inquiries
Name of Creditor
1234 Main Street, #100
Any town, USA 10021

Dear Sir or Madam:

I am writing to dispute a billing error in the amount of $_____ on my account. The amount is inaccurate because (describe the problem). I am requesting that the error be corrected, that any finance and other charges related to the disputed amount be credited as well, and that I receive an accurate statement. Enclosed are copies of (use this sentence to describe any enclosed information, such as sales slips, payment records) supporting my position. Please investigate this matter and correct the billing error as soon as possible.

Sincerely,
Your Name

Enclosures: (List what you are enclosing.)

you have an overview of processes like foreclosure, repossession, and the steps that unsecured creditors can and cannot take in their attempts to collect what you owe them.

But for some of you reading this, it may already be too late for measures such as those we've discussed. You have already tried to work something out with your mortgage holder, you've been unsuccessful, and foreclosure is proceeding. Or you've already been notified that a creditor has filed a lawsuit against you.

Even if such dire circumstances confront you, don't despair. There is still a way for you to resolve your debt and have legal protection from creditors while you do so. It's called the U.S. Bankruptcy Code, and it is the subject of the next part of the book.

STEPS IN THE RIGHT DIRECTION

1. Get a free copy of your credit report and check it for errors.

2. Know what bill collectors can and cannot do in their collection efforts.

3. Take notes on all conversations with creditors, including names, phone numbers, dates, amounts of money discussed, etc.

4. Check your credit card statements to make sure all charges were authorized by you or according to your contract.

PART TWO

"IN CASE OF EMERGENCY, BREAK GLASS"

"WE DON'T HAVE TO KEEP UP WITH THE JONESES ANY MORE... THEY'VE FILED FOR BANKRUPTCY."

NOTE: In the sections following, certain legal concepts and practices are discussed. This material is presented for informational purposes only; you should not use it as a basis for making legal decisions. You should consider legal options only after consulting a qualified bankruptcy attorney.

Chapter 5

UNDERSTANDING BANKRUPTCY

GUIDEPOSTS

In this chapter, you'll learn

- Why your credit rating may not be the main thing you should worry about right now

- How the U.S. Bankruptcy Code provides a fresh start

- Bankruptcy myths

- The protections from creditors and collection activity provided by the U.S. Bankruptcy Code

Remember Doug, the guy in the introduction who got a call from the collection agency? Well, as it turns out, Doug realized he either had to take some sort of action regarding his debt or wind up in court with no lawyer, no plan, and very little hope of any sort of good outcome.

Feeling desperate and with no idea of where to turn, Doug got on the Internet and googled "bankruptcy lawyer." There were a number of links to law firms offering free consultations for people considering personal bankruptcy.

Doug stared at the screen and thought about everything he had heard regarding bankruptcy: It would kill his credit rating; he wouldn't be able to borrow money for ten years. After a few more minutes of soul-searching and thinking about the collector sending somebody to repossess his car if he didn't pay, Doug decided he had very little to lose by simply exploring his options. He clicked on the link to a bankruptcy attorney's website and dialed the phone number that appeared on his screen.

Doug spent about half an hour speaking to the representative who took his call. He gave her as much information as he could about his financial situation and especially his debts. He also asked a few questions about the process of bankruptcy. The representative was very helpful and seemed understanding about his situation. When he hung up the phone, Doug realized that for the first time in quite a while, he felt hopeful.

Personal bankruptcy, in its simplest terms, is a court-ordered and court-protected plan to help those in financial crisis satisfy their creditors to the extent possible. It provides a way for individuals to protect themselves from foreclosure, repossession, and other legal actions that creditors might take. Under the court's approval and protection, you can work out a plan that, if approved by the court, will permit you to satisfy your creditors as much as possible and get a fresh start with your finances. Think about it like this:

- About how much are all of your monthly payments right now, if you could make them? As an example, let's say they are $3,200.

- What if an agreement could be put in place that would let you legally pay about 60 percent of that each month, or about $2,000. Would you be able to do that?

That is basically a description—although very oversimplified—of how Chapter 13 personal bankruptcy works (which I discuss in chapter 7).

Certainly, bankruptcy is a difficult decision with far-reaching ramifications for your financial future. However, if the alternative is losing your home, your car, or other assets that are crucial to your and your family's well-being, it may be a course of action to which you should give serious consideration.

WHEN DOES YOUR CREDIT RATING CEASE TO MATTER?

Like Doug, one of the first things that many people associate with filing bankruptcy is its negative implications for their credit rating. That's not completely unreasonable, because bankruptcy can stay on your credit history for up to ten years. Any lender who sees a bankruptcy on your record is going to think long and hard about loaning you money, and if he or she decides to go ahead, you probably won't get the same interest rate on your loan that would be extended to someone with a good credit score and a clean payment record.

But is your credit rating the main thing you need to worry about right now? Think about it: Do you really believe it would be wise for you to borrow in the near future, even if you could find a lender willing to extend you a loan in your current circumstances? On the other hand, if you were to get sued because of nonpayment and lose the suit, that would also have a negative effect on your credit rating, wouldn't it? And if that happened, you could be deprived of some of the assets that are very important to you, such as your house or your car.

Not only that, but bankruptcy is far from the only item that can harm your credit score. Late payments, over-limit balances, foreclosures, court judgments, liens, and repossessions are all events that end up on your credit history and can stay there for up to seven years. Most of the people I talk to who are considering bankruptcy have enough of these types of items already showing on their credit histories to make them a high-risk proposition for almost any lender. In chapter 10, I'll discuss how to review your credit report to verify its accuracy and request removal of any inaccurate negative information. But right now, we need to concentrate on protecting the assets you still have. At this point, bankruptcy may very well be your best option to accomplish that.

The fact is, people who are already in enough trouble with debt to be considering bankruptcy probably shouldn't be as worried about their ability to borrow as their ability to continue living in their houses and driving their cars. By the time your circumstances have deteriorated to the point that you need the court's protection from your creditors, getting a loan should be close to the last thing on your mind. And honestly, it's not exactly like bankers are going to be lining up to loan you money anyway.

Borrowing more money when you're already drowning in debt is like using an anchor for a life preserver.

Let's face it: borrowing more money when you're already drowning in debt is a little bit like using an anchor for a life preserver. About the only entity that can successfully employ such a strategy is the federal government—and only because they own the presses that print the money.

Instead of worrying so much about bankruptcy's effect on your credit rating, you need to take a careful look at your situation in the cold, hard light of reality. Set aside your pride and consider how you can best protect the assets that you and your family depend on. Have you tried working with your creditors but have run out of money, time, and second chances? Have you tried credit counseling and, like so many—up to 80 percent of enrollees, by some estimates—have been unable to complete the program? Have you attempted to work through a debt negotiation firm and failed, either because a creditor decided to sue or you couldn't keep up with the program payments? Or, like many people I've worked with, have you done nothing except get farther behind on your obligations until a creditor finally filed a suit or the bank started foreclosure proceedings on your home? Then it may be time for you to seriously consider the protections afforded you by personal bankruptcy. The bankruptcy laws were written to give you a chance at a fresh start. Perhaps it's time for you to seriously pursue this option.

BANKRUPTCY MYTHS

If you've read this far, I might reasonably assume that you believe bankruptcy may be the way for you to go, but if you're like a lot of people I talk to, you may still have some serious misgivings. You may be thinking, "If I file bankruptcy, I'll never be able to get a loan again," or "Bankruptcy is for dishonest people," or "Bankruptcy is the same as admitting I'm a failure."

If some of these thoughts are going through your head right now, join the crowd. Such negative associations exist for many people and can hold them back from giving bankruptcy the serious consideration it deserves, even though they may have few other options available. Most of the fears people have about the effects of bankruptcy are based on incomplete information. Let's take a look at a few of the major myths surrounding bankruptcy and shine a little factual light on them.

Myth #1: Bankruptcy Is Shady

Based on my conversations with hundreds of debtors from all parts of the country, I believe this is the number one bankruptcy myth that needs to be dispelled. Let me say it as clearly as I can: the purpose of bankruptcy is to give honest, but unfortunate people a chance to have their debts reduced, and to get a fresh start. Some may have the perception that people file bankruptcy because they lived foolishly and bought lots of stuff they couldn't afford, but the fact is that the majority of individuals who file for bankruptcy protection are doing so because of the financial fallout from one of the "big four" discussed in the introduction: unexpected expenses and bad financial habits, job loss, grave illness, and divorce or death of a principal wage earner

Remember what I said at the beginning of the book: you are not your debt. We could also extend that even further by saying, "You are not your bankruptcy." Although it is true that some dishonest people have used the bankruptcy laws as a way to get out of paying legitimate debts that they could have paid but simply chose not to, for the vast majority of Americans seeking bankruptcy protection, this is their last hope at retaining control of the assets most critical to their families: their homes, their vehicles, and in some cases, their retirement savings. Another way of looking at it is this: Bankruptcy is like the ejection seat on a fighter airplane; you hope you never have to use it, but if you do, it can save your life so that you can live to fly another day.

As a matter of fact, significant protections against abuse are written into the U.S. Bankruptcy Code to prevent, as far as possible, its misappropriation by greedy and dishonest people. Judges take a very dim view, for example, of people who max out all their credit cards, then file bankruptcy as a means of avoiding paying for their spending binge. Further, the Bankruptcy Abuse Prevention and Consumer Protection Act of 2005 adds additional protections against what some have considered "frivolous" filings in the past, including the requirement that you must submit tax return information in order to have your petition proceed. Of course, like any law, the bankruptcy code can be flaunted and even cheated by persons who are inclined that way, but that in no way changes

Bankruptcy protects honest people who have fallen on hard times.

the fact that sometimes honest people, either because of poor decisions or circumstances beyond their control, need the protection afforded by the bankruptcy laws. Most of the people who file for bankruptcy are doing it to give themselves a much-needed fresh start.

It is certainly true that your creditors would prefer that you not file bankruptcy—it interferes with their attempts to collect what you owe them—but remember that bankruptcy is primarily meant to protect you, not them. Credit counselors, for example, will often advise potential enrollees about the evils of bankruptcy—the damage it does to your credit, future difficulties it will cause you, and other dire predictions—to discourage consumers' consideration of this alternative. When you think about it, that makes sense, because most credit counseling agencies receive the bulk of their income from the banks and credit card companies. Likewise, debt negotiators will discourage bankruptcy because if you file bankruptcy, you don't need the services for which they charge their fees. Even though both credit counseling and debt settlement are options that people can use successfully—as we saw in chapter 3—that doesn't mean bankruptcy might not better serve the needs of some individuals.

The bottom line is that only you can decide, in the final analysis, if bankruptcy is the best option for you. And, as I've already said several times, that is a decision you should make after careful consideration of all factors and only *after* consultation with a qualified bankruptcy attorney. But you should make your decision on the basis of the facts, not on the belief that you will be branded as a cheat, a deadbeat, or any other of the labels attached to bankruptcy filers by people who either don't know any better or who have reason to wish you didn't.

Myth #2: Bankruptcy Is for People Who Are Flat Broke

As we've already seen, bankruptcy is actually a way for you to *protect the assets you do have*, so that they won't be taken away from you without your consent, after careful consideration of your best interests and the nature of your debts. Many people who file bankruptcy have significant assets that they are seeking to maintain control over rather than giving up control to their creditors. Usually, bankruptcy is more about protecting what is most important to you rather than giving everything you have to creditors.

Related to this myth is the idea that bankruptcy automatically results in losing everything you have to satisfy creditors. This is simply not the case. Remember our earlier discussion of the exemptions allowed by state and federal law for certain assets during bankruptcy proceedings? These exemptions typically cover things like your house, your car, and certain personal belongings that are considered crucial to resuming a normal life after bankruptcy. For the majority of people who file, these assets are retained throughout the process. Let me say that again, for emphasis: most people who file bankruptcy don't lose any of their stuff.

Myth #3: Filing Bankruptcy Makes You a Loser

If this one is true, we need to redefine what constitutes being a loser. Here's a partial list of some people who have filed bankruptcy and gone on to lead productive—and, in some cases, history-changing—lives: Walt Disney, Ulysses S. Grant, L. Frank Baum (author of *The Wizard of Oz*), Mark Twain, actress Kim Basinger, Charles Goodyear (inventor of the process for vulcanizing rubber), H. J. Heinz (founder of the ketchup company), Larry King, Abraham Lincoln, Stan Lee (creator of Spider Man), and Mickey Rooney. By anyone's measure, these people were not and are not losers—and neither are you just because you make the decision to file bankruptcy. Remember: you are not your debt. Your personal worth is not measured or negated by how much you owe or by what you do to deal with your debt, as long as your actions are within the law. Believing this fact is one of the keys to overcoming the paralyzing emotional effects of financial difficulty. Don't think of bankruptcy as the end—think of it as a fresh beginning.

Myth #4: Filing Bankruptcy Means Your Credit Is Gone Forever

As we will discuss in detail in the final portion of this book, bankruptcy gives you the ability to rebuild your finances—including your creditworthiness—over time. It takes discipline, a healthier set of financial habits, and patience, but you *can* make a new and improved credit reputation for yourself, even after coming out of bankruptcy.

As a matter of fact, many individuals have reported success in obtaining credit long before the expiration of the ten-year period during which their bankruptcy appeared on their credit report. Obtaining and responsibly using credit will allow you to make steady improvements in your credit rating.

The key word in that last sentence, of course, is *responsibly*. Many of us have heard horror stories about people who come out of bankruptcy, grab a fistful of those credit card offers with come-ons like "Bad credit? No problem!" printed on them, and quickly run up tens of thousands of dollars' worth in brand-new unsecured debt, landing themselves right back in the same predicament they entered bankruptcy to escape. That is behavior that any reasonable person would want to avoid.

Rest assured: if you pay your bills on time and don't apply for or use all the credit someone is willing to give you, you will begin to build the kind of record that will make you a "good customer" again in the eyes of lenders. And that is true, even if you just came out of bankruptcy. In fact, chapter 10 will go into detail about the steps you can follow to rebuild your credit rating after bankruptcy.

Myth #5: Filing Bankruptcy Means You Can Never Buy a House or a Car

This myth is closely related to Myth #4. Remember that although bankruptcy is a serious step to take, it's not the same thing as financial suicide. And when you think about it, how could it be? If the purpose of the bankruptcy code is to give you the chance for a fresh start, it stands to reason that people who use this means would again be able to enjoy many, if not all, of the same rights and privileges as other consumers, including the ability to purchase a home or a car.

As I'll discuss in more detail later, it is very important, especially after bankruptcy, that you review your credit report and correct any inaccurate information you find there. As I said in chapter 4 in the section on the Fair Credit Reporting Act, mistakes do show up on credit histories. For example, it is not uncommon for individuals who have just emerged from bankruptcy to find that one or more of the debts included in the bankruptcy filing is still listed as "open" on the credit report. In that case, the individual should contact the credit bureau in writing and direct that the entries be changed to show "included in bankruptcy." Taking care of such details is an important part of the post-bankruptcy rehabilitation program for your finances. Again, we'll discuss this process in detail in chapter 10.

It should probably go without saying that you should be completely truthful with prospective lenders regarding your bankruptcy. Having a bankruptcy on your credit history is a significant negative factor; lying in order to get credit *is against the law*. Don't risk it.

Myth #6 Filing Bankruptcy Will Cause You to Lose Your Job

Unless you are in certain military, law enforcement, or national security–related jobs, your employer is prohibited from terminating your employment simply because you filed for bankruptcy protection, period. Also, holders of certain types of licensing such as securities dealers or investment brokers may require specialized assistance from a qualified bankruptcy attorney.

FINANCIAL GPS

Bankruptcy Myths

Myth #1: Bankruptcy is shady.

Myth #2: Bankruptcy is for people who are flat broke.

Myth #3: Filing bankruptcy makes you a loser.

Myth #4: Filing bankruptcy means your credit is gone forever.

Myth #5: Filing bankruptcy means you can never buy a house or a car.

Myth #6: Filing bankruptcy will cause you to lose your job.

BANKRUPTCY FACTS

Thinking back about all the people I've talked to about their finances, I'd be hard-pressed to recall anyone who was eager to file bankruptcy. You will hear me repeat what I'm about to say several times during the course of this book: The decision to file personal bankruptcy should be considered only after you believe you have exhausted all other reasonable options; furthermore, you should file bankruptcy only after speaking to an attorney who is experienced in personal bankruptcy cases similar to yours. Bankruptcy can help you get back on your feet; it can give you the fresh start you desperately need. But it is also a serious matter, with long-term implications for your ability to borrow and other aspects of your financial life, as we'll discuss in a later chapter. As a matter of fact, one of the reasons the bankruptcy code contains strict requirements for filers to receive financial counseling is so that those who seek bankruptcy protection address the underlying financial behaviors that may have contributed to their bankruptcies. This is serious business, and, as with any other major financial decision, you should carefully weigh all the factors, both positive and negative, before opting to proceed with personal bankruptcy.

In its simplest terms, bankruptcy is a process under federal law that permits debtors who owe more than they can pay to either eliminate their debts or work out a plan to pay back all or some of their debt over time. During the term of your bankruptcy filing, you are protected by the courts from the claims of most creditors.

SURVIVAL TIP:
UNDERSTAND THE UNITED STATES CODE TITLE II (BANKRUPTCY)

To download the entire text of the U.S. Bankruptcy Code or one of the individual forms (such as Chapter 7 or Chapter 13), go to uscode.house.gov/download/title_11. shtml.

As I discuss in detail in chapter 7, the two divisions of the U.S. Bankruptcy Code that deal with most individual bankruptcies are Chapter 7 and Chapter 13. Deciding which of these options is best for you is a choice you should make after receiving the advice of a qualified bankruptcy attorney. To help you better understand what bankruptcy can do for you, following are the most critical facts about bankruptcy that you should know. These basics may also help you work through your discussions with an attorney.

Fact #1: Bankruptcy Makes the Creditors Stop Calling

When you file your bankruptcy petition with the court, creditors are enjoined (barred by the court) from further attempts to contact you. From that point on, any contact by creditors must be only with the court that is administering your bankruptcy or with your attorney. When you properly file your petition with the court, an automatic stay goes into effect the moment the clerk of the court time-stamps your document. According to the U.S. Senate Committee on the Judiciary,

> The automatic stay is one of the fundamental debtor protections provided by the bankruptcy laws. It gives the debtor a breathing spell from his creditors, stopping all collection efforts, all harassment, and all foreclosure actions. It permits the debtor to attempt a repayment or reorganization plan, or simply to be relieved of the financial pressures that drove him into bankruptcy (Senate Report No. 95-989).

The automatic stay requires no hearing, no prior notification, not even the signature of a judge. Furthermore, if a creditor willfully contacts you after it has been notified of the existence of the automatic stay, you may have grounds for a legal complaint. For these reasons, you can see why some have likened the automatic stay to a "pause" button for creditor activity.

In certain situations, creditors may request relief from the stay. If the request is granted, the creditor would have the right to resume attempts to collect the debt or take possession of the collateral. However, this usually occurs only in cases where the creditor has reason to believe the collateral is being exposed to undue risk that might unfairly harm the creditor's interest. One example of this might be a vehicle that is subject to a loan, but on which the owner has allowed the insurance to lapse.

However, the automatic stay effectively halts most collection attempts, including calls, letters, repossession of vehicles, and foreclosure on mortgages, during the term of the bankruptcy petition. In addition, it halts lawsuits and other legal actions toward the petitioner. In fact, even if a lawsuit over an unsecured debt has resulted in a wage garnishment, bankruptcy, in most cases, will stop the garnishment in its tracks while you work out a plan to address your debts.

SURVIVAL TIP:
END WAGE GARNISHMENT

Bankruptcy's automatic stay halts wage garnishment. If your wages are being garnished by a creditor, filing bankruptcy will usually put a stop to this while you work out a plan.

Notable exceptions to the protection of the automatic stay are court-ordered obligations such as alimony and child support. We will discuss these in more detail later in this chapter.

Fact #2: Bankruptcy Halts Foreclosure

A bankruptcy filing halts foreclosure, though not necessarily permanently. Depending on which bankruptcy option you choose (more on this later), you will either work out a plan to make up the back payments—sometimes, over as long as five years—or perhaps arrange for the mortgage holder to take back the home and, in exchange, cancel any remaining mortgage debt. This is an area where you need the advice of an experienced bankruptcy attorney because the type of petition you file has a large bearing on what you will need to do to stay in your home, if that is your goal. I will discuss these options more fully in chapter 7.

At this point, it might be helpful to answer a question some homeowners pose: which looks worse on your credit history—foreclosure or bankruptcy? This is a valid question because, if you're considering bankruptcy, you're already trying to choose among the best of several unappealing options.

Foreclosure stays on your credit report for seven years and bankruptcy for ten, but that doesn't automatically mean that future potential lenders prefer to see foreclosure instead of bankruptcy. Especially in cases where the bankruptcy filer opted to keep the house and even continue making payments on the mortgage during the bankruptcy process—a choice we will discuss more fully later—a mortgage loan officer may look more favorably on the bankruptcy than on a foreclosure, where the house was taken away from the debtor and auctioned off for a price that may or may not have been sufficient to satisfy the indebtedness.

Having said all that, I need to remind you that right now, at this point in the process, you probably need to worry less about how your credit report will look and more about protecting your assets. Leaving aside the question of what does or doesn't look best on your credit history, in foreclosure you actually lose something of great value—your home. In fact, one of the primary reasons many people seek bankruptcy protection is to prevent this exact scenario. Whereas allowing foreclosure to proceed—and taking advantage of every right and delaying tactic allowed by law—may make sense for some debtors, most would greatly prefer to be able to stay in their house and even get the loan back in good standing, either through making up back payments or restructuring the loan. Both of these options may be pursued as a part of a bankruptcy proceeding.

For this and other reasons, and as negative as bankruptcy can be, it may not be the "kiss of death" for your financial future that many people assume.

FINANCIAL GPS

In certain cases, bankruptcy doesn't look as bad on your credit report as foreclosure.

Fact #3: Bankruptcy Allows You to Keep Certain Assets

In most cases, successful completion of a bankruptcy plan can permit you to retain your most important assets, such as your home, your car, and much of your personal property. In fact, as I mentioned earlier, in most of the personal bankruptcies I've seen, debtors have been allowed to keep all their possessions. However, different state and federal laws govern which types of assets are protected—"exempt," in legal terms—and which are not.

Always keep in mind that exempt doesn't mean you don't have to pay what you owe on the loan for which the assets are collateral. The exemption only applies to *other* creditors' abilities to use these assets to satisfy your obligations to them. If you intend to keep such secured assets as your car and your house through bankruptcy, you must have in place a plan to satisfy the lienholders who have those assets as collateral for your loans.

The principle behind the exemption of certain assets from being used to satisfy creditor claims goes back to the reason for bankruptcy: to give someone who is hopelessly in debt a fresh start. The laws recognize that in order to start over, you must have something to start with. However, state and federal laws vary widely in what they consider as exempt assets. You may remember, for example, in the discussion of homestead laws and exemptions in chapter 4, I mentioned that each state has its

You can represent yourself in bankruptcy court—but why would you?

own standards of what may be protected under its homestead laws. In a similar way, the laws determining what you may list as exempt property on your bankruptcy petition differ depending on where you live. As we'll discuss later, you may be able to choose which rules apply to the exemptions in your case—the federal or the state. For many people, the federal exemptions are more favorable, but in some cases the governing state's rules could have advantages. This is another reason I strongly recommend that you consult a qualified bankruptcy attorney in your state if you are considering bankruptcy as an option.

Fact #4: You Shouldn't Go It Alone!

In fact, let me make the point even clearer, if I can. You can legally file bankruptcy on your own, using a packet of forms that you can probably order over the Internet. You can even legally represent yourself in court. But the question remains, why would you? In most cases, the time you will spend in self-representation—often, time you could spend being gainfully employed—and the potential cost of the legal mistakes you are likely to make would more than cover the relatively modest fee most attorneys charge for filing a simple personal bankruptcy case.

Go back to the medical analogy we used at the opening of chapter 1. If you were sick enough to go to the emergency room, you probably wouldn't try to treat yourself, would you? If you needed surgery, would you try to perform it yourself, using a "self-surgery kit" you ordered on the Internet? If you are seriously considering bankruptcy, your financial health is every bit as threatened as your physical health would be if you had a major illness or injury. Don't try to "play doctor" with your financial recovery—find a qualified bankruptcy attorney you trust and hire him or her. You'll save money in the long run.

SURVIVAL TIP:
FIND A LAWYER

For a referral to a qualified bankruptcy attorney in your area, visit www.ASurvivalGuidetoDebt.com or do a Google search of the term "bankruptcy lawyer."

Fact #5: Bankruptcy Can Give You a Fresh Start

This may be the best news of all. For debtors who have no hope of paying back everything they owe, bankruptcy really can give you a financial do-over. The bankruptcy code is written so that you can draw a line under your downwardly spiraling resources, gain some time free from creditor demands to figure out a plan, and have the blessing of the courts for your approved plan and your new beginning.

We are fortunate to live in a time and a society where debtor's prison no longer exists. Don't get me wrong: bankruptcy is certainly no picnic, and the decision to file for bankruptcy protection is often a difficult emotional bridge for individuals to cross. After all, none of us likes to admit failure, even if the circumstances that bring it about are—like illness and unemployment from downsizing—beyond our control. However, once the decision is made, many of the people I've worked with report an almost immediate sense of relief. At last, they have some time to make careful, reasoned decisions about which of their available alternatives make the most sense in their circumstances. When you've exhausted all other reasonable options, bankruptcy really is a way to start over.

FinanciaL GPS

Bankruptcy Facts

Fact #1: Bankruptcy makes the creditors stop calling.
Fact #2: Bankruptcy halts foreclosure.
Fact #3: Bankruptcy allows you to keep certain assets.
Fact #4: You shouldn't go it alone!
Fact #5: Bankruptcy can give you a fresh start.

Now that you have a basic overview of what bankruptcy can and can't do for you, it's time to look in more detail at some of the implications of filing.

Bankruptcy is a scary word for most people, but as is true with many scary words and concepts, part of the fear stems from having a few facts mixed in with lots of fiction. Once you know the facts, you'll be able to make a decision that is right for your situation. In the next chapter, we'll consider some of the real-world consequences of filing bankruptcy that you need to be aware of as you approach this important decision.

STEPS IN THE RIGHT DIRECTION

1. Do not place more importance on your credit rating than on keeping your most critical assets.

2. If you are at risk of losing your home or other critical assets, consider bankruptcy as a viable solution.

3. If you are considering bankruptcy, learn the facts rather than make a faulty decision based on myths and assumptions.

4. If you think bankruptcy may be advisable in your situation, talk to a qualified personal bankruptcy attorney.

Chapter 6

"YOU MIGHT NEED TO FILE BANKRUPTCY IF . . ."

GUIDEPOSTS

In this chapter, you'll learn

- The principal indications that you should seriously consider bankruptcy to solve your debt problems

- Some things that bankruptcy cannot do for you

- The real financial, career, and emotional consequences of bankruptcy, and how to anticipate them

As we continue to move closer to the bankruptcy decision, it's time to start looking at the specifics of your situation to evaluate the ways that bankruptcy can help you—and also the ways it can potentially hurt you. Weighing the advantages against the disadvantages is part of any important choice, and bankruptcy is no different. In addition, this sort of careful, cost/benefit analysis can remove a lot of the emotion from the equation, which can help you be more certain you're making your evaluation based on facts rather than what you wish were true or what you're afraid might be true.

WHEN BANKRUPTCY CAN HELP

Following are the hallmarks of a situation where bankruptcy should be considered as a viable option.

You're "Upside Down" and Behind on Your Payments

Get out your personal net worth statement, completed according to the instructions in chapter 1. Look at the total value of all your assets, then subtract from that number the sum of all your liabilities including amounts owed on those assets. If the resulting number is negative, you are what is commonly known as "upside down": your debts total more than your net worth. If you could sell everything you own today, you still wouldn't have enough money to pay back everything you owe.

Note that being upside down, in itself, may not be a compelling reason to file *as long as* you are handling your obligations in a timely manner. After all, most of us started out in life with few if any assets; we've all been upside down at some point, and most of us worked our way out of it. But many of the people I've talked to are not keeping up with their debt; instead, they are steadily losing ground every month in terms of their net worth because of rising debts, driven by late fees and punitive interest.

As I said in chapter 1, this is not an unusual situation for debtors in the United States. Especially if you refinanced your home with an adjustable rate mortgage to use your equity to improve your property, finance education, or pay off other debt, you could easily owe more than you could sell your home for. To make matters even worse, in falling real estate markets like the one that prevails as I'm writing this in early 2009, many homes won't appraise for as much as they did when you applied for the loan—your principal asset has actually lost value. If you owe more on your mortgage than your home is worth but you are still able to keep the payments current, you'll probably be all right in the long run, even without filing bankruptcy. But if your home payments have gotten beyond your ability to maintain, either because of an unfavorable provision in an adjustable rate mortgage, second liens, or some other reason, you should probably take a close look at bankruptcy.

And, as we mentioned in chapter 1, assets like automobiles tend to depreciate in value much more rapidly than loan balances on them, so unless your car is paid off or nearly so, you probably owe more on it than you could sell it for. Add to that the burden of lots of unsecured debt like credit cards, and it's no wonder that so many Americans find themselves in the unenviable position of having a net worth written in red ink.

Obviously, you may not want to completely liquidate all your assets any time soon, and even if you did, you'd still find yourself in debt at the end of the process—without your assets. So, unless you're expecting a financial bonanza in the very near future that will permit you to either pay off much of what you owe or at least become current with your payments, bankruptcy is probably your best option, both for the short and longer term.

You've Already Tried Other Alternatives

If you've already attempted to work with your creditors and have not been successful, either because your creditors were inflexible or because you were unable to follow through on what you agreed to do to settle your debt, it may be time for you to seriously consider bankruptcy. Also, if you enrolled in an approved credit counseling program but were unable to maintain the terms of your debt management plan (remember what I said in chapter 3: as many as 80 percent of those who enroll in credit counseling are unable to complete their programs), or if you tried to work with a debt negotiation or debt settlement firm and were unable to settle your debts, you may need the protection of the bankruptcy court.

As I also noted in chapter 3, not all debt negotiation or debt settlement attempts have a happy ending. Sometimes creditors get tired of waiting for their money and file a lawsuit anyway. Sometimes unsecured creditors who learn you are working with a debt negotiation firm will file a preemptive lawsuit because they know that the outcome of debt settlement is that they will receive less than 100 percent of what you owe them. They may decide the expense of a lawsuit is a cheaper alternative than taking what your debt settlement company offers.

Perhaps you tried to get a debt consolidation loan or to borrow from family members and friends, but these alternatives proved impossible. For whatever reason, your other attempts to take care of your debt without resorting to bankruptcy may have been unsuccessful. You gave it your best shot, and you exhausted all possibilities, but you're still facing debt you can't pay and possible legal sanctions. If so, bankruptcy can afford you some protected time and space to figure out what you should do next.

You've Already Been Notified of Pending Legal Proceedings

If you've gotten a formal Notice of Deficiency from your mortgage lender or, worse, notification of the date the lender plans to sell your home on the courthouse steps, you need to take a careful look at bankruptcy, especially if you intend to keep your house. If you're way behind with your car payments and you think the repo man is in his tow truck, trolling for your vehicle, bankruptcy will hold him at bay until you can figure out what to do. If an unsecured lender has filed a lawsuit and you are potentially facing a judgment lien or garnishment of wages, the automatic stay of bankruptcy can halt such efforts and give you the time you need to come up with a plan for satisfying as many of your creditors as possible.

The fact is, if you are facing legal proceedings, you have likely run out of time for most other courses of action. Although speaking with your creditors to explain your situation and asking for more time may sometimes help, bankruptcy protection guarantees that whatever action your creditor has instituted against you will be halted, at least for some period of time, while you formulate a plan of action. For many of the people I've worked with, the problem is not any single debt; it's the cumulative, overwhelming effect of trying to keep too many financial plates spinning at the same time. When the legal clock is ticking, time becomes your enemy. Bankruptcy can give you a "pause" button on the countdown.

You Want to Protect Your IRA

The Bankruptcy Abuse Prevention and Consumer Protection Act of 2005 stipulates that many types of retirement plans, including IRAs, are exempt assets in bankruptcy proceedings, and they may not be used to satisfy creditor demands (as long as the assets in the plan do not exceed $1 million in value). Although some states exempt assets in retirement plans from the claims of creditors, others do not. If you have significant assets in plans such as these, and you want to be certain that no creditor forces you to liquidate your retirement plan to pay off debt, bankruptcy will, in most cases, enable you to accomplish this objective. However, as I've said before, you should proceed only after consulting with a qualified bankruptcy attorney.

You're Unemployed or Have Had a Drastic Reduction in Income

By some measures, this is the reason given most frequently for filing personal bankruptcy. In fact, according to figures cited in a 2004 government study, two-thirds of Americans filing for personal bankruptcy listed "job-related financial stress, with layoffs being identified as a major factor" (see www.gao.gov/new.items/d04465r.pdf).

Even though we've all heard how we're supposed to have six months' worth of our salary in savings in case of emergencies like unemployment, the fact is that if you're like the vast majority of Americans, a serious interruption in your income will very quickly result in a large backlog of unpaid bills. Most of us simply don't have that savings cushion in place, even though we know we should.

Even with the meager safety net of unemployment benefits, few of us could survive long without our monthly paycheck. If that situation continues long enough, personal bankruptcy can often be the only way to stave off the loss of your most important possessions until you can find new work and get back on your feet. Of course, if you have no income and no prospects of any on the horizon, even the bankruptcy court may not be able to prevent the loss of some of your assets because debtors must be satisfied to the extent permitted by law. But at the very least, bankruptcy will give you the time you need to make careful decisions about your situation, in consultation with your attorney.

SURVIVAL TIP:
BANKRUPTCY COULD HELP YOU IF . . .

- You owe more than you own and you're behind on your debt
- You've already tried other methods unsuccessfully
- You are already facing legal proceedings
- You want to protect your retirement funds from creditors
- You are unemployed

WHAT BANKRUPTCY CANNOT DO FOR YOU

For all the good and worthy things about it, of course, bankruptcy also has limitations and liabilities. Some people are surprised, for example, when told that bankruptcy doesn't entitle them to keep their houses and cars without making payments. As I said at the beginning of chapter 5, you should never file bankruptcy lightly, or without considering all the ramifications—especially the negative ones. So, with that in mind, let's take a look at the other side of the bankruptcy coin.

Bankruptcy Cannot Give You an Immediate "Clean Slate"

Even though your bankruptcy filing will give you immediate relief from most creditors and will allow you the time to form a plan for rebuilding your finances, you shouldn't confuse this with a clean bill of financial health. Surprisingly, I have heard some attorneys use this exact term— *clean slate*—when describing what bankruptcy does for debtors. As a matter of fact, filing bankruptcy will probably make you an unlikely prospect for most lenders, and the legal fact of your bankruptcy usually stays on your credit history for ten years. As long as the bankruptcy appears on your credit report, you will find many lending doors closed or, if open, only at interest rates you would not have previously considered competitive.

When you file bankruptcy, the reality is this: you owed money, but you didn't pay it back. Even though you had the legal right to file bankruptcy, and even though the court has approved the plan for your repayment or other satisfaction of your debts, creditors don't like it when they don't get 100 percent of the debt repaid—with interest. So, as far as they are concerned, you are no longer a good customer.

When you emerge from bankruptcy, one thing you will want to begin to do is prove your former creditors wrong. How can you do that, when you just emerged from bankruptcy? By establishing good financial habits and building a record of timely payments on your obligations. As we will discuss more fully in the final chapters of the book, you will probably have to start small and slowly.

Even though you are emerging from bankruptcy, it probably won't be long before you begin receiving credit offers in the mail. You may even be able to find a local lender who is willing to extend credit to you for a car loan or some other purpose—though, as I said earlier, the interest rate and terms may not be what you are accustomed to. You certainly should not go on a spending and credit binge, but you may wish to consider how you can, very selectively, reestablish yourself as a creditworthy borrower. Over time, by exercising discipline and good judgment, you can rebuild your credit rating. But it won't happen overnight, and it won't happen by accident.

Bankruptcy Cannot Eliminate Certain Types of Secured Debt

The court cannot decree that you no longer have to make house payments if you plan to keep your house when you emerge from bankruptcy. Secured debt is still secured debt, and if you intend to maintain your right to keep and use the collateral—your house and your car, for example—you must work out a plan for repayment of the debt and the court must approve your plan. Depending on your situation when you file bankruptcy and your intentions for these assets, there are several options for filing bankruptcy and still keeping your house and your car. But—here it comes again—you should thoroughly discuss your situation and goals with a qualified bankruptcy attorney. The attorney will then be in a position to advise you about how to proceed with bankruptcy and still retain the use of the assets.

As we will discuss in more detail in chapter 7, in order to retain the use of the assets providing collateral for loans during and after bankruptcy, you must have in place a repayment agreement that the court will approve. When you are discharged from bankruptcy protection, the liens on your secured debt are still intact unless you chose, as part of your chapter 7 case, to surrender the asset. So, for example, if you want to stay in your house and keep your car, you would need to continue making payments on the loans and also gain agreement with your lender on a way to make up any missed payments.

For many consumers, gaining relief from massive unsecured debts through bankruptcy enables them to get caught up with their important secured debts.

Bankruptcy Cannot Relieve You of Certain Other Obligations

There are some debts or payments that even bankruptcy cannot protect you from. These include student loans, some back taxes, and court-ordered child support or alimony payments.

Student Loans. Most courts are very reluctant to discharge student loans, according to the Student Loan Marketing Association (Sallie Mae), the quasi-governmental organization that administers the government's insurance program for education lenders. If your student loan is causing most of your financial problems, bankruptcy may not make sense for you. You may be able to obtain a discharge on your loans if you can demonstrate that paying them creates an "undue hardship," but this is difficult to prove in bankruptcy unless you have become disabled to the point that you can't work or otherwise have no prospect of being able to earn money. Even then, you must file a separate motion with the court and present your case before the judge. I have spoken with many bankruptcy attorneys who have, collectively, represented clients in tens of thousands of bankruptcy proceedings, and I have heard very few of them say they were successful in getting student loans discharged in bankruptcy.

Back Taxes

Unless the due date for the return was three years or more before you filed bankruptcy, the return was actually filed two years or more before you filed, and the assessment is at least 240 days old, your tax debt cannot be discharged in bankruptcy. Oh, and you can't be guilty of tax fraud or tax evasion either.

SURVIVAL TIP:
TAX DEBT MAY BE DISCHARGED IN BANKRUPTCY IF

- The due date on the return is at least three years before your bankruptcy filing
- The return was filed at least two years before your filing
- The assessment from the IRS is at least 240 days old
- You aren't guilty of tax fraud; you aren't guilty of tax evasion

In other words, if you got slammed with a big tax bill last year and you can't pay it, don't file bankruptcy as a way to avoid it; if it isn't at least three years old, the court will have nothing to say about it.

Another note on taxes and bankruptcy: according to the Bankruptcy Abuse Prevention and Consumer Protection Act of 2005, all tax returns must be filed and copies furnished to the court and requesting creditors in order for your bankruptcy petition to proceed successfully. In addition, if you file Chapter 13 bankruptcy, you must provide tax returns for the four years preceding your petition in order for your repayment plan to be approved.

SURVIVAL TIP:
WHAT IF I CAN'T PAY MY TAXES WHEN THEY ARE DUE?

1. File your return on time, even if you can't pay. This will limit your liability for penalties and will prevent any appearance of tax evasion.

2. Request an extension of time to pay. In some cases, the IRS will grant up to 60 extra days to pay the full amount due.

3. Request an installment agreement. Approval by the IRS is automatic if:

   a. Your tax liability, including interest and penalties, is $10,000 or less;

   b. You can pay the amount due in three years or less;

   c. You have no other installment agreements in effect with the IRS;

   d. You have not had an installment agreement within the past five years;

   e. Your returns have been filed on time.

4. Consider filing an offer in compromise (OIC), which essentially is an offer to settle with the IRS for an amount less than the amount owed. The IRS will not likely accept an OIC if they think an installment payment plan is possible or reasonable. Go to www.ASurvivalGuidetoDebt.com for a list of companies that can help.

(For more information, see the latest revision of IRS form 9465, available at www.irs.gov. Also visit www.ASurvivalGuidetoDebt.com and review the listed resources for getting help with tax debt.

Child Support and Alimony

The laws are very clear: if you owe child support or alimony payments to an ex-spouse, bankruptcy will not alleviate your responsibility to continue paying these obligations. As a matter of fact, an ex-spouse who is owed such payments may intervene directly with the court administering the bankruptcy petition—usually at no cost to themselves—to ensure that payments disbursed to other creditors do not harm the right of the ex-spouse to continue receiving child support or alimony payments. Furthermore, if you got behind on child support or alimony payments, you must still make up that deficiency, even if you have filed for bankruptcy.

The U.S. Bankruptcy Code specifically exempts child support and alimony from discharge in bankruptcy proceedings. The automatic stay that prohibits other creditors from continuing efforts to collect from you does not apply to child support and alimony. If you owe these payments, you must continue making them—bankruptcy or not.

Financial Consequences of Bankruptcy

In addition to the limitations just discussed, there are some long-term implications of bankruptcy for your financial future. Remember, the purpose of this book is not to convince you to file bankruptcy or not to file it; it is to give you all the facts—positive and negative—so that you can make an informed decision about whether bankruptcy is an option you should consider. With that in mind, let's look at some of the consequences of bankruptcy that extend long after your case is closed and you have emerged from bankruptcy protection.

Getting Loans after Bankruptcy. Whereas it is usually possible to obtain loans after bankruptcy, they may not be offered at the more favorable interest rates reserved for borrowers with better credit histories. The underwriting of loans (a lender's evaluation of the amount of risk involved in lending to you) takes into consideration not only a prospective borrower's current ability to repay the loan but also the past payment performance of that borrower; therefore, a bankruptcy on the credit history raises a major red flag with most lenders. If lenders agree to do business with you at all, and if they believe they must assume a higher risk in order to do business with you, they will charge extra—in the form of higher interest rates—to compensate themselves for this increased risk.

We will discuss such situations in more detail in chapter 10, but for now, suffice it to say that just because you have a bankruptcy on your record, all bankruptcies are not viewed the same way by all lenders in all situations. Particularly if you can demonstrate a good payment record on some of your debts, a lender may be willing to work with you on a similar type of obligation.

Higher Interest Charges. As mentioned, if you can find lenders who are willing to work with you following your bankruptcy, they will usually factor the increased risk of loaning you money into the price they charge—the interest on the loan. Especially with auto loans following recent bankruptcies, these rates can be way, way above what you used to think was the norm.

You shouldn't automatically assume you should shun credit until ten years after your bankruptcy.

However, you shouldn't automatically assume you should shun credit until ten years after your bankruptcy, when it drops off your credit history. In fact, as discussed under Myth #4, obtaining and carefully using small amounts of credit is one way to begin rebuilding a good credit history. For many consumers, this may mean getting a secured credit card: a card with a charge limit backed by a deposit with the issuing bank. The limits on such cards are typically small—in the $200 to $500 range—but it's a way to get started. We'll talk more about establishing healthy habits for credit use in the last part of the book.

Some Insurance May Be Harder to Get. Like potential lenders, insurance companies may decide that you are less likely to pay your monthly premiums on time once they see a bankruptcy on your record—and yes, insurance companies do review your credit history. Like lenders, they may decide—if they agree to insure you at all—to charge you higher premiums to compensate for the higher risk they associate with doing business with you.

Bankruptcy Stays on Your Credit History for Ten Years. There is a reason why just about every credit application you will ever see asks some version of the question, "Are you now or have you ever been personally involved in a bankruptcy filing?" In most cases, your bankruptcy filing will appear as part of your credit history for ten years. That's a long time, and a very sizable blot on your creditworthiness. This is perhaps the most important reason why you should carefully consider all other options before deciding to proceed with bankruptcy.

Career and Emotional Consequences of Bankruptcy. Even though Title 11 (Bankruptcy) of the United States Code specifically prohibits employers from discriminating against someone who has filed for bankruptcy, employers can request and review credit history information on current or prospective employees. If any such information is used to justify a negative employment decision, you are entitled, under the Fair Credit Reporting Act, to be informed of the nature and source of the information (see chapter 4). However, sometimes, by then, the damage has already been done.

Persons working for or applying for work with a governmental entity that could have classified or national security aspects may encounter difficulties if they have negative credit histories or a bankruptcy on their records. Also, for persons employed in financial services and banking, employers may be wary of hiring, promoting, or even retaining someone whose personal finances may be perceived as placing them at higher risk of being untrustworthy or financially irresponsible, especially if their responsibilities include handling or overseeing large amounts of cash, securities, or other valuable commodities.

Even if you are not dismissed because of bankruptcy, you may find yourself passed over for promotions or other opportunities, especially if you are in competition with someone of equal qualification without such blemishes on his or her credit record.

It's worth mentioning in this connection, however, that, once again, all bankruptcies are not created equal. A bankruptcy brought on by serious illness or divorce may not be of as much concern to a current or prospective employer as one caused by a load of credit card debt that became unmanageable. Here is another case where honest communication can pay off.

In any case, because most employment applications either ask whether you have ever declared bankruptcy or, at the very least, request permission to pull a credit history, you should be truthful and forthcoming. Trying to conceal the facts from an employer will certainly not do anything to increase the organization's opinion of your trustworthiness.

Even as negative and potentially unfair as the career consequences of bankruptcy can be, however, for most people the emotional fallout is the worst. As I said previously, no one likes to admit failure. Obviously, no one files bankruptcy because things are going great. No matter whether your filing was instigated by unemployment you didn't deserve and couldn't control, a divorce you didn't want, a death or an illness, or poor decisions and bad habits that got you in financial trouble, bankruptcy still means one thing at its core: you owed more money than you had any way of paying. That fact is a hard thing for anyone to accept. And, as I mentioned, our American culture, with its idealization of self-reliance and independence, makes things even worse.

Some people struggle with depression because of their bankruptcies. For some, the anxiety and shame of bankruptcy can put an unbearable strain on relationships, resulting in divorce and estrangement of other types. The embarrassment of seeing friends and acquaintances after your filing becomes a matter of public record can feel paralyzing and debilitating. What can you do about the emotional baggage that can come with bankruptcy?

Remember, you are not your debt; you are not your bankruptcy. The fact is, bankruptcy is a tool. It is not a comment on your honesty, your intelligence, or your work ethic. I have written this book because in making important financial decisions like whether to file for bankruptcy, people need all the facts. If you come to the conclusion that you should file for bankruptcy, you should do so after having considered all the facts, both positive and negative. You should be completely convinced that filing bankruptcy is the best way to protect the assets your family depends upon until you can rebuild your affairs and get back on track. If you are absolutely persuaded by the facts that what you are doing is in your best interest, much of the negative emotional backwash can be controlled or eliminated.

It also helps to know that chances are, unless you are a celebrity, a public official, or otherwise prominent in your community, very few people are likely to know about your bankruptcy. Even though bankruptcy filings, as proceedings of the court, are part of the public record, very few individuals outside the legal system will ever look through the files. In many areas of the country, bankruptcy information is not published in any newspaper, and even if it is, only those who habitually read the tiny print in the "public notices" section of the classifieds will see it. Often, the only people who will know about your bankruptcy are those you choose to tell, the court officials involved, and your creditors.

Finally, I will again say that in most of the cases I have been involved with, once the decision to file bankruptcy has finally been made, many individuals report a great sense of relief, as though a weight has been lifted. Certainly, none of them were joyful about the circumstances that forced them to file, but once they weighed all their alternatives, reviewed all the pros and cons, spoke with an attorney, and concluded that bankruptcy was the best way left to them to begin their financial rebuilding process, they felt something they may not have expected: better.

For many people, the decision to file bankruptcy brings a sense of relief.

The act of making a decision, of exerting some control in what had been an out-of-control situation, of reclaiming the right to some say in their financial futures gave them the strength and determination to begin the recuperation process.

We're now ready to begin looking more closely at the two main types of bankruptcy petitions filed by individuals: Chapter 7 and Chapter 13. As we'll see in the next chapter, each type has advantages and disadvantages, depending on your specific situation and what you want to accomplish through your bankruptcy plan. Learning a few basic facts will move you well along the way to understanding which type of bankruptcy is best for you.

STEPS IN THE RIGHT DIRECTION

1. Consider talking to a bankruptcy attorney if

   - you owe more on your assets than they are worth and you can't make the payments
   - you've already tried other methods of resolving your debt
   - you are concerned about protecting your retirement savings
   - you are already being sued by creditors

2. If you have problem student loans, find out whether you can qualify for temporary forbearance, an adjusted or deferred repayment schedule, or other hardship provisions.

3. If back taxes are causing some of your problems, contact the taxing authority to find out about hardship provisions, installment repayment plans, and other alternatives.

4. Learn about the financial consequences of bankruptcy before filing.

Chapter 7

TYPES OF BANKRUPTCY

GUIDEPOSTS

In this chapter, you'll learn

- Main characteristics of Chapter 7 bankruptcy (liquidation) and Chapter 13 bankruptcy (reorganization, repayment)

- Advantages and disadvantages of each type

- Overview of the process for each type

- Why you need a qualified attorney

- How to begin evaluating which type is best for you

Especially in difficult financial times, it's likely that you've heard the word *bankruptcy* on the news or seen it in large type in the headline of an article in the financial section of a newspaper or a magazine. We often hear of large corporations filing Chapter 11 because they were in financial trouble and needed protection from creditors.

The U.S. Bankruptcy Code is divided into sections called "chapters." Each chapter is devoted to a specific aspect of the code. Some chapters, like Chapter 11, are intended to govern the procedures for large, complex business organizations such as corporations that are seeking the protection of the courts while they work out a plan to satisfy their debts and resume operating normally—reorganization—or, if that proves impossible, for selling the company's assets and distributing the proceeds to creditors until the money runs out—liquidation.

For most individuals, the two chapters of the bankruptcy code that are applicable are Chapter 7, which governs a personal bankruptcy in which assets are sold and the proceeds paid out to creditors, and Chapter 13, which contains the rules for a bankruptcy in which a repayment plan is worked out to allow the debtor to retain assets and still satisfy creditors over time. Another section, Chapter 12, governs bankruptcy by family farmers and is fairly similar to Chapter 13.

In this chapter, we'll cover the main characteristics of Chapter 7 and Chapter 13 because these are the parts of the law that are of most relevance to the majority of individuals who will file for bankruptcy protection.

YOU SHOULDN'T GO IT ALONE!—PART 2

Before we go any farther in our discussion of personal bankruptcy, you need to understand that the following material is presented for informational purposes only; it does not constitute legal advice. I am not an attorney—though I work with a number of them—and you should not base any decision to proceed or not proceed with a bankruptcy filing on what is said in this book. My purpose is to give you enough solid information to get you pointed in the right direction. You should not assume, after reading this or any other book on a similar topic, that you know enough to practice bankruptcy law. There's a saying popular among attorneys: "A lawyer who represents himself has a fool for a client." If you try a do-it-yourself bankruptcy, you will probably fall into the same category.

Along this same line of thinking, I want to spend a little more time on a theme that I've been sounding since the beginning of the book: if you believe a bankruptcy best serves your interests, you owe it to yourself to hire a qualified bankruptcy attorney who has experience in cases similar to yours. Bankruptcy law is far from simple, and every case is different because every person's situation is different. The best strategy for you to pursue in your bankruptcy depends on a number of factors including, but not limited to, your particular mix of assets and liabilities; your income level, its sources, and its reliability; how far behind you are with certain creditors; whether you owe back taxes, child support, or alimony; whether any of your debts involve cosigners; and even where you live. The answers to these questions will determine whether you should file Chapter 7 or Chapter 13, will impact the assets you seek to have exempted from the bankruptcy estate, will influence the terms of your repayment plan if you file Chapter 13, and a host of other matters you must decide about during the course of your case.

You owe it to yourself to hire a qualified bankruptcy attorney who has experience in cases similar to yours.

Would you really want to try strolling through this legal and financial minefield without an experienced guide?

A little later, we'll talk in general terms about the legal costs associated with filing personal bankruptcy. But remember what I said in chapter 5: the money you might save by trying to handle it on your own could be a drop in the bucket compared with the amount you could lose because of failing to file a motion, missing a deadline, or not knowing the most advantageous way to prepare your documents for the judge and the bankruptcy trustee.

To find an attorney, you can always do a general search on the Internet or look in your local Yellow Pages. But it's important that you not simply hire the first lawyer that happens to answer the phone or return your email. You need to have representation by someone who is qualified and knowledgeable in personal bankruptcy and who has experience in handling cases of similar size and complexity to yours.

Ideally, you'd want to talk to some people who had filed bankruptcy to find out who represented them, what their experience was like, and how well they felt their attorney met their needs. However, as you probably know, the attorney-client relationship is protected by confidentiality, so no bankruptcy attorney is going to give you a list of clients and invite you to call them for references. If you happen to know people who filed for bankruptcy, and if you know enough about their situations to know that they were similar to yours, it's possible that the attorney who represented them could effectively represent you too.

Another method is for you to offer some preliminary information about yourself to a prescreened list of attorneys, such as those you can find by going to www.ASurvivalGuidetoDebt.com. By filling in a few simple Internet forms, you can request information and contact from bankruptcy attorneys who have experience in helping people in situations similar to yours. You won't have any obligation, and the initial evaluation is usually free.

FINANCIAL GPS

To contact a bankruptcy attorney for a free evaluation, do a Google search of the term "bankruptcy lawyer" or go to www.ASurvivalGuidetoDebt.com.

CHAPTER 7 PERSONAL BANKRUPTCY: LIQUIDATION

Often called "regular bankruptcy," "straight bankruptcy," or "liquidation," Chapter 7 is bankruptcy in its most basic form. Chapter 7 discharges all of your unsecured debts, and there's no repayment plan. Under Chapter 7, you must give up any nonexempt property (see the definition of *exempt property* in the list of terms in appendix II). The trustee (see definition) assigned to your bankruptcy may sell this property and divide the proceeds among your creditors. Debts that aren't discharged include secured loans like cars, homes, and some merchant credit card purchases. You can choose to forfeit the assets that provide security for these loans in order to discharge the debt. Most of the time, however, people who file a Chapter 7 bankruptcy don't lose any assets by filing.

Given the choice, most people will want to file Chapter 7, if possible, because the bankruptcy is shorter, and more debts may be discharged without repayment. If you and your attorney determine that in your situation it's a toss-up between Chapter 7 and Chapter 13, it's almost always a good idea to go with a Chapter 7.

The Chapter 7 Process

In most cases, the Chapter 7 process goes like this:

1. Talk to an attorney
2. Analysis of your financial affairs by an approved credit counseling agency
3. Completion of an approved credit counseling course
4. Filing the case with the bankruptcy court
5. The 341 (creditors') meeting (see definition in appendix II)
6. Completion of a pre-discharge debtor education course
7. Discharge

Each of these steps is described in more detail in the following pages.

1. Talk to an Attorney. By now, I hope I've made the point that your first step, once you've concluded that bankruptcy could be advisable in your situation, is to consult with a qualified bankruptcy attorney. It is absolutely essential that you have someone in your corner who knows the applicable law, is familiar with the procedures and forms, and can represent your interests to make sure you receive every possible benefit and consideration.

2. Analysis of Your Financial Affairs. Before beginning any kind of bankruptcy proceeding, a detailed analysis of your current financial situation must be completed. It includes the following:

- Systematic documentation of your average monthly income

- Your average monthly expenses
- Your financial goals

This analysis will also determine which chapter of the U.S. Bankruptcy Code best meets your needs and protects your interests. Also, depending on which state they live in, some people who file for bankruptcy have the option to choose whether they want to follow the state or federal rules for exemption. Because some states allow for different property exemptions than the federal guidelines, this decision can have a significant impact. For this reason, choosing which set of exemptions best fits your case is a decision you should make in consultation with a bankruptcy attorney. Once all the filing documents are in place, the legal proceedings can begin.

Means Test for Chapter 7 Another important reason for this step is that by analyzing your finances, your attorney can help you determine whether you meet the "means test" for filing Chapter 7 now required by the Bankruptcy Abuse Prevention and Consumer Protection Act of 2005. This law requires that individuals with monthly incomes above their state's median income who have at least $166.67 of monthly income above living expenses ($10,000 over five years) available to repay debt must file Chapter 13 instead of Chapter 7.

To calculate whether you meet the means test for filing Chapter 7, first find out the median income for your state (these figures are available at the U.S. Census website: www.census.gov). If your income is lower than the median, you can file Chapter 7. If it's higher, however, you need to calculate how much income above living expenses you have available for debt repayment. The allowance for living expenses is established by using the IRS-approved schedules for tax calculation and collection. If, by applying this schedule, you have $166.67 or more per month above living expenses, you will probably be required to file Chapter 13.

If your income is above the median and you have less than $166.67 per month after living expenses, there is still one more hurdle you must clear to meet the means test for Chapter 7. You must determine whether the amount of excess income above living expenses available over a five-year period equals 25 percent or more of your debt. If it does, you will probably have to file Chapter 13. If it doesn't, you meet the final means test and may proceed with filing Chapter 7.

3. Completion of an Approved Credit Counseling Course. Before you
can proceed with any bankruptcy filing, the law stipulates that you must
complete a credit counseling course offered by an approved agency. To
get information about approved courses that may be completed online,
you can do an Internet search for "approved debtor education courses."
You can also get a list of all approved providers in your state at the U.S.
Justice Department's website (www.usdoj.gov). Or you can simply sign
up for the approved program available online at www.debt-foundation.
org, the website of the Debt Education and Certification Foundation, the
organization I help run. Note that approval does not ensure the quality of
a provider's services, so choose carefully.

4. Filing the Case with the Bankruptcy Court. The legal portion of the
bankruptcy process begins when you and your attorney file an official bankruptcy petition with the bankruptcy court. Once the filing is complete,
the automatic stay goes into effect. As you may remember from chapter 5
and from the definition given in appendix II, the automatic stay protects
you from all collection activities, lawsuits, and foreclosure proceedings that
your creditors would otherwise attempt. They must stop all collection efforts at once and cannot contact you in any way other than through the
court and your attorney.

5. The 341 (Creditors') Meeting. Approximately thirty days after filing
your bankruptcy petition with the court, you and your attorney will attend
a meeting, known as the "341 meeting" (named for the section of the U.S.
Bankruptcy Code that regulates it), with your creditors and the appointed bankruptcy trustee. Once your financial information is confirmed, the
trustee will review your bankruptcy petition. This usually takes between
fifteen and thirty minutes.

At the 341 meeting, the bankruptcy trustee will ask you a number
of questions, under oath. These include questions about the schedule of
exempt and nonexempt assets you have submitted with your bankruptcy
petition, whether you understand your rights under the bankruptcy code,
and whether you understand various courses of action available to you.

Financial GPS

Even though creditors are advised of the 341 meeting and may attend, they often do not. You, on the other hand, should attend this meeting.

One thing that the trustee usually asks about is a procedure called "reaffirmation of debt." This is an important topic for people who are in bankruptcy but who have certain assets they intend to keep, such as houses or cars. Even in Chapter 7, where your nonexempt assets will be sold to satisfy creditors, you must continue to make payments on secured assets like your house and your car if you intend to keep them. For many debtors, the main reason for filing bankruptcy is because they are behind on unsecured debt, like credit cards. However, they may still be current—or nearly so—on secured obligations like mortgages and car payments. For these people, it can make sense to reaffirm a mortgage or car loan debt and simply continue making payments on the debt during the bankruptcy and beyond. Some secured creditors do not require formal reaffirmation of the debt, as long as you remain current on payments.

Reaffirmation of debt can have a couple of benefits. First and most important, it allows you to keep the assets and continue using them. Second, any debt for which you continue making timely payments will show on your credit history and will be a factor in rebuilding your credit rating. If you anticipate needing another home or car loan prior to ten years following your bankruptcy, a record of timely payments on a similar obligation can go a long way toward encouraging a prospective lender, if not to completely overlook your bankruptcy, at least to take other factors into consideration.

You should discuss debt reaffirmation with your attorney, however. Depending on how much or how little equity you have in your home or you car, reaffirmation of the debt may still not be in your best financial interest. For instance, reaffirmation results in mandatory repayment of the loan, even if default occurs. The point is, reaffirmation of a debt means that it will survive your bankruptcy and becomes ineligible for discharge. Before you give up this important protection with respect to any debt, talk to your attorney.

FINANCIAL GPS

Reaffirming a debt in bankruptcy means agreeing to continue making payments on it.

---

6. Completion of a Pre-discharge Debtor Education Course. Under the new bankruptcy code in place since the passage of the Bankruptcy Abuse Prevention and Consumer Protection Act of 2005, you'll also be required to complete an approved credit counseling course in order to have your bankruptcy petition approved and your debts discharged. Usually, this course is between two and four hours long. The course provides additional information on how to stay out of debt and establish better financial habits after your bankruptcy is complete. (For a look at an approved online course, go to the DECAF site previously mentioned: debt-foundation.org.)

7. Discharge. When the trustee liquidates your nonexempt assets and distributes the proceeds to unsecured creditors under the terms of your plan, and when the bankruptcy judge discharges any remaining debts included in your petition, your Chapter 7 bankruptcy is complete and you are no longer responsible for the debts discharged in your bankruptcy. The court has eliminated all of your remaining eligible debts, and your creditors are satisfied. You are now out of bankruptcy and have complete control over your money.

JENNY'S STORY

To get an overview of how the Chapter 7 process looks in real life, let's take the example of a young woman we'll call Jenny. Typical of many Chapter 7 filers, Jenny was in way over her head with all kinds of debt. Recently divorced and facing reduced hours at work, she had no equity in her home because the value of her home had declined and her adjustable rate mortgage had recently reset to a new, higher rate, resulting in payments that became impossible for her to keep current along with her other obligations. She had lots of credit card debt too. She was still paying on her car and was behind, but not overwhelmingly so. Jenny had few additional assets other than some furniture and jewelry.

Jenny met with her attorney, who helped her analyze her financial situation in light of her goals. Because her income was below the state's median rate and she had no real assets available to satisfy her creditors, her attorney advised Jenny that a Chapter 7 filing was probably in her best interest. In cooperation with her attorney, she prepared a plan for her bankruptcy. After completing an approved online credit counseling course, she filed with the court.

Jenny had no equity and her home loan was one of the prime culprits in her inability to stay current with her debt; as a result, the house just wasn't a true asset in Jenny's case. Her attorney told Jenny that her jewelry's value was within the exemption allowed in her state for personal property, so none of it would likely be sold to satisfy creditor claims.

Her car, however, was a different matter. True, she was a bit behind on the payments. But she needed transportation to continue getting to work, and if she could get free of the stranglehold on her cash flow posed by the mortgage and some of her other debt, Jenny thought she could get caught up on her car loan fairly quickly. For that reason, her attorney advised her to reaffirm her vehicle loan. Part of her plan involved making extra payments for several months to bring her car loan current.

Over the past few years, Jenny had accumulated about $30,000 in credit card debt on four different cards, and she had fallen way behind on all of them. With the penalties and 20 percent interest the banks began charging her when she started getting behind, it didn't take long for the balances to snowball—along with the minimum required payments. Jenny's attorney reviewed the accounts with her and concluded that it was in Jenny's best interests to have the credit card debt discharged in Jenny's bankruptcy.

At the 341 meeting, about thirty days after Jenny's bankruptcy petition was filed with the court, the bankruptcy trustee went over Jenny's listing of assets and liabilities. She reviewed the asset list and asked Jenny some questions about various items. Then she wanted to know if Jenny understood her rights under the U.S. Bankruptcy Code and also what would happen to her assets if she proceeded with the filing. Jenny answered all the trustee's questions, and the meeting was over in about twenty minutes.

Next, Jenny attended a required debtor education course offered by an approved credit counseling provider. In the course, which took about four hours to complete, Jenny learned budgeting and other financial management methods. She also learned about the problems caused by having too much debt and too little savings. She filed a certificate of course completion with the bankruptcy court.

Not long after that, Jenny's case was closed and her debts were discharged. The bank took back her house, according to the terms of her bankruptcy, and canceled her remaining mortgage debt. The credit card debt was discharged by the court, since Jenny had no assets to use for repayment. She was out from under the high mortgage payments and the credit card bills, and so Jenny was able to catch up on her car loan. She rented an affordable apartment and, using the budget she had developed as a part of her pre-discharge financial counseling, began rebuilding her life, free from the crippling load of too much debt.

CHAPTER 13 BANKRUPTCY: REORGANIZATION AND REPAYMENT

Because this type of bankruptcy involves a reasonable, court-approved repayment plan designed to pay back all or part of your debt over a five-year period, the first eligibility requirement for filing Chapter 13 is that you have a means of income that is relatively dependable. The repayment plan will be based on your income level and covers both secured and unsecured debt.

FinanciaL GPS

To successfully file Chapter 13, you must have sufficient monthly income to maintain your repayment schedule for the entire term of your plan.

As a part of your plan, you will establish a monthly budget that allows for all your necessary monthly expenses: food, clothing, shelter, transportation, utilities, education, health care, court-ordered payments like child support and alimony, and other needs. This filing is very detailed and specific, and, like the means test for Chapter 7, is based on national standards used by agencies like the Internal Revenue Service for collection and reporting of income and expenses; in fact, the form on which you will file your report looks quite a bit like a tax return.

SURVIVAL TIP:
REVIEW CHAPTER 13 STATEMENT OF CURRENT MONTHLY INCOME

To see a copy of the Chapter 13 Statement of Current Monthly Income on the U.S. Federal Court website, go to www.uscourts.gov/rules/BK_Forms_08_Official/ B_022C_0108v2.pdf.

After you have completed this form with your attorney's advice and assistance, your attorney will file it with the court. This is the basis on which the court will establish the amount of your monthly disposable income. You'll typically have to pay all of your disposable monthly income to the trustee, who then disburses the money to your creditors.

The Chapter 13 repayment plan must pass two tests: the "best interest" test and the "best efforts" test. The best interest test states that unsecured creditors must be paid at least as much as they would have if you had filed for Chapter 7. The best efforts test requires that you pay all disposable income to the trustee for up to sixty months.

Under law, Chapter 13 cannot last longer than five years. As long as you make your payments under the payment plan, creditors can't contact you. This plan is an excellent solution as long as you have regular income and you can create and follow a budget.

The Chapter 13 Process

Usually, the Chapter 13 process goes like this:

1. Talk to an attorney
2. Analysis of your financial affairs by an approved credit counseling agency
3. Completion of an approved credit counseling course
4. Filing the case with the bankruptcy court
5. The 341 (creditors') meeting
6. Approval by the court
7. Repayment period
8. Completion of a pre-discharge debtor education course
9. Discharge

Each of these steps is described in more detail in the following pages.

1. Talk to an Attorney. We probably don't have to belabor this point any more; obtaining qualified counsel should always be the first step.

2. Analysis of Your Financial Affairs. As with Chapter 7, the first step is carefully deciding, on the basis of your individual situation, which bankruptcy procedure is in your best interests. If you have a stable source of income, and especially if you have a number of assets that you wish to retain control over during your bankruptcy, you and your attorney may conclude that Chapter 13 best serves your needs.

3. Completion of an Approved Credit Counseling Course. As with the Chapter 7 process, this is required before you are allowed to file with the court. Go to www.debt-foundation.org or a similar approved agency to complete your pre-bankruptcy credit counseling course.

4. Filing the Case with the Bankruptcy Court. As in Chapter 7, the legal portion of the bankruptcy process begins when you and your attorney file your official bankruptcy petition with the appropriate bankruptcy court. With Chapter 13, you also have up to fifteen days from the day you file the petition to file the payment plan and details of your financial situation. Again, as in Chapter 7, once the petition is filed, an automatic stay is in effect. Arising as a matter of law, the stay protects you from all collection activities, lawsuits, and foreclosure proceedings. Your creditors must stop all collection efforts and cannot contact you in any way.

5. The 341 (Creditors') Meeting. Approximately thirty to forty-five days after you file your petition with the court, you and your attorney will attend a 341 meeting. Under oath, the trustee will ask you questions to confirm facts about your filing, your assets, and your documentation. Once your financial information is confirmed, the trustee will review the repayment plan that you and your attorney have prepared. Your plan must be reasonable, the trustee must conclude that you're likely to meet your payment requirements, and the plan must show that you are making a good faith effort to repay your creditors.

6. Approval by the Court. Once the 341 meeting is completed, your Chapter 13 plan is sent to the bankruptcy judge for approval at a confirmation hearing. The judge makes sure all court costs have been paid, determines whether your plan complies with the law, decides whether it was made in a good faith effort to repay your creditors, and confirms that you're able and likely to meet the requirements of the payment plan.

FInancIaL GPS

The purpose of the 341 meeting is to establish the facts in your bankruptcy case, not to hold a test to prove your need for bankruptcy. The questions you'll be required to answer will be about the information you have provided and your rights under the law; you will not be required to justify your filing.

7. Repayment Period. Within thirty days of filing, you start making plan payments (if you haven't already done so) to the trustee. The trustee then disburses the payments to your creditors in accordance with your plan. The repayment plan may be structured over a three- or a five-year period. Also, many filers appreciate that they have to make only a single payment to the trustee—not the five or ten payments they were previously making to various creditors. In some areas, you can even arrange to have your payment automatically deducted from your checking account.

8. Completion of a Pre-discharge Debtor Education Course. As with Chapter 7, before you receive your discharge from bankruptcy, you'll have to complete a debtor education course from an approved provider. Go to www.debt-foundation.org for more information.

9. Discharge. Once your plan has been approved and you have made all required payments, your Chapter 13 repayment is complete. The court will eliminate or discharge all your remaining eligible debts, and your creditors are satisfied. Now you are out of bankruptcy and once again have complete control over your money.

If for some reason after you begin your Chapter 13 repayment plan, you are unable to make your payments as scheduled, you will need to explain the circumstances to the court. The court can choose to amend your plan, give you a grace period to make up for missed payments, extend the payment period, or, if the circumstances preventing you from making payments are genuinely beyond your control, to discharge your debts on the basis of financial hardship.

Quick Comparison of Chapter 7 and Chapter 13 Processes

Form of Bankruptcy	Chapter 7	Chapter 13
Analysis and credit counseling	Yes	Yes
Filing with the court	Yes	Yes
341 meeting	Yes	Yes
Repayment plan approved by court	Not applicable	Yes
Repayment period	Not applicable	Yes
Debtor education course	Yes	Yes
Discharge	Yes	Yes

If the court won't allow any of these alternatives, you may be able to convert from a Chapter 13 to a Chapter 7 filing. In order to qualify for this, you must not have received a discharge for a Chapter 7 filing within the eight years prior to the date you filed your chapter 13 case or a discharge from a Chapter 13 filing within the six years prior to the date you filed your current case. You must also have paid at least 70 percent of your unsecured creditor claims in any previous chapter 13 case (which must have been filed in good faith). You must also meet the means test, discussed on page 148.

DOUG'S STORY—PART 1

Doug, whom we met in the introduction and again at the beginning of chapter 5, had his first meeting with his attorney. Though his wife, Carol, was still unemployed, she was collecting benefits, and Doug's job, thankfully, was pretty stable. Unlike Jenny, Doug and Carol had a good amount of equity in their home, and they really hoped to retain control over it through the bankruptcy. Furthermore, he had been able to make most of the payments on his mortgage, though lately there had been some late fees assessed because of missed deadlines for timely payments. Doug and Carol also had some nonexempt assets that they were hoping to keep including a coin collection, some jewelry, and a small rental property.

Other than the immediate problem with his car and the lender's recent threats of repossession, Doug's biggest trouble was unsecured credit card debt. After Carol had lost her job, the minimum payments became impossible. When they had finished a complete review of his finances with the assistance of an approved financial counselor, Doug and his attorney concluded that it made the most sense, given his income level and his goal of keeping property that would otherwise be nonexempt from creditors' claims, for Doug to file his bankruptcy under Chapter 13.

Doug and his attorney developed a plan for Doug to pay back all his creditors—including the credit card companies—over a five-year period. The attorney helped Doug devise a schedule that included payments on his mortgage and vehicle, plus an amount to be paid to his unsecured creditors. Because of the protection of the bankruptcy court, Doug's unsecured creditors had to accept reductions in the amounts of Doug's balances and drastically lowered interest rates, resulting in much lower payments on Doug's unsecured debt. The attorney explained to Doug that as long as he made the agreed-upon payments on his plan, he would retain his vehicle, his house, and all his other assets—including his rental property.

Once Doug and the attorney had completed his repayment plan, they filed it with the court. About forty-five days later, Doug and his attorney attended the 341 meeting, at which the bankruptcy trustee asked Doug questions under oath about his listing of debts and the particulars of his repayment plan. He also queried Doug about whether he understood his rights and obligations for making his payments on the plan he had submitted to the court. In about fifteen minutes, the meeting was over.

For the next five years, Doug faithfully made the agreed-upon payments on his bankruptcy reorganization plan. Each month, he sent his payment to the trustee, who disbursed the funds to creditors as stipulated in Doug's plan. During this time, Doug completed an approved debtor education course that helped him learn some better financial habits to improve his chances of avoiding future money problems.

Once Doug completed his scheduled payments, his case was closed and all his remaining debts were discharged or eliminated by the court.

He still had the nonexempt assets with which he had entered Chapter 13 protection and was able to resume his life, free from creditor calls and an impossible load of debt.

CHAPTER 7 OR CHAPTER 13: WHICH ONE IS RIGHT FOR YOU?

As you can see from the previous discussion and case studies, the particulars of your situation, your future earning power, and your financial goals have a direct bearing on whether you would be better served by filing Chapter 7 or Chapter 13. For this and many other reasons, before seriously considering bankruptcy, you should hire an attorney you trust who has experience in personal bankruptcies similar to yours.

The objection that first occurs to many people at this point is fear about the cost of hiring an attorney. As I've already said a couple of times, though, what you'll pay a qualified bankruptcy lawyer is nothing compared to the amount you could cost yourself by not having competent counsel during the legal proceedings of bankruptcy. As we close this chapter, let's take some time to talk about court costs, legal fees, and the questions you should ask of any attorney you are considering for your bankruptcy case.

For basic bankruptcy representation, you can often expect to pay between $2,000 and $3,500.

Hiring an Attorney: What You Need to Know

One of the unavoidable costs of filing bankruptcy is the expense of actually filing the legal forms and having them processed by the clerk and officers of the court. Bankruptcy court fees vary by state and by type of bankruptcy, but generally, the court costs for filing personal bankruptcy range from $200 to $500. Attorney fees are harder to estimate; they are calculated based on the attorney's experience, the complexity of your case, whether problems with creditors are anticipated, and other factors that vary with each situation. However, for basic bankruptcy representation, you can often expect to pay between $2,000 and $3,500.

Does that mean that if an attorney quotes a figure lower than this range he or she is either incompetent or apt to do a poor job? Not necessarily, any more than a higher fee guarantees good representation. As with many important purchases, the price tag may not be the most important part of this decision. In fact, there are several things other than price you should definitely consider as you determine who will represent you in bankruptcy court.

Experience. Does the attorney have experience with personal bankruptcy? How much? Even more important, does the attorney have experience in representing clients whose bankruptcies were similar to yours in asset mix and complexity? How many cases did the attorney handle during the previous year (or other period) that were similar to yours, and were all of the cases brought to a successful conclusion?

Scope of Service. What are you getting for the fee you will pay? Will the attorney go to the 341 meeting and all other necessary court appearances with you? How much access to the attorney will you have during the process? If you have questions during your bankruptcy, who will answer them, and is that included in the fee you will pay, or will you be billed for extra time? Will the attorney assist you in preparing your financial information, and if so, will you pay extra for the time?

Client Relations. Perhaps most important of all, you should work with someone you feel you can trust. The bankruptcy process can be intimidating and is often emotionally draining; don't attempt it unless you can establish a comfortable working relationship with your attorney. In this connection, you might want to ask the attorney how he or she will help you decide whether you should file Chapter 7 or Chapter 13. The attorney should show evidence that he or she will carefully consider the details of your situation and help you take every possible advantage of the law to bring your case to a favorable conclusion.

There are also some things you can do to contain attorney costs, regardless of whom you hire. At the top of this list is having all your information current and organized before you meet with the attorney. Certainly the attorney's paralegal assistant or secretary could go through everything for you and arrange it in a logical order, that won't happen for nothing. Furthermore, having your information in order will give you a level of familiarity with your situation that will also be helpful for your attorney in giving you the best possible representation. Don't assume that your responsibility for your situation or the need for your close attention ends when you hand your attorney a check. Stay engaged and involved, as you would in any business relationship. Your attorney will do better work, and you'll be more satisfied with the result.

SURVIVAL TIP:
GET ORGANIZED

To save time and effort, organize your financial information before your initial meeting.

Let's assume that, like Jenny and Doug in the stories you just read, you've decided the only way out of the bad situation you're in is by filing personal bankruptcy. I hope that by carefully considering the information presented in this and the preceding chapters—and especially by retaining the services of a qualified attorney—you have successfully completed or are on course to complete the bankruptcy process and are ready for your fresh start in life, free from the burden of excessive debt.

As good as it probably feels to be rid of nagging creditors and an impossible debt load, this is not the end of the story. As a matter of fact, if you're emerging from bankruptcy, in a very real sense you are back at the beginning. So, how will you take advantage of the fresh start afforded you by the bankruptcy system? In fact, even if you were able to handle your situation by using some of the ideas presented in chapters 1 through 4, without resorting to bankruptcy, it still remains for you to establish healthier patterns of financial behavior in order to keep from getting back in the same kind of debt trap you just escaped.

In the final section of this book, we'll look at ways you can establish and maintain sound financial practices in your everyday life. If you follow the advice I'm about to present, I can promise you that you will not only survive your debt problems—you will thrive.

STEPS IN THE RIGHT DIRECTION

1. To save time and money, gather and organize your financial information before you speak to a bankruptcy attorney.

2. Obtain a free consultation with a qualified bankruptcy attorney at www.ASurvivalGuidetoDebt.com.

3. Write down a list of questions you plan to ask the attorney before you agree to representation.

4. Educate yourself on the differences between Chapter 7 and Chapter 13 bankruptcy filings so that you can work with your attorney to determine which is the most appropriate for your situation.

PART THREE

BLOCKING, TACKLING, AND DIGGING DITCHES

"Al, I haven't seen you for ages! — Where have you *been*?"

"Living within my income."

Chapter 8

ATTITUDE, PERSONALITY, AND MONEY

GUIDEPOSTS

In this chapter, you'll learn

- How your personal characteristics affect the way you think about and handle money

- How to start changing bad financial habits into good ones

- How to improve your family's "money culture"

As I said at the beginning of the book, I believe this final section contains the most important information you'll need as you begin building your own personal financial recovery. Whether you've just emerged from bankruptcy or were able to handle your money problems some other way, you are now poised to make a fresh beginning, free of the worry and financial burden of an unhealthy load of debt. But unless you do some things differently from what you did before, you could wind up in the same place you were when you started reading this book. You do not want that to happen, and this final section will show you how to avoid it.

There's a saying popular with psychological counselors: "Wherever you go, there you are." All of us carry some invisible baggage with us on our journey through life, baggage packed with the experiences, beliefs, habits, assumptions, and tendencies that go into making us who we are. Some of the items in our personality suitcases are positive and helpful, and some aren't. How we deal with our baggage, both the good and the bad, depends to a large degree on how aware we are of what is packed in our luggage. But one thing is certain: wherever we go in life and whatever we do, we take this baggage with us. You can change jobs, change addresses, change marriages, or even change your name, but it's still you in there, making choices and reacting to circumstances.

In this final section, we'll address some of the financial baggage you're carrying. We're going to open the suitcases and take a look at the attitudes, assumptions, beliefs, and habits that determine your financial behavior. We'll identify the good and bad decisions people make about their money and lay the groundwork for making smart choices in the future. I hope you'll think of this as an opportunity instead of as something you'd rather avoid. Remember: avoiding problems rather than dealing with them may be one of the behaviors that landed you in debt trouble to begin with. Now that you've wiped the slate clean, it's time to form some new habits. It probably won't be easy. Like the "ditch digging" alluded to in the title for part 3 of this book, it involves some hard work that most of us would rather not do. On the other hand, it will enable you to enjoy a much more secure future, one less likely to be clouded by the problems of debt that has gotten out of control. So let's get started.

UNDERSTANDING YOUR "MONEY ATTITUDES"

It may not surprise you when I say that people tend to be very emotional about money. As I stated in an earlier chapter, many individuals would be just as willing to talk to a stranger about their sex lives as about their money. The fact is, our decisions about money, whether conscious or unconscious, are often driven primarily by emotion. We buy things because owning them makes us feel successful; we sock away money in savings because it makes us feel secure; we risk our life savings on a business deal because we have a burning desire to "hit it big"; we purchase expensive gifts for friends or loved ones because we think it will demonstrate our love or our respect. Sometimes, of course, we spend money because we must: we need groceries, clothing, a place to live. However, even for those "necessary" expenses, most of us have some sort of underlying emotional response that governs the way we feel about what we do with our money.

Year after year, surveys by groups like the American Psychological Association tell us that worries about money are close to the top of the list of stressors for most of us. The latest survey, completed in September 2008—the same month that the stock market was in freefall and Congress was debating a $700 billion financial bailout—showed that almost half of those surveyed were "increasingly stressed about their ability to provide for their family's basic needs" (www.apa.org/monitor/2008/12/money.html). Money is definitely an emotional subject for most people.

Understanding that the topic of money is fraught with emotion—whether consciously recognized or not—is an important first step to gaining understanding about the proper use of money. The truth is this: money, at its most basic level, is nothing more than a tool. If you can reach this basic understanding,

> **Money, at its most basic level, is nothing more than a tool.**

you can begin to get a perspective on your financial life that will help you make wiser decisions in the future.

It's also important to realize that your attitude about money—like your attitude about almost everything in your life—was partially formed when you were very young. Most of us acquired at least some of our attitudes about money from the financial management styles of our parents.

Your "Money Biography"

For example, I have a friend whose father was a farmer. Every year, he watched his dad go to the bank and borrow money to buy seed, fertilizer, fuel, equipment, and other necessary expenses involved in planting and harvesting a crop. At the end of the year, after the harvest, he watched his dad take the money from the crop and pay off his loans—at least in a good year it worked that way. He grew up in a household where debt—usually, significant amounts of it—was a normal way of life; thus, it might not surprise you to learn that this person has a fairly accepting attitude toward the idea of incurring debt.

On the other hand, I know another person whose father was a blue-collar laborer and mother worked as a secretary. Her parents paid cash for everything and avoided debt at all costs. They were also committed and zealous savers, putting every dollar they could in the bank for "a rainy day." My friend, as a result, has a very different attitude toward debt than the guy in the first example. She works hard, lives a fairly simple life, and has a sizable amount of money in her savings account and her retirement accounts. Credit card debt? No way! Like her parents, she pays cash for almost everything.

Which model is the right one? The answer may surprise you: neither. On the other hand, neither one is wrong. There can be good reasons to incur certain types of debt, and there are times when it makes more sense to focus on saving. The key to finding the right response at the right time is being conscious of why you spend, why you save, why you borrow, and what motivates you to do any of the three.

Take a little time to think about what you remember about the financial culture in your family of origin. Was your dad always bringing home a new toy: a boat, a new car, a motorcycle, the latest sporting equipment? Did your mom work, and if so, did she have "her" money, separate from the household income? Did your folks frequently complain about bills and expenses? Or did they discourage family money discussions, perhaps by treating money as a taboo subject unsuitable for children?

Your childhood experiences have probably formed some portion of your emotional patterns with regard to money. Either you approved of the behaviors and attitudes exhibited by your parents and have adopted many of them for yourself, or you disapproved and have reacted by going as far as you can in the other direction. For example, if your mom was a scrupulous saver who pinched every penny, you buy what you want, when you want—whether you can pay for it or not; if your dad believed in "having the best" and "keeping up with the Joneses," you question and agonize over every purchase that is not absolutely necessary to sustain life.

As if that weren't complicated enough, people who live together must also be aware of the inherited money attitudes of their partners, because they come from different backgrounds and probably have different assumptions, attitudes, and beliefs about financial matters. As with every other area of human relationships, your partner probably experienced different financial behaviors during childhood than you did. For that reason, what "just makes sense" to you may very well not be intuitive to him or her. Dealing with the differences caused by such diversity of experience is an important part of understanding your household's "financial culture."

WHAT IS YOUR "MONEY PERSONALITY"?

At the simplest level, your money is doing one of two things: coming or going. Similarly, there are two primary financial personality types: spenders and savers. Although there are many different ways to subdivide and refine these basic definitions—and you can buy a library full of books to help you do just that—most of us will tend to lean one way or the other: either we derive the greatest emotional satisfaction from saving or we derive it from spending. As you review your financial history and your current situation, ask yourself whether you are a spender or a saver.

For most of the people reading this book—unless your financial troubles were caused by circumstances utterly beyond your control or ability to anticipate—the answer is probably "spender." Most people who get into financial trouble do so, at least in part, because they have accumulated an unmanageable load of (mostly) unsecured debt by using credit cards to buy things they didn't have the cash to purchase. And I'm not just talking about conspicuous consumption–type items like fancy vacations, the latest electronic gadgets, furniture, or designer clothes. You may be in debt trouble because you used a credit card to pay a chunk of college tuition that wasn't covered by your daughter's financial aid package. You might have run up a load of unsecured debt because you tried to keep a business afloat by using plastic. Whatever the reason, you decided, by consummating a transaction using credit instead of cash, that making the purchase right then was better or more advisable than waiting until you had enough money in the bank to cover it. That, at its core, is "spender" behavior. It can happen a little at a time or in one big wallop, but the end result is the same: you end up owing more than you own.

IMPORTANT TIPS FOR SPENDERS

If you are a spender, it's probably not realistic to assume that reading this book is going to fundamentally change your financial personality. However, by adopting some of the ideas I will present, you may very well be able to adapt your spending behavior in ways that make it manageable. You may even be able to build in some rewards for your need to spend—rewards that will help keep you motivated to make the long-term changes necessary to get your financial house in order and keep it that way.

Cash vs. Credit: "The Pain of Paying"

According to four studies whose results were announced in September 2008 by the American Psychological Association, persons who pay with cash tend to spend less than those who use noncash methods, including credit cards and gift certificates. The researchers concluded this was true partly because when consumers use cash to complete a transaction, the outflow of resources is readily apparent. It is easier for them, in the researchers' words, to feel "the pain of paying."

In one study, participants were asked to read a list of the specific contents of a meal in a restaurant. Then they were asked how much they would be willing to spend in cash, and how much they would be willing to spend if using a credit card. The results demonstrated that people tend to spend more when using credit than when using cash.

Maybe this study just proves what many merchants have known for years: people will buy more and make larger purchases when they can use credit. The credit card companies know this, for sure; in fact, they count on it. So do the casinos; that's why they use chips at the gaming tables instead of letting you take money out of your wallet. If that comparison makes you a little uncomfortable, good.

Use cash instead of credit.

What does this mean for you as you begin assessing your spending plans for a more debt-free future? Simply this: When you do need to spend, use cash instead of credit; you'll spend less, and still probably get what you need. Not only that, but you just might discover the satisfaction of actually being able to pay for something without having to worry about what your next credit card statement is going to look like.

People will buy more and make larger purchases when they can use credit.

The other benefit of using cash instead of credit is that sometimes, the inconvenience of it causes you to stop and think before buying. If you've got to make a trip to the ATM to get the money to pay for something, you're more likely to carefully evaluate whether you really need it. Once you get in the habit of making this judgment before you spend money, you'll probably notice that you tend to spend less. I probably can't overemphasize this point: paying with cash instead of credit is the single best way to make sure you don't overspend.

In a later chapter, I'm going to talk some more about the ins and outs of credit use and its place in your financial recovery plan. But for now, remember that as long as you are paying cash for the things you need, it's much less likely that you are digging yourself back into a money pit.

"Keep Yourself Poor"

This heading may not sound like good advice, but it is. In fact, this principle is one I use in my own personal finances. I use it because I learned it from watching several millionaires. These aren't the people you read about in *Forbes* or the financial section of *USA Today*. Instead, they are what might be called "the millionaires next door": people who worked as teachers, blue-collar laborers, or in some cases, small business owners. They don't drive flashy cars or vacation abroad. Their houses are often modest. But through the years, they developed the habit of paying off debt early (especially unsecured debt, but also vehicle loans and mortgages), keeping some money in savings, and using cash for almost everything they bought.

When they got an unexpected influx of money—from a tax refund or an inheritance, maybe—they used it to pay down debt instead of spending it. Over the years, they started earning more interest than they paid. They contributed the maximum to their retirement plans, and upon their retirement, their net assets were in excess of a million dollars. They achieved this by keeping themselves poor: keeping only the cash balances they needed to live on, and putting everything else toward paying off debt and, later, to accumulating savings.

The key to keeping yourself poor is to make getting at the money more difficult than writing a check or using a debit card. Money that you put "into savings" should not be in your checking account. You should have a separate savings account. You will see that over time, using this strategy can be fun and curiously addictive.

As you begin your financial makeover, you really need to take a moment to understand the opportunity you have to completely change the way you approach your finances. You can become one of the millionaires next door if you apply these principles—especially if you are committed to learning from your past mistakes. Like ditch digging, it won't be easy, and it's definitely not automatic, but it is possible.

TYPES OF SPENDERS

As I said earlier, I imagine that most people who read this book are probably dominated by the "spender" tendency, so it might be helpful to do a little more analysis of the different ways this behavioral style plays out in everyday life. Understanding your financial personality and behavior is the first step in gaining better control of your money. It's also important to remember, as I mentioned earlier in the chapter, that spending isn't always wrong. There are times when we need to be not only willing but also happy to part with our hard-earned cash in order to do what's best for ourselves and our families. But understanding is the key. Making financial decisions based on planning and priorities looks very different from impulse buying or binge spending. The first will usually keep you on track to meet your financial goals, and the second will usually get you in debt trouble.

"Splurge" Spenders

Variously classified by financial behavior analysts as "high rollers," "pleasure seekers," "happy-go-lucky," and various other similar labels, spenders of this type tend to engage in expensive, even lavish buying habits with little thought for future consequences. Spenders in this category like the finer things, and they will gladly incur debt—often, lots of it—to have them. Splurge spenders are not to be confused with bargain shoppers; for them, the name of the game is getting it now and letting tomorrow worry about itself. The fact is, splurge spenders get deep, emotional satisfaction from the act of spending money.

If you think you may fall in this group, the best advice I can offer is to seek long-term value in your spending behavior rather than short-term excitement or gratification. You will probably always feel the urge to spend money, but if you can learn to ask yourself, "Do I need it, or do I just want it?" and answer honestly, you may be able to start reining in your spending habit to something more manageable and helpful for your long-range financial security. By limiting your spending—especially your big-ticket items—to things that will provide value for a long time, you will also get the maximum benefit for those times when you do spend money. Finally, you really should try to discipline yourself to save at least something on a systematic basis. Who knows? You might decide you like that feeling of always having a little something in the bank. I'm not saying you'll ever turn into a full-fledged saver, but taking a couple of steps in that direction wouldn't be a bad thing for you to consider.

FINANCIAL GPS

Splurge spenders should look for long-term value and begin building savings

Sale Spotters

Whether you call them bargain hunters, shop-till-you-droppers, clearance sale queens (or kings), discount divas, or some other descriptive name, these are the spenders who honestly believe if they're buying it below normal retail, it's got to be good. Somewhat like the splurge spenders, these folks are very focused on what's on sale today and not too worried about how the purchase will affect their bottom line tomorrow. For sale spotters, the thrill of the chase is the main motivation. Never mind that they'll end up throwing out half of the stuff they bought in that bulk quantity—after all, they got it for half as much a pound as you'd pay at the grocery store!

Sale spotters love to shop; it makes them feel better. They will always use store loyalty cards and incentive programs, even to the point of buying things they don't really need, simply in order to get the discount.

Getting personal for a moment, this is the spending behavior that generates the most interesting discussions between my wife and me. I'm not necessarily saying she's a sale spotter, but I can't tell you how many times she has opened a conversation with the words, "You won't believe how much money I saved you today . . ." My initial impulse is always to respond with, "But can I put it in the bank?" Usually, I try to be a little more tactful.

For the sale spotters reading this book, my main piece of advice is to go with your strengths and, following the principle mentioned above, use cash, not credit, to bring down your bargain-hunting big game. Even if it's an unbelievable markdown, using credit to buy it will usually add loads of interest to the eventual purchase price, turning your good deal into dead weight. By all means, keep looking for those bargains. But focus your energies on things you really need, not on add-ons or options. Just because it's in the sale circular doesn't mean you need it.

Another thing to consider is that prices are almost always negotiable. Whether it's a bargain you located on eBay or in the sale bin at Target, there's almost nothing you can't haggle for and get a little cheaper if you're willing to take the trouble. If you're a dyed-in-the-wool sale spotter, why not take it to the next level and ask for an even deeper discount? And if you get it, buy it with cash.

FiNaNCiaL GPS

Sale spotters should use cash and focus on needs vs. wants.

The Giver: Spending as Caring

This spending pattern is tricky, because this type usually derives little, if any, personal financial benefit from his or her spending behavior. Instead, this person spends in order to give it away because that's what makes him or her feel good inside, or because the giver believes or senses that the gift will make the recipient feel loved, respected, or appreciated. Givers can be motivated by guilt, insecurity, poor self-image, or a simple need for recognition, but the thing they have in common is that their spending, though ostensibly for the benefit of someone else, is really undertaken to meet their emotional needs.

Now, I'm not necessarily talking here about the doting grandmother who can't pass a children's clothing store without buying something for one of her angels—though such a person may also be a giver. Nor am I trying to suggest that anytime someone financially helps out a loved one or friend who is in a tight spot they should be classified in this category. However, givers will continue to buy things—often, quite costly things—for the objects of their attentions, even when the giver can't afford it and couldn't be reasonably expected to incur the expense. They will run up debt with little thought of the consequences, simply because of their need to give something to someone they care about. In this respect, they actually have much in common with the splurge spenders and the sale spotters: their need to spend (for someone else) is greater than their ability to consider the consequences. For givers, love and money are so deeply intertwined that they are almost the same thing.

If you think you may be a giver, my primary caution to you is this: if you don't take care of yourself, you will soon be unable to take care of anyone else. Think of it this way: by saving your gifts for really special occasions or for things that are truly necessary for the people close to you, you can get the maximum bang for your giving buck. Always keep in mind that for the people you really care about, the greatest gifts you can give may not involve money. Instead, think about giving gifts like your time and understanding.

Another caution: if you are a giver who is trying to change to a healthier pattern, you may need to have some honest communication with the people who have been on the receiving end of your spending pattern. They may have grown dependent on you, and they may even feel that your new lifestyle means you are neglecting them. You need to explain that just because you aren't spending money on them doesn't mean your feelings toward them have changed. You must convince them—and yourself—that money and love are not the same thing. It won't be easy, but you must address this underlying misperception for yourself and any other people who might be involved in the cycle. Otherwise, you won't be able to escape this self-defeating pattern.

Finally, remember that, as with the other spending types I described, if you can discipline yourself to use only cash to fund your giving, your need to give is less likely to land you in financial straits.

FINANCIAL GPS

Givers should save their financial generosity for times of genuine need and remember that the most meaningful gifts may not be financial at all.

The Ostrich

Spenders in this category, like the proverbial animal, keep their heads in the sand as far as their financial circumstances are concerned. They probably haven't opened a bank statement in years, and if they are in credit card trouble, they probably have a pile of sealed envelopes containing account information they would rather not see. They usually have no idea how much debt they have or how much it's costing them. For that matter, they probably couldn't tell you how much cash they have on hand at any given moment. Budgets? Balance sheets? Forget it! They don't know, and deep down, they don't want to know. They just want to go about their business without having to worry about things like due dates, minimum payments, and late charges.

Oddly, ostrich spenders don't necessarily get in trouble because of big-ticket spending. They are as likely to overspend on eating out, designer coffee, and other trifles. If they consider such expenditures at all, they are likely to persuade themselves by thinking, "It's just one dinner," or, "I really need my extra-tall mocha cappuccino with two espresso shots in the afternoon," until the cumulative effect of all those "reasonable" and "just-this-once" expenditures eventually becomes too much for them to handle. They usually have a big load of unsecured debt and may even go to nontraditional sources such as payday loans, loan companies, or even pawnshops, making their problems even worse.

Obviously, this is a very dangerous financial attitude. Until an ostrich spender realizes that he or she alone is responsible for his or her financial behavior and well-being, there's not much that any advice, training, or book can do for them. They frequently feel helpless in financial matters, but that is mostly because of their unwillingness to educate themselves and take charge of their own affairs.

Ostriches' biggest need is to pull their heads out of the sand and begin asserting some control over their financial behavior. Unfortunately, spenders of this type often will not take action unless they are forced to, either by the legal system or by friends or family members who can practice financial "tough love." If you are an ostrich and you recognize yourself in the description above—congratulations! You've taken the first step toward self-awareness, and you may be on your way to a better money attitude. But it will take focus, determination, and discipline. You also might want to keep this book handy and reread it a few times.

FInanCIaL GPS

Ostrich spenders should spend some time facing up to exactly where they are, then form a plan to get where they need to be.

Now that you've looked at a few of the "spender" personality types, you may be recognizing yourself or a family member in one of the descriptions. These are not by any means every type of spending behavior that exists, and some people may at various times exhibit characteristics of more than one type, but these are somewhat indicative of the primary behaviors that get people into debt trouble.

I hope that by now you are more aware of your financial attitudes and the implications they have for the decisions you make. The next step is to convert this awareness into action, exchanging your less healthy impulses for some new habits that will keep you moving in the right direction with your money.

However, many of you live in households with other people who will have a huge impact on what you decide and what you actually do. For that reason, it's important as you begin your journey toward financial health to have some open, honest family conversations about money matters.

FINANCIAL COMMUNICATION FOR FAMILIES

As any marriage counselor or divorce attorney can tell you, family friction over money plays havoc with relationships. It can't be stated with certainty that money actually causes the majority of divorces, but you can be sure that if any relationship problems do exist, money will factor into the equation somewhere almost every time.

Think money doesn't have emotional strings tied to it? Try telling that to the hard-core saver who married a spender; every time she manages to build the savings account to within a few dollars of a level she's comfortable with, he comes home with a new rod and reel, home theater system, or top-of-the-line power tool. The conversation that follows will usually be anything but calm and reasoned. And it's not much better, sometimes, if two spenders marry each other. Especially if they are of contrasting styles—say, a giver married to an ostrich—you can bet there will be some heated discussions over whose fault it is that the credit cards are always maxed out.

The fact is, financial strain, like any other stressor, can create an environment that is corrosive for relationships. Whereas relationship coaching is not the purpose of this book, I can tell you nevertheless that many of the people who come to me for financial counseling or help with their debt are feeling the strain in their marriages, their parenting, and in just about every other area of their lives. Frequently, one of the contributing factors to the debt overload faced by households is poor communication: He spends money on things that he thinks are none of her business; she intercepts the credit card statements so he won't know how much she charged last month. Such behaviors are not only self-defeating but also destructive to relationships.

Tips for Family Financial Communication

One of the best things you can do, especially now that you're beginning your financial do-over, is to establish a pattern of open communication about money matters. Your family's financial attitudes and expectations are inseparable from the everyday decisions you will make—decisions that add up to form your financial future. Talking openly and honestly about money matters—budgeting, spending, and saving—will help you form a healthy financial culture for your household. When everyone is on the same page—or at least reading from the same book—you've got a much better chance of establishing the practices that will keep you out of the kinds of trouble you bought this book to escape. It's also vital to acknowledge with your family that "this is *our* problem; we have to solve it together." Until everyone involved acknowledges the fact that change is necessary and takes ownership of the process, it will be difficult for any real progress or change to occur.

Involve the Kids. It's a mistake to think that family finances aren't an appropriate topic for children. Remember your money biography from earlier in this chapter? Whether or not you speak openly with them about money, your children are acquiring financial assumptions and attitudes. Why not make it a proactive process rather than accidental? I don't think it's necessary to share all the details of your financial life with younger children, but I do think it's certainly a good idea to begin teaching them at an early age about topics like saving money for future needs. If you are a contributing member of a religious group, encourage your kids to give their offerings from a portion of the money they've saved. When important financial decisions are being made—such as a potential job change for one of the parents or the planning of a special vacation—involve the children in the conversation. They certainly can't be expected to make the final decisions in such matters, but they should feel that their opinions and feelings matter.

Set Goals—Together. If there's something that you really want to accomplish, you need to set a goal. For most people, setting a goal means writing it down, forming an action plan, and breaking the ultimate objective into monthly, daily, or even hourly increments. For others, goal setting is less formalized; it may be limited to a firm intention for a particular outcome—including the steps needed to achieve it—that is kept in mind consistently until it becomes a reality. Whatever your style and however you go about it, goals are what provide you with direction and purpose.

> **Goals are what provide you with direction and purpose.**

Goals are important in your financial life as well. As you begin your money makeover, take some time to sit down with your spouse or partner and talk about where you'd like to be in your finances in six months, a year, five years, or even at retirement. Even though your focus may need to be more on the short term right now, it doesn't hurt to have a long-range objective in mind. You can always adjust your goals to make them work for you, but establishing a target is important. It's important that you agree on your financial intentions and commit to working toward them together.

I keep my financial goals in front of me. For example, one of them is the login on my computer; every time I use my computer, I'm reminded of my goal. You might want to write your four or five most important financial goals on an index card and stick them on the refrigerator door. The point is that the goals should be something everyone agrees on, and they should be talked about on a regular basis—say, once a month.

Here are some examples of goals you might consider:

- Have $1,000 in savings by [date].
- Pay off student loans in the next thirty-six months.
- Fully fund my 401k (or IRA account) this year.
- Pay cash for a new refrigerator (or other necessary major purchase).
- Be debt-free within the next five years.

Hold Regular "Finance Committee" Meetings. Most of us tend to avoid the unpleasant whenever possible. If you only talk about money when there's a crisis, guess what? You'll eventually avoid talking about it altogether. Instead, why not establish regular times—maybe around the first of the month, or whenever you're paying bills—to discuss family finances? Don't just focus on problems; share the success stories too (yes, there will be some). When you keep each other informed about what's going on with your money, you reduce the chances that someone will make a rash or ill-informed decision.

Talk About Major Purchases—Before You Commit to Them. I realize that all of us have varying opinions about what constitutes a "major" purchase, but because most of you reading this are in the position of starting over financially, I would advise erring on the side of safety. Especially if you or your partner have had a tendency in the past to make large impulse buys, it's important to commit to the discipline of getting mutual agreement before committing to any large purchase that is not necessary to the immediate health or safety of your family. As mentioned earlier, these types of decisions might even be appropriate for a family meeting, where everyone has a chance to hear the alternatives and express opinions and feelings. By making yourselves accountable for bringing such decisions to the other involved parties for consideration, you will avoid many of the blunders that can get you back in financial trouble.

Make some commitments about what constitutes a major purchase for your family: anything over $100, $500, $1,000—whatever works best in your situation. Make an agreement that no purchase above this amount will be made unless both partners—or the entire household, if that works better for you—have discussed and agreed to it. Agree that large purchases will not be made for any purpose—because "it was on sale," to demonstrate love or appreciation, on impulse—unless everyone involved has carefully considered its impact on household financial goals.

If this process seems like it takes all the fun and spontaneity out of life, recall how much fun it was the last time you bought a "surprise" for someone, and instead of being grateful for it, they yelled at you for spending too much money. This is another situation where open communication makes everyone's life easier.

By the way, this principle also applies to allocating large infusions of cash—tax refund checks, for example. You should think carefully and strategically about how to use these resources. Rather than running out and blowing the whole wad on the new laptop you've been wanting, talk to your spouse or partner about how to use the money in a way that is most beneficial for the entire household. You might be better off limping along with that slightly shopworn desktop computer and using the cash to make an early payoff on a loan. I know this idea doesn't sound like nearly as much fun, but remember: we're learning to dig ditches. Once the hard work is done, you'll be able to afford to reward yourself with some more enjoyable expenditures. Recall the millionaire next door who kept herself poor and reaped the rewards later in life.

Avoid Blaming. Inevitably, mistakes and mishaps will happen: a checking account will get overdrawn because of a math error; someone will get a traffic ticket at the worst possible time; the electric bill will be double what it was the previous month—the list is endless. Accept that these things happen and try to avoid pointing fingers. You may win the argument and still lose the war.

Keep your goals in mind and realize that even when mistakes or unexpected barriers arise, you're staying on the right course for eventual success. As long as everyone is continuing to strive to reach a mutual goal, you shouldn't allow yourselves to get bogged down by the inevitable temporary delays.

Also, an atmosphere of faultfinding is hardly conducive to the type of open communication you need in order to be successful. As I've said before, money can be a very emotional topic. Try not to add fuel to the flames; keep your conversations about money calm, reasoned, and confined to the facts. Don't assign motives, don't second-guess decisions, and don't lay blame.

Share the Load. Part of open communication is sharing available knowledge. One of the best ways to do this is by dividing up the financial tasks so that everyone is involved in the ongoing financial functioning of the household. If one of you pays the bills, let the other balance the bank statements. Alternatively, divide up the responsibility for paying the monthly bills. However you do it, try to arrange the workload so that every responsible person can be involved in knowing the process by which the money flows into the household accounts and out to pay necessary expenses.

SURVIVAL TIP:
FAMILY FINANCIAL COMMUNICATION

- Involve the kids
- Set goals—together
- Have regular financial discussions
- Talk about major purchases before buying
- Avoid blaming
- Share responsibilities

Now that you've gotten an idea of your money personality and laid the groundwork for effective financial communication in your family, it's time to start taking some concrete action steps. Here again, you've got to begin with the basics. To get started, let's turn to the next chapter.

STEPS IN THE RIGHT DIRECTION

1. Know your "money personality."
2. Use cash, not credit.
3. Use unexpected income to pay down debt.
4. Only give if you can afford it—in cash.
5. Form a family financial communication plan.
6. Share the responsibility for various financial tasks with your spouse, partner, or other responsible household member.

Chapter 9

ASSESS YOUR
FINANCIAL SITUATION

GUIDEPOSTS

In this chapter, you'll learn

- The basics of financial goal setting

- How to budget to reach your goals

- How to keep yourself "on course" with your budget

- Smart insurance strategies to protect against the unexpected

From 1959 to 1967, Vince Lombardi coached the Green Bay Packers, who had gone from 1-10-1 the season before his arrival to five NFL championships and victories in Super Bowls I and II. It is said that Lombardi would begin the first day of practice every season by holding up a football as he stood in front of his seated players. "Gentlemen," he would announce, "this is a football."

This was Lombardi's way of reminding his team that no matter how good they were and how many victories they had achieved, they still had to focus on the fundamentals—the foundational principles of the game—if they wanted to be great. To continue to win championships, they had to excel at the basics: blocking and tackling.

It's the same with your finances. You may not aspire to financial greatness, but you probably would like to reach the point where you don't dread the final week of the month—or more—because there's not enough money for basic needs. You'd probably like to stop feeling that your paycheck is completely spoken for before you even get it. You'd probably like to actually earn interest for a change, instead of paying it to a credit card company. Well, if you want to get to that point, you've got to heed the advice of Vince Lombardi: you need to get good at the basics. In fact, there's another quote from another famous football coach—Bear Bryant—that applies here: "It's not the will to win, but the will to prepare to win, that makes the difference." In other words, everybody says they want to win the game, but not everybody is committed to doing what it takes to prepare to succeed.

In order to succeed with your finances, you must focus on the financial equivalent of blocking and tackling. Will this be a fun process? Probably not. But it will be rewarding, once you learn a few simple principles that can help you set and maintain your course to financial stability.

FINANCIAL GOAL SETTING

As stated in chapter 8, setting financial goals—and, if you have a family, involving everyone in the process—is one of the basic components of financial communication. It's also the first necessary step to getting from where you are now to where you want to be. It just makes sense: you have to know where you're going in order to know if you're headed in the right direction.

Before you begin this first step, however, you should keep in mind some basic principles of financial goal setting. The following points are drawn from "Building Wealth: A Beginner's Guide to Securing Your Financial Future," an interactive online course offered by the U.S. Federal Reserve Bank of Dallas (www.dallasfed.org):

- Goals should be realistic. If you've just emerged from bankruptcy, buying a vacation home in the Rockies may not be a very workable or practical objective for you—at least, not in the short term (more on this in a moment). Instead, you might want to focus on something a bit more basic, such as saving enough cash to help your sixteen-year-old buy her first car.

- Goals should have time frames. You will probably want to establish long-term goals (the house in the Rockies, maybe) as well as more short-term targets (paying off that balance on the flat-screen TV). If all your goals are long-range (or, worse, start with the words "Someday, I'd like to . . ."), they may be too vague to motivate you to action.

- Make a plan. If you want to pay off the second lien on your home five years early, figure out how much extra you need to pay on the loan each month (you can find an online calculator to help with this task at www.AsurvivalGuidetoDebt.com). Next, by looking at your budget (more on this a bit later), decide how you will reallocate your monthly expenditures to allow you to make the extra loan payments. A goal without specific action steps for achievement is really just a wish.

- Stay flexible. Remember that a goal gives you direction; this doesn't mean that your direction can never change. In fact, circumstances beyond your control may dictate that you rethink your goals from time to time. For instance, you may have a goal of retiring at age forty-five, but a weak stock market could suck away a big chunk of the retirement funds you were counting on to fund your post-employment lifestyle. In that case, you might need to reevaluate your goal and work a few more years in order to make your objective of secure retirement a reality. The point is that your goals should work for you, not the other way around.

Short-term Goals

At www.ASurvivalGuidetoDebt.com, you can find information about goal setting for your finances. When I work with people who need help in learning how to manage their finances, I usually encourage them to think in terms of short-term, mid-range, and long-term goals. As you begin formulating your financial objectives, you should think of short-term goals as those that take a year or less to accomplish. They also normally involve smaller amounts of money and often have very specific deadlines. Short-term goals could include things like paying off a small credit card balance in the next three months or saving enough cash to buy a new couch in the next six to nine months.

Short-term goals are important because they can get you focused on your progress. If you are successful in meeting them, they can also provide great motivation for staying on course financially. Even if you aren't 100 percent successful with your short-term goals, however, you shouldn't become discouraged. In fact, you probably accomplished more with a near miss on a short-term goal than you would have by continuing to just spend on the spur of the moment, with no future objective in mind.

SURVIVAL TIP:
PRINCIPLES OF FINANCIAL GOAL SETTING

- Be realistic
- Set a time frame
- Make a plan
- Stay flexible

Mid-range Goals

I encourage people to think of their mid-range goals in terms of what they want to accomplish in the next one to three years. These can include objectives such as paying off a car loan or saving enough to pay for a kitchen remodel. Typically, such goals require larger amounts of money and may be somewhat less time specific than short-term goals.

The importance of mid-range goals is that they cause you to begin thinking more strategically. Instead of focusing only on getting through the month or making it past tax season, you begin to consider the longer-term ramifications of your financial decisions. If you have a choice between buying that new cordless drill you've been eyeing and making the next deposit into the remodeling savings account, you may find it easier to resist the urge to scratch a short-term itch to the detriment of a mid-range goal.

Long-term Goals

These goals will take three years or more and will require the largest financial outlays to achieve. They will also require the most careful planning. However, because long-term goals often include some of our most dearly held dreams—owning a home, financing a child's education, buying a business, or even an early retirement—they can be powerful motivators.

MAKING IT REAL

One simple way to get yourself organized toward meeting your goals is to construct a simple chart. It should include your goals, the date by which you intend to achieve them, how much they will cost, any amounts already saved toward the goal, and how much you need to set aside each month to stay on track. As suggested in chapter 8, you might even want to write this down and put it somewhere so that you'll see it often. The chart might look something like the figure at the top of page 192.

You'll notice that the above chart contains a long-term goal (paying off a car loan in about four years), a short-range goal (buying a TV in less than a year), and a mid-range goal (saving enough for a down payment on a house within three years).

Even if you're more of an informal goal setter, you'll find it helpful to have a written record of what you want to accomplish, when you want to accomplish it by, and the monthly (or other regular incremental) steps

needed to stay on track. As a matter of fact, recent surveys indicate that as
little as 3 percent of the population keeps written goals. That may indicate
why so few of us achieve what we say we intend to achieve.

Goals as of 2/1/2009

Goal	Target Date	Total Cost	Saved/Paid	Needed Per Mo.
Pay off car	02/15/2013	$16,700	$5,000	$260
Buy new TV	12/31/2009	$1,200	$200	$100
Down payment for house	06/01/2011	$15,000	$2,500	$446

For an interactive version of this chart that you can tailor to your situation,
go to www.ASurvivalGuidetoDebt.com. You can fill it in and print out
hard copies, and you can update it as your goals and needs change.

A written plan keeps your goals in the forefront of your mind, so that
the next time you're tempted to make an impulse purchase that could delay
your progress toward your objective, you'll be more likely to weigh the
benefits versus the drawbacks. At the very least, if you decide to go ahead
and spend the money on something besides your goal, you'll do it from a
position of knowledge. Even that is better than spending money with no
plan or strategic purpose in mind.

Now that you've spent some time thinking about your financial goals,
it's time to take the next step toward making them a reality. It's time to set
up your budget.

CREATING A BUDGET

There it is: the dreaded "b" word. For many people in or recovering from
debt trouble, making and sticking to a budget is one of the toughest tasks
on the To Do list. I include myself; trust me, making and sticking to a
budget is as tough for me as it is for you.

For some reason, many folks hate the thought of budgeting. This distaste is stated in a variety of ways:

- "I don't know how to get started."
- "I hate thinking about how much money I have (or don't have)."
- "I don't understand finance."
- "Budgeting makes me worry about my money."
- "I don't have time to budget."
- "I can't keep up with all those receipts and categories."

And the list goes on.

There are probably as many reasons given for not budgeting as there are people in financial trouble. Unfortunately, there's really no shortcut on this one. Like the Green Bay Packers working on blocking and tackling at every practice, you've got to get past your distaste, fear, anxiety, or any other negative emotions that may be preventing you from learning how to set up a budget, and get started doing it. As you'll see once we get going, budgeting doesn't have to be complicated or even very time-consuming. But it does have to be done.

Why? Simply because your monthly budget is the self-correcting internal guidance system for your journey to financial health. Think of it like the horizon indicator on an aircraft: your budget is what tells you if you're right side up or upside down. You can also think of it as a financial compass: if you're following your budget consistently, it means you're staying on course for your desired financial destination. Or, you might think of your budget as the bathroom scales you use when you're trying to lose weight. Like your scales, your budget is objective; it doesn't lie.

If you'll keep these images in mind as we work together on setting up your budget, maybe it won't seem like such a (scary, boring, nitpicky, you

Your budget is the self-correcting internal guidance system for your journey to financial health.

fill in the blank) thing. In fact, I'll give you some even better images to help you stay motivated during the budgeting process:

- What if you never again had to worry about making excuses to one creditor so you could pay another?
- What if you could take a quick weekend getaway at a first-class destination and know—with complete certainty—that you already had the money in the bank to cover it (without skipping out on any bill payments)?
- What if you never had to have another argument with your spouse or partner about unplanned purchases?

Got those images in your mind? Okay, now let's take our first steps into the Great Budgeting Adventure.

Money In, Money Out

Remember the monthly cash flow statement we created in chapter 1? You will probably find it very helpful as you begin preparing your budget. As a matter of fact, at its simplest level, that's what a budget is: a plan for making sure that money coming in matches favorably with money going out during the same period. However, at this point, we're going to get a little more detailed in the information we include.

Take a look at the worksheet on page 195. You may want to make several copies of it to use as rough drafts, and another to keep as your final version, after you're certain you've made all necessary adjustments and corrections. Alternatively, you can use the online budgeting worksheet at www.ASurvivalGuidetoDebt.com by clicking on the online forms link. You can either fill it out as you go or enter the information from your hard-copy rough draft and then print a copy to keep in your files.

Income. Get out your most recent monthly pay stub (hard copy or online) and find the amount listed as your "gross pay." This is your monthly income before your employer deducts taxes, insurance, or other costs. Write down this amount in the field indicated on the worksheet. If you have the capability of working overtime for extra money (as discussed in chapter 2), estimate as closely as you can the amount of money you receive for overtime during an average month. Enter this amount in the space provided. Next, look at each of the deductions listed on your pay stub. They will probably include items like payroll taxes, Social Security, Medicare deductions, insurance (perhaps both life and medical), union dues, and pension or retirement deductions not paid directly by your employer. List these deductions in the appropriate fields, and list the total of any other deductions in the space indicated as "other."

Monthly Budget Worksheet

INCOME

Monthly gross pay	$
Monthly estimated pay	$

Deductions

Payroll taxes	−$
Social Security	−$
Medicare	−$
Life insurance	−$
Medical insurance	−$
Union dues	−$
Pension/retirement	−$
Other	−$

Other Monthly Income

Income for real property	$
Social Security	$
Pension/retirement plan payment	$
Alimony	$
Child support	$
Other monthly income	$
Total monthly income (net income)	$

If you have rental property that generates income (an amount of money in excess of any payments and taxes on the property), enter that amount as "income from real property." If you are receiving payments from Social Security, enter that monthly amount in the space provided. If you receive pension payments or regular income from other retirement plans, enter those amounts as indicated. If you have other monthly income (from work you perform as an independent contractor, freelancer, a second job, etc.), enter this amount on the line labeled, "other monthly income." Add up the income, subtract the amounts of any deductions listed, and enter the result on the bottom line marked "Total monthly income." This could also be called your "net income."

SURVIVAL TIP:
PREPAY YOUR TAXES

If you receive income as a contractor or freelancer (if the person for whom you do the work does not deduct taxes from your pay), you should subtract the amount of estimated taxes from this income before including it in the "other monthly income" category.

Expenses. Now we need to look at the other side of the ledger. A good place to start is by separating your expenses into three categories: fixed, variable, and periodic expenses. In the first category, place items like your mortgage or rent, car payments, insurance premiums, and other monthly expenses that do not change. In the second category you should group expenses like utility payments, entertainment, clothing, food, and other costs that change each month. Periodic expenses are items like vehicle registration, taxes, and holiday expenses that come around regularly, but less frequently than monthly.

Monthly Budget Worksheet

EXPENSES

Fixed Expenses

Rent/Mortgage $ _____
Car payment $ _____
Home insurance $ _____
Renter's insurance $ _____
Health insurance $ _____
Life insurance $ _____
Auto insurance $ _____
Other insurance $ _____
Internet $ _____
Cable $ _____
Alimony $ _____
Child support $ _____
Other fixed expenses $ _____

Variable Expenses

Utility payments $ _____
Clothing $ _____
Food $ _____
Gas $ _____
Other transportation $ _____
Reading material $ _____
Entertainment $ _____
Body care $ _____
Other variable expenses $ _____

Periodic Expenses

Vehicle registration and inspection $ _____
Income taxes $ _____
Property taxes $ _____
Holiday expenses $ _____
Charitable donations $ _____
Subscriptions $ _____
Other periodic expenses $ _____

Savings

Monthly savings $ _____
Vacation fund $ _____
Remodeling account $ _____

Total monthly expenses $ [_____]

Another way to categorize expenses is by priority. High-priority expenses are those that carry serious consequences for nonpayment. If you don't make your mortgage payment, you risk foreclosure. If you don't pay your utilities, you lose electric, water, gas, or Internet service. Low-priority expenses do not carry such severe consequences if unpaid. If you don't go to the movies as much as you did previously—or at all—the only consequence is, perhaps, having to deal with boredom.

Using the online worksheet or a copy of the one that appears on page 197, list your monthly expenses. You may need a recent checkbook register or, if you pay your bills using an online service, a listing of your recent account activity. Be sure to include expenses for categories such as entertainment, charitable contributions, and clothing, especially if these types of expenses tend to recur regularly. For your variable expenses, as suggested in chapter 1, you may need to take an average of several months' payments to calculate a monthly amount for budgeting purposes. Using your check register or online record, combined with the receipts you kept for cash purchases, add up your last three months' expenditures for these items and divide by three. The resulting average is a pretty good figure to use for budgeting purposes.

One way to make your budget work for your lifestyle is to personalize your expense categories to match the way you tend to spend. For example, if you prefer reading books over going to movies as a mode of entertainment, you might want to have a separate category for "books" in your expense column. The point is to make the budget a true reflection of what happens to the money you make. It's also a good idea, as we'll discuss further in chapter 11, to create a budget line item for savings. If you commit to a periodic amount for savings, you're much more likely to accumulate money rather than just spending it. It might even help to call the savings line item "vacation fund" or "remodeling account," if these are goals you have set for yourself and your family. The point is that systematic deposits into such an account are more likely to lead to success than only putting money into savings "when I have something left over." Unless you have a plan for savings, you probably won't ever have anything left over.

When you have all your expenses listed, total them and enter the result on the line titled "Total Monthly Expenses." If things are working properly, this number should be the same or, even better, smaller than the amount you entered as "Total Monthly Income." If it's not, you've got to figure out why your expenses are more than your income and adjust accordingly.

FINANCIAL GPS

Instead of putting money into "savings," think of it as making a deposit into a vacation account, a remodeling fund, or some other label related to your financial goals.

Don't Use Credit as a Budgeting "Slush Fund"!

This brings me to an important point: you may notice that the "Expenses" list has no category for "credit card payments." For many people, this represents the way overflow expenses are handled: they're simply charged to the plastic and put out of mind—that is, until the minimum monthly payments have overtaken just about all the other expense categories. Now that you've gotten a new lease on your financial life, either through bankruptcy or by working with your creditors to get rid of your debt, you know that this type of undisciplined use of credit leads right back into the kind of trouble you just escaped.

In a later chapter, we'll discuss "smart" uses of credit versus—well, the other kind. For now, you should avoid, at all costs, the temptation to use credit cards to "balance" your monthly budget. This creates a false sense of security ("We got everything we needed and we still have cash left!") that will come back to haunt you in the form of mushrooming payments and punitive interest. In order for budgeting to work for you, you must figure out a way to make your monthly expenses match your monthly income. You must not rely on unsecured debt to take care of your living needs—or wants.

MAKING THE TOUGH CHOICES

If your expenses are more than your income, you must figure out ways to do one of two things: either earn more or spend less. It's just that simple. Without a balanced budget, no household, no business, not even a government can operate.

In chapter 2, we talked about putting together a better offense (maximizing income) and a better defense (minimizing expenses). It's time to revisit that discussion now that you've constructed your budget. You may recall that we discussed several ways of increasing your monthly income: working overtime, taking on a second job, finding freelance work, selling unneeded items to raise cash, and other ideas. If you've already explored these options as far as you can and your expenses are still outstripping your income, you must figure out ways to reduce your monthly costs.

You may also recall that in chapter 2 we discussed the importance of distinguishing between needs and wants. Take a look at the budget you've just created and identify areas where your wants are greater than your ability to pay for them. Can you reduce housing costs by moving into a smaller apartment, or selling your house and downsizing? If your transportation expenses are wrecking your budget, you may need to consider selling a vehicle or perhaps trading down to a less expensive model. What are you spending on entertainment? Clothing? Is it time to cancel the cable or downsize to the basic package? Are you really reading all the magazines to which you've subscribed? Do you use Netflix, a landline telephone, the deluxe plan for your cell phone, a gym membership, or other "options" enough to justify the cost, or is it time to eliminate some of these expenses from your monthly obligations? Now that you have a budget and know where your dollars are going each month, you should be in a position to answer these questions. You should also be able to determine the areas where you can pare back on what you're spending to satisfy wants, instead of needs.

THE MAP IS NOT THE TERRITORY

At this point, assuming you've recorded accurate information in your income and expense categories, and making the further assumption that your expenses are equal to or less than your income, you have before you a budget: a map that will lead you toward financial security. However, as the heading of this section indicates, holding the map and understanding what it tells you are not the same thing as making the trip successfully. As you make the journey toward financial health, you must still steer straight, avoid dead ends, and watch out for obstructions in the road.

What this means is that you must compare your actual expenditures and income with the budget you've just developed. If you're new to budgeting (and I assume that many who are reading this book fit that description), this will involve keeping a record of all expenditures during the month, placing them in the appropriate categories, totaling them, and comparing the totals with what is shown on your budget. You will probably need to do this every month, at least until living within your budget starts to become a habit.

If this sounds like a lot of work, that's because it is. I know very few people who jump out of bed in the morning, excited about the prospect of tracking their expenses throughout the day. Nor do I know many individuals who relish the thought of adding up columns of figures at the end of the month to see how much or how little they strayed from their budgetary guidelines.

But you've got to remember: this is blocking and tackling—the basic skills you need to improve as you prepare for success. To use our other analogy: digging a ditch isn't glamorous or amusing, but if you need to move water from one place to the other, it's about the only method that works. These are the financial basics that are going to take you from where you used to be—in debt over your head—to where you want to be—financially secure and not having to worry every month about where the money for the bills is going to come from.

You can use any of several methods to track monthly expenses. They vary from simple to complex, and from free (or nearly free) to expensive. Some people simply carry a notebook (or use an expense recording program on their handheld device) and note out-of-pocket expenses as to type and amount. Other people use an envelope system: they label envelopes according to the expense categories in their budget, get receipts for all expenditures, and drop them in the proper envelope for totaling at the end of the month. Or, you can use the envelopes for allocating cash at the beginning of the month to various expense categories: when the envelope is empty, you stop spending in that category. Various computer software programs also promise to make budgeting and expense tracking easy and fun. If you enjoy working on a computer (and assuming the expense of the software is within your budget!), you might want to investigate some of these programs to see if they can help you.

The point is, use something! Don't leave your spending to chance. Whatever system you use, consistency and accuracy are the keys to success.

At the end of the month, compare your actual expenses with your budget. Note the categories where you were successful and those where you strayed off the map. It's important to communicate the successes and failures to the other responsible persons in your family or household. In fact, closing the communication loop is one of the principal purposes and advantages of budgeting: it allows you to make corrections in your spending habits in order to stay on track. It also makes you acutely conscious of how you spend your money. For example, a few months of overspending your entertainment allocation because of all those extra-tall mocha cappuccinos with two espresso shots will demonstrate to you that even seemingly insignificant $4 and $5 purchases here and there really do add up on a monthly basis to more than you realized. But you won't know the effect of these or any other purchases on your finances until you make a budget and track how well you stay within it.

Let me emphasize this point a little further. You must continue to track your expenses and compare them to your budget *each month*. As I said earlier, you need to continue doing this until keeping your spending within your means and staying within your budget become a habit. And even then, you will probably want to do a detailed comparison of actual spending to budgeted amounts once a quarter or so, just to be certain you're staying on track. This is how successful businesses remain successful, and the same rules apply for personal finance. Unless you know where your money is going, you can't know whether it's going to the right places.

HOW DOES YOUR BUDGET STACK UP?

It might surprise you to learn that there are guidelines and recommendations that can tell you how your budget and expenses compare to recognized standards for other households. In fact, banks and other lending institutions have measurements of recommended financial ratios for making these comparisons that they use when deciding whether or not to lend money to consumers. When you hear people talk about "qualifying for a loan," they are referring to the process of submitting their financial information to a bank or other lender so that the lender can compare the prospective borrower's financial measurements with these standards.

Debt-to-Income Ratio

You may remember that we discussed the debt-to-income measurement of financial health briefly in chapter 1, in the section on preparing your statement of income and expenses. Simply put, your debt-to-income ratio, or DTI, is the percentage of your monthly income that must go to pay your recurring debt obligations. To obtain this number, total up the amount you're paying each month on your debts (don't include expenses such as groceries, gasoline, or utilities; only amounts you are paying on loans) and divide this number by your monthly income. The result is your DTI. For example, if you bring home $4,000 per month and your debt payments total $1,440, your debt-to-income ratio is 36 percent (about the highest number bankers like to see when evaluating your loan application, by the way). If you don't have a calculator handy or don't trust yourself to do the math, you might want to use an online aid such as the "debt evaluation calculator" at www.ASurvivalGuidetoDebt.com.

For mortgage lending, bankers use your gross income (your income before taxes and other deductions, as entered in your budgeting worksheet, above) to calculate your DTI. They will usually not consider you for a home loan that requires a monthly payment—including insurance and taxes—of more than 28 percent or 29 percent of your gross income. However, unless you are actually trying to qualify for a mortgage loan, at this point you should be more concerned with evaluating your real month-to-month financial health. For this reason, using your actual take-home pay ("net income") is a more practical measure, of course, because you must pay taxes, and your pretax income is not the amount you will have available to pay bills.

Financial GPS

- Gross income = your income before taxes and other deductions
- Net income = your income after taxes and deductions ("take-home pay")

Take a look at your debt-to-income ratio. As I just mentioned above, bankers like to see a DTI in the range of 36 percent or less to consider you a creditworthy prospect for a loan. But 36 percent is by no means the "gold standard." If you are really serious about trying to save money, you want your DTI ratio to be as low as possible. It is probably not realistic for most of us to adopt a "zero debt" policy, but having as a goal the elimination of all your debt is a pretty smart idea. In other words, a DTI ratio of 0 percent might be thought of as representing perfection in the world of consumer budgeting. Certainly, though, you need to work toward reducing as much as possible the amount of your income that must go toward paying debts. The lower your DTI ratio (see "Financial GPS" on the opposite page), the more flexibility you'll have and the less susceptible you'll be to bumps in the road, whether your annual income is $25,000 or $250,000.

INSURANCE: A NECESSARY EVIL OR AN INDISPENSABLE TOOL?

As you construct your budget, it is essential that you build in and account for the cost of maintaining insurance protection for yourself and your family. You need adequate insurance to cover the cost of repair or replacement of your home and any vehicles you own, to provide protection against catastrophic medical and health care costs, and to provide for your family in the event of the death or permanent disability of a wage earner.

I know very few people—except, of course, for those selling it—who enjoy talking or thinking about insurance. Let's face it: the connotations for insurance are usually pretty negative. The only time you need it is

FinanciaL GPS

Debt-to-Income Ratios: A Quick Comparison

If your debt-to-income ratio (excluding your mortgage) is

- 15 percent or less—You're doing well; your DTI is below average.
- 15-20 percent—Be careful! Your debt may be getting too high to handle easily.
- 20 percent or more—Look out! You should not consider taking on any more debt at the present time.

when something bad has happened, and the rest of the time it's just an expense for something you hope you never need. The inescapable fact is, however, that the cost of insurance, whether you think of it as a necessary evil or an indispensable tool, is something you must include as a part of your overall financial plan.

By the way, we've developed a great online insurance planning resource at www.ASurvivalGuidetoDebt.com; as you continue to read this section, you might want to refer to it, using the data from your personal financial situation.

Property and Casualty Insurance

In some cases, of course, you have no choice. When you buy a house, the lender requires you to obtain and maintain property insurance sufficient to protect against a loss of the property due to fire, "acts of God," or other types of casualties. The same is true when you buy a car, whether you do it with a loan or with cash: you must insure the vehicle's repair or replacement value to protect the lender's investment (and to make sure you've got a means of transportation), and if you own the vehicle outright, your state will still require you to maintain minimum liability coverage to guarantee that if you cause damage to someone else's health or property with your car, the victim will be compensated.

Even when you do have a choice, insurance is usually a good idea. For example, if you rent an apartment or house rather than owning your residence, you may still want to consider renter's insurance to protect against the loss of your possessions in the event of a natural disaster or theft. Most of us would not be able to bear the expense of replacing those items most important to us if we had to do it all at once. Renter's insurance can help you avoid this type of financial calamity.

One way of controlling property insurance costs to some degree is by carefully evaluating the deductibles on your coverage. A deductible is the amount of money you must pay in the event of a loss before your insurance company begins paying. In simple terms, if you have, for example, a $500 deductible on your automobile insurance policy (the highest amount many car lenders will allow, by the way) and you are in an accident for which you are at fault, the first $500 of expense for repairing your car is your responsibility, and the rest is paid by your insurance company (of course, if the accident is your fault, your company pays 100 percent of the cost for fixing the other party's car, but that's a different matter). The higher the deductible on your policy, the lower the premium (the amount you pay to maintain the coverage).

This means that you may have some choices if you own a vehicle outright. You may wish to consider carrying a higher deductible or even carrying liability coverage only (your insurance company pays only if you damage someone else's property). As you make these decisions, you must balance your budgeting needs with the requirements of your lenders, if any, and with the rules of prudence for protecting yourself against financial loss due to accidents and other events beyond your control.

Health Insurance

In the case of health insurance, you have a few more options. Many of us are fortunate enough to work for employers who provide a certain amount of health insurance as a benefit of employment. In fact, U.S. labor laws require employers of certain types to provide minimal health insurance coverage.

This means that one of the best places to start looking for affordable, worthwhile health insurance is at the HR department of your employer.

Health insurance is almost always less expensive if provided through your employer, even if you must pay all the cost from your wages (some employers pay part of this cost). In fact, health insurance coverage is one of the principal benefits that employers offer in order to retain quality employees. And buying it on your own, unless you have access to group plans through a professional or special-interest association, can be both expensive and frustrating; the coverage is sometimes not that great compared with what you must pay in premiums.

Health insurance is a critical component of smart financial planning. Although it can be costly, not having it can jeopardize your financial security. If you don't believe you can afford a regular health insurance plan, you should consider getting at least a catastrophic health insurance plan. The deductible (what you will have to pay in medical expenses before the insurance kicks in) may be high (more than $1,100 for an individual), but the premiums (the monthly cost) are affordable and at least you won't be stuck with six-figure medical bills if something dreadful happens.

Life Insurance

As with health insurance, a good first place to start looking for life insurance is with your employer: Does your employer offer it and can you get additional coverage beyond any that may be covered by your employer? Depending on the particulars of your employer's plan, it may make sense for you to purchase additional amounts of life insurance (usually called "voluntary life insurance") above that provided in your employer's basic benefit package. Often—though not always—this coverage is less expensive than what you could get on your own. Another benefit of this type of insurance—and not the least advantage, for many of us—is that the cost is deducted from gross pay before you get your check; it's almost painless.

The central purpose of life insurance is to provide for a family's financial needs in the event of a breadwinner's death. How much you need is a function of several variables particular to your family. If you live in a two-income household with young children whose needs must be provided for a number of years before they become self-sufficient, your coverage need is greater—and you should provide coverage on both wage earners. However, even if you live in a single-income household, the wage earner isn't the only person whose death would create a financial burden. Aside from the obvious emotional impact of the death of a spouse, partner, or parent, there are real financial implications for the death of a non-wage-earning spouse, especially when there are young children in the home. Even though the deceased parent was not earning income, someone would be needed to provide the child care and perform the other household duties previously managed by the deceased parent.

It's inaccurate to assume, even in a two-person household, that expenses will be halved in the event of the death of one of the partners.

It's also inaccurate to assume, even in a two-person household, that expenses will be halved in the event of the death of one of the partners. Housing costs will not usually be halved, nor will utilities, clothing costs, or insurance. Additionally, there may be other financial consequences to the surviving family members. For example, psychological counseling may be advisable, especially in the case of young children who are trying to deal with the incomprehensible loss of a parent.

Because each situation is so different, I encourage you to take advantage of some estimating tools, such as the online insurance need calculators at sites like BankRate.com and SmartMoney.com. Using an online insurance calculator (like the one at www.ASurvivalGuidetoDebt.com), you can input your financial and family data and receive a calculation of the financial need created by the death of one or more wage earners.

But knowing how much insurance you need is only part of the equation: you must then provide the coverage needed. In the life insurance world, there are basically two choices: term life and some sort of cash value life insurance.

Term Life Insurance. Term insurance is by far the least expensive method of providing a payment to your beneficiaries (usually called the "death benefit" or the "face amount") upon your death. In fact, I would go so far as to say that for most of the people reading this book, term insurance is the only type of life insurance that should be considered.

With term insurance, you pay only for the risk assumed by the insurance company to insure your life. For this reason, term insurance is much less expensive when you are young, but it becomes progressively more expensive as you get older because the likelihood of illness and death increases with age. As the name implies, term life insurance is temporary: you pay the specified premium for the specified coverage term, and at the end of that time, the policy terminates with no value. Insurance companies offer a number of variations on this basic design, with some term policies that last five, ten, or more years, and with premiums that are averaged out in cost so that they may stay the same as long as the policy is in force. Some term life insurance is renewable annually, which means that you can continue paying the premium each year as long as you want it, without having to prove that you are still in good health. Once you stop paying the premium, however, the policy terminates and has no further value.

For many young wage earners with children, some amount of term insurance is usually advisable: it provides the largest amount of financial benefit for the smallest expense. In many ways, the life insurance offered through your employer functions like term: it provides a death benefit but usually has no value once you leave employment.

Cash Value Life Insurance. This form of insurance, which offers both a death benefit and a savings or investment component, can be divided into two basic types: whole life insurance and universal or variable life insurance. The idea behind both types is that you pay an amount of money above what is needed for the company to simply assume the risk of the policy's face amount, and in return you can build up either a guaranteed savings amount (in the case of whole life) or a non-guaranteed investment amount that usually depends at least in part on the investment experience of the insurance company. The advantage of cash value life insurance, of course, is that it can offer you a type of savings for your future in addition to providing a death benefit for your family in the event of your passing. The disadvantage is that it requires a larger premium—often, much larger—to provide the same death benefit as term insurance because some of your payment goes toward the investment or savings portion.

For most of the people reading *A Survival Guide to Debt*, paying the extra premium for cash value life insurance may not be the best use of your insurance dollars. There are other ways to accumulate long-term savings that are probably more practical for you, and if you need death benefit protection for your family, you can probably obtain it much less expensively with term insurance. If you believe you need life insurance with some form of cash accumulation built into it, you should consult a financial planner before making a purchase decision.

FINANCIAL GPS

For young wage earners with children, term life insurance usually offers the highest face amount (death benefit) for the lowest premium.

Finding the Right Mix. It is beyond the scope of this book to give you advice about how much or what type of life insurance will best provide the amount of financial protection your family requires. The introduction in these few paragraphs may enable you to ask some intelligent questions, however, and get the answers you need to make a wise purchasing decision. If you have done your homework, your budget will indicate to you how much you can afford to pay for the coverage you need. I also advise you to be sure to include in your calculations any life insurance benefits provided by your employer; be sure you are taking maximum advantage of any low-cost coverage that may be available to you through your workplace, professional association, union, or other organization. To review a list of quality providers of term life insurance, go to www. ASurvivalGuidetoDebt.com.

THE BIG PICTURE: YOUR NET WORTH

You may remember the discussion of net worth—your balance sheet—in chapter 1. In that section, we discussed the various types of assets you might own and the liabilities—debts—that you might owe. As you probably recall, your net worth is simply the value of your assets when compared to your liabilities. If you own more than you owe, you have a positive net worth; you're in the black. If it's the other way around, you're in the red, or upside down as we noted in chapter 1.

Especially now, as you begin your financial makeover, it's important to know your net worth. In fact, you may want to calculate this important financial benchmark and use it to set one or more of your financial goals, as discussed earlier in the chapter. Additionally, if you've just emerged from bankruptcy or another major alteration in your financial circumstances, you need to know where you stand. You should also review your net worth regularly to be certain you are staying on course toward your goals.

Let's take a look at the net worth worksheet Doug constructed just after emerging from Chapter 13 and see if we can identify where he might be on the financial health scale. The figure on the next page shows Doug's balance sheet.

One thing to notice is that the only debts on Doug's balance sheet are the balances he owes on his home and his rental property. Of course, prior to his Chapter 13 filing, he had a pretty large unsecured debt balance due to all the credit card debt he had run up. However, according to the terms of his plan, Doug paid off those balances—at reduced interest rates and with some balance reductions as well—along with the amount he owed on his car. At the end of the five years that his plan lasted, Doug still had his personal property and real estate: according to the terms of his bankruptcy, he kept his home and rental property because he reaffirmed those debts and continued making the payments on them during his bankruptcy.

Doug's Balance Sheet

Liabilities		Assets	
Mortgages		*Cash and Equivalents*	
Home	$63,475.00	Cash	$55.00
Rental Property	$27,000.00	Checking/Savings	$788.00
		Life Ins. Cash Value/ Annuities	$1,100.00
		Real Estate	
		Home	$80,000.00
		Rental Property	$35,000.00
		Personal Property	
		Car	$3,200.00
		Jewelry	$1,800.00
		Coin Collection	$1,500.00
		Retirement Accounts	
		Pension Fund	$32,000.00
Total Liabilities	$90,475.00	*Total Assets*	$155,443.00
		Net Worth	$64,968.00

What are some things we might infer from looking at Doug's net worth statement? Well, first of all, it's pretty easy to see that the vast majority of his assets are illiquid: it would be time-consuming for Doug to use them to raise cash. Selling his home or his rental property, for example, might be difficult to do in a short period of time, especially if he wanted to get the best price possible. Likewise, Doug's pension plan is not a good place for him to look for quick cash. Most pension plans have very severe restrictions about access prior to retirement. In fact, even private retirement accounts like IRAs carry penalties for withdrawals prior to age 59 ½ (in addition, the withdrawals are taxed as ordinary income in the year they are made). One goal for Doug and his family, then, might be to work on increasing their liquid—easily available—assets. It's a good idea to have an emergency fund equal to several months' income, so it would probably make sense for Doug to focus on this as a goal. This effort would also be beneficial to Doug's overall net worth.

Another thing Doug's balance sheet suggests is that he needs to look at his life insurance coverage to make sure it's adequate. Presently, he's the only income-generating member of the household, yet he still owes significant balances on two of his principal assets: his home and rental property. Doug may want to consider ensuring that his family would have the money to take care of these loans in the event his income was no longer available. Wiping these two debts off the balance sheet would give Doug's family a great deal of financial flexibility in the event of his premature death or disability.

There are other things you can learn from your own net worth statement, once you've constructed it. As I said previously, you should take this important financial snapshot on a regular basis—once a year, at least, and more often if your financial situation is changing frequently, either positively or negatively—and use it to reevaluate your financial situation and form goals for the future.

DOUG'S STORY—PART 2

Doug took to heart the principles he learned during the mandatory financial counseling he had to complete for his Chapter 13 bankruptcy. He sat down with his family and had a long discussion about their finances, including the need to develop a realistic and responsible budget for monthly income and expenses. He used the budgeting worksheet he found online at AsurvivorsGuidetoDebt.com to develop the basic income and expense categories that were applicable to his family's lifestyle, and each month he and his wife faithfully tracked their expenses, comparing them to the amounts indicated by the budget they had developed together. After the comparison, they made the adjustments necessary to get back on track, and lately there have even been a few occasions when they got to the end of the month with a few hundred extra dollars left over.

It hasn't always been easy. There were a few times, for example, when the kids really wanted the newest video gaming system or the latest Internet-ready cell phone. In the old days, Doug realized, they would have just gone out and gotten it with a credit card. Especially at first, Christmas and birthdays were more meager than in the old, free-spending days. But with the budget in hand, Doug knew there wasn't always money available for wants. Furthermore, because he had begun openly sharing the family's financial goals and what was necessary to achieve them, the kids had started—grudgingly—to agree that the only way to make it work was to spend less than they made. And the only way to do that, Doug knew, was to stick to the budget.

Like Doug and his family, you may now be in the position of taking those early steps out of bankruptcy, a debt settlement program, or a debt management plan. You've got your budget, and you've made the commitment to master the basics of household financial management: you're ready to work on blocking and tackling. You know your net worth, and, even more important, you're committed to improving it.

But you know that at some point in the future, in order to continue meeting the goals you've set for yourself, you are probably going to need the ability to borrow money. Your credit rating is not good at this point, in all likelihood, and you wonder how to improve it to the point that you can walk into a bank or credit union, sit down in front of a loan officer, and not break out in a cold sweat.

In the next chapter, we're going to discuss how you can begin rebuilding your creditworthiness: the best avenues to attempt and the dead ends to avoid. Over time, you *can* rebuild your credit reputation. To start learning how, turn to chapter 10.

STEPS IN THE RIGHT DIRECTION

1. Set short-, mid-, and long-range financial goals.

2. Communicate these goals to your family.

3. Create a realistic and detailed monthly budget that will help you meet your goals.

4. Compare actual expenses to your budget and adjust accordingly.

5. Get in the habit of sticking to your plan.

Chapter 10

CREDIT DOS AND DON'TS

GUIDEPOSTS

In this chapter, you'll learn

- When and how to apply for credit

- How to begin rebuilding your credit score

- How to get and keep your credit report clean and accurate

- The top five mistakes people make with credit cards and how to avoid them

By this point, some of you may have decided that if you never see a credit card again for the rest of your life, it will be too soon. You were hopelessly in debt before, and now that you've gotten rid of that heavy load, the thought of being saddled with debt again gives you the shakes.

Although this attitude might certainly keep you out of debt trouble, it's probably not completely realistic. Depending on your age and earning power, it might not be reasonable to believe that you can take care of all your future needs—buying a house, purchasing an automobile, paying college tuition for yourself, a spouse, or children—with current earnings or cash from your savings and investments. If you're serious about doing things that way, though, more power to you! Your low debt-to-income ratio may give you the flexibility to accomplish everything you have in mind without resorting to borrowing from anyone other than yourself.

However, some of you realize that at some point you will probably need to be able to borrow again. On the other hand, like Doug, who just emerged from Chapter 13 bankruptcy, you also suspect that most loan officers wouldn't touch your file with a ten-foot pole. And if they did, they'd charge you premium rates for the privilege. So what can you do? You've got a serious blemish on your credit record, but you want to rehabilitate your reputation as a creditworthy borrower. How can you get started?

There are several steps you can take, and several mistakes you should definitely avoid; in this chapter we'll discuss both sides of the coin. But at the beginning, I want to stress a basic concept that I will return to several times during this chapter: you didn't get in debt trouble overnight, and you won't reestablish a good credit rating overnight either. Just as your money problems were likely caused by a series of decisions and habits that formed and took place over a number of years, your return to creditworthiness will also require the formation of better habits and a consistent history of responsible decisions and actions. Now that you are emerging from bankruptcy, debt settlement, or a debt management plan, you must take a long-term, patient, and methodical approach to persuading lenders that you deserve favorable treatment as a borrower. So let's get started.

> **You didn't get in debt trouble overnight, and you won't get out overnight either.**

WHAT'S CREDIT FOR, ANYWAY?

Don't be too quick to answer the question posed by this section's title. If your first impulse is to answer, "to get the stuff I need," you may not yet be ready to stick your toe back into the credit pool. Credit has its proper uses, for sure, but now, more than ever, you need to be discerning about how you use this financial tool that has the perplexing capability to transform into shackles on your legs.

In previous chapters, we've covered a good deal of information about the different types of credit and their implications for your finances. Now that you have developed a budget and are using it to keep your monthly expenses on track (at least, I hope you're doing that), I want to pose the idea for you that if you never used credit again, you would always stay within your budget. Right? Think about it: If you are using only cash to pay for what you need, that means that when you don't have money, you don't buy anything; by definition, this means you aren't spending money you don't have, which, in turn, means you are adhering to your budget.

Using credit changes the picture for the simple reason that credit allows you to spend money you don't really have. In this sense, credit is what creates the possibility of overspending your budget. In other words, credit is a two-edged sword: it can be your best friend, allowing you to take advantage of opportunities that would be impossible for you if you had to depend only on current income or savings. But if credit is mismanaged, you also know that it can be your worst enemy, bringing with it the stress of bills you can't pay, creditor calls you don't want, and the potential loss of possessions you can't do without.

Having said all that, it's still true that credit isn't always bad. But how do you know when it's appropriate to use it and when it isn't? What are some of the appropriate uses of credit? Are there times when using credit for a purchase makes more sense than using cash? Let's take a look at some scenarios and see if we can come up with some guidelines for when using credit might actually be a good idea.

Purchasing an Asset That Increases in Value

One appropriate use of credit would be using it to take possession of an appreciating asset—one that will increase in value over time. The financial principle behind this is that the asset should increase sufficiently in value to offset the cost of obtaining the credit needed to buy it.

A common example of this credit strategy is the home mortgage loan. For most of us, our home is our principal appreciating asset. In a normal real estate market, we can generally expect the value of our property to increase over the years so that by the time the mortgage is paid off, our property has acquired a value much greater than the amount we paid for it, even after including the interest paid on the loan. In fact, homeowners are frequently able to realize a profit on their purchase long before the mortgage is paid off; many of us have had the experience of buying a house with a mortgage loan, then selling it at some point a few years later for enough money to pay off the mortgage and have money left over to use as a down payment on another—usually larger— house. In such situations, using credit for the purchase can make a lot of sense. We are using the lender's money to make a purchase we couldn't manage with our cash resources in order to acquire an asset that we can potentially sell for enough to pay off the obligation and still have money left over.

At this writing, however, the real estate markets have been anything but normal for the last several years. For the first time in decades in many parts of the country, home values are actually falling. In such times, using credit—even for purchasing a home—may not be a wise decision. The type of mortgage loan used also makes a big difference. Recall our earlier discussion of adjustable rate mortgages that have locked some homeowners into escalating payments that are becoming unmanageable. If the only way you can obtain credit for a home purchase is by resorting to a loan containing provisions that can come around to bite you in the future, you may be unwise to consider using it, even for an otherwise worthy purpose such as buying a home. A bit later, we'll talk about some of the things you need to think about when shopping for a mortgage loan, but right now I want to remind you that in this, as in all other spending decisions, you must keep in mind needs vs. wants. Do you really need the big house with the pool in the backyard? If it comes at the cost of a mortgage payment you can barely make, it might make more sense to buy a less expensive house that you can live in without feeling the monthly stress of figuring out how to stretch your income around too many expenses.

Purchasing a Necessary Item when Your Cash Resources Are Insufficient

There are times when something you really need is beyond the reach of your checking and savings accounts. Although the argument could be made that everyone should budget enough savings to take care of needs like car purchases, college tuition, and other big-ticket expenses, everyone isn't always able to allocate such sums to savings and still maintain current obligations.

Car Loans. Should you borrow money to buy a car? After all, as I pointed out in chapter 2, an automobile can usually be counted on to lose value much faster than the balance on the loan. So, in the case of a car loan, you really can't make the argument that you're borrowing money to buy an appreciating asset.

However, transportation is a basic need. Especially if you live in an area where public transportation is nonexistent or undependable, you must have a means of getting to and from your place of employment and going other places that you need to go. Does that mean a car loan is a justifiable expense?

You can find the answer in your budget. Is there sufficient money left after other expenses to make the monthly payment needed for a car loan? Online loan calculators like the one at BankRate.com can help you decide if you can afford to borrow enough money for the car of your dreams, or if you need to set your sights on a more economically priced model. If the extra cash isn't presently available to support the payment, you shouldn't go forward with the loan. By the way, I included the phrase "presently available" in that last sentence for a very specific reason: I've seen too many people who based borrowing decisions on some anticipated favorable event—a big tax refund, a long-sought raise or promotion, a large business profit—only to be left high and dry when the looked-for windfall blew the other way. Don't obligate yourself today based on money that's coming tomorrow; it's a recipe for financial failure.

Education Loans. Without a doubt, adequate education is absolutely essential for success in just about any field you can think of. Investing in your education or that of your children is one of the best ways to assure a bright future. Unfortunately, over the past several decades, education costs have consistently risen faster than the core rate of inflation. That means that it now takes a larger percentage of current or future earnings to pay for college or other training than it did ten, twenty, or thirty years ago. And the future prognosis isn't too much better. For more and more Americans, paying for higher education means taking out some amount of student loans.

Is it worth it? Probably. And because the U.S. government has programs that insure lenders against borrowers' defaulting on education debt, these loans can usually be obtained at more favorable rates and with more lenient terms than other types of debt. But you should still exercise discretion. Make sure you're getting the best deal possible on your student loan, and also consider ways to contain the overall cost of your education. For example: can you take some courses at a local community college, then transfer the credits to the university that will be granting your degree? If you're trying to choose between a public and a private college, have you carefully analyzed the difference in tuition and other fees? Finally, be very sure that the degree being sought is one that will open up real opportunities. I've listened to many people who went into debt to get a certificate from a vocational school that "guaranteed employment," only to find out that the jobs promised just weren't there. Don't pay that price. Make sure you're getting the education you really need to achieve your objectives.

Remember, also, that in our discussion of different types of debt in chapters 1, 2, and 6, student loans fall into the category of "must-pay" obligations. Even though they are not secured by collateral, because of their government backing they carry stiff consequences for nonpayment, and they cannot be discharged in bankruptcy except under very limited conditions. When you borrow money for college or other education, you must consider how you plan to pay it back from your current or future earnings.

The intent, of course, is that your degree or advanced training will position you to make enough extra income to more than cover the expense of your student loan payments. Unfortunately, things don't always work out as planned. If you are concerned about your ability to keep your student loan payments current, you may wish to review some of the strategies for working through student loan difficulties that are mentioned in chapter 6.

Shopping for the Best Rate

If you conclude that getting a loan for one of the above purposes is in your best interest, it is important for you to do enough comparison shopping to assure yourself that you are getting the most competitive interest rate possible for your circumstances. Of course, at this time your credit history is probably not pristine or anywhere close, so you should prepare yourself for the likelihood that you won't have access to the most favorable rates (for a comparison of rates for various credit rating [FICO score] ranges, see the discussion and charts on pages 96 and 97).

On the other hand, that doesn't mean you should just take the first loan offer that comes along. Even though your credit rating is not good, there are still companies out there willing to compete for your business. If you don't do your homework, you could end up needlessly paying thousands of dollars in interest. Especially with the Internet as a tool, doing some basic research on available rates has never been easier. Before you sign loan papers for any purpose (and especially before you get a credit card, as we'll discuss more fully in a moment), make sure you're getting the best rate possible.

Unsecured Debt

Of course, the credit decisions that most of us will make from day to day usually involve whether or not to use a credit card to pay for something, instead of using cash. Most often, we must make this decision because we need or want something that we don't have enough cash to buy outright. Should you use a credit card?

Recognize first, as I have said before, that you will probably begin receiving credit card offers fairly soon after you begin emerging from debt trouble. Even if you have recently had your Chapter 7 or Chapter 13 bankruptcy closed, marketers will begin sending you "pre-approved" credit card applications with all kinds of encouraging phrases calculated to persuade you to complete them and send them in. Carefully review these offers before obligating yourself.

You may also wish to consider obtaining a secured credit card. Secured credit cards, offered by many major banks and credit card companies, require you to make an initial deposit into an account with the issuing institution. This deposit then becomes your "available credit" for the card. Over time, as you reestablish a record of timely payments, you can qualify for a normal, unsecured credit card account.

So, let's say you applied for and received a credit card after your bankruptcy. You find yourself in the situation just described: needing or wanting an item that you don't have enough cash to pay for. Under what circumstances is it okay for you to take out that plastic and hand it to the salesperson?

1. Emergencies That You Can't Handle with Cash. First of all, you shouldn't risk a deviation from your financial plan for something that you really don't have to have. Unexpected, emergency needs do occur, of course. Maybe it's a car repair that you can't cover with current cash. Maybe it's a trip to the minor emergency clinic. Whatever the situation, you should first satisfy yourself that the need is genuine and that the purchase cannot be deferred until the cash is in the bank to cover it. It should go without saying that really good clearance sales, "special, time-limited offers," and other similar marketing enticements do not, in the vast majority of cases, constitute a genuine need or a valid reason to use plastic.

2. You Have a Plan to Pay Off the Expense in Three Months or Less. Ideally, you should pay off all credit card charges each month to avoid having interest added on top of your unplanned purchase. But there can be situations, such as the car repair scenario above, where the expense can't be digested in a single billing cycle. If you have sufficient extra cash flow to liquidate the charge in three months, the interest you'll pay won't be that significant. As with the prior discussion on car loans, your payoff plan for the expense should not depend on "future money," unless it is coming to you subject to the terms of a legally binding contract or some other agreement or relationship—such as a merit-based or cost-of-living raise from your employer—you can depend on.

3. You Are Attempting to Reestablish Your Credit History. This can be a valid reason for careful, sparing use of credit. You may wish to charge a small amount—perhaps even an amount that you could cover with cash—and pay the entire balance off when the statement comes. By doing this, you will begin building a history of timely payments on a credit account that will begin the process of rehabilitating your credit history. Please note the deliberate use of the words *careful* and *sparing* in the first sentence of this section. The last thing you want to do, when you are trying to regain your status as a creditworthy borrower, is use all or even most of the credit available to you. In fact, overuse of credit and high balances on charge accounts are factors that will decrease your credit score.

If your contemplated use of a credit card doesn't meet at least one of the conditions I've described, I strongly advise you to put it back in your wallet or purse and either use cash or delay the purchase until you have the funds to pay for it outright.

SURVIVAL TIP:
YOU CAN USE YOUR NEW
CREDIT CARD IF

1. You have an emergency expense you can't handle with cash, *and*

2. You have a plan to pay off the expense in three months or less, *or*

3. You're making a small, affordable charge that you will pay off in full at the end of the month in order to establish a history of timely payment.

REBUILDING YOUR CREDIT RATING

Item #3 described in the previous "Survival Tip" serves as a good transition into a discussion of how to go about the process of "credit rating rehab." Basically, improving your credit score from its (probably) dismal current level involves three factors: establishing a history of timely payments, keeping your balances well within your means of payment (zero, if at all possible), and verifying the accuracy of the entries on your credit report.

The other indispensable ingredient for the credit rehab regimen is time. Remember what I said earlier: your debt problems didn't happen overnight, and your bad credit score won't vanish that way either. Time is your best ally in your credit repair efforts. As a matter of fact, you should be very wary of any individual or organization that promises quick credit repair or something similar. According to no less an authority than Experian, one of the three principal credit reporting agencies, "there is no quick fix for bad credit" (www.experian.com).

1. Check Your Credit Report for Errors

This might be a good time for you to review the information on the Fair Credit Reporting Act (FCRA) that we covered in chapter 4. You may recall that this act guarantees you the right to receive a free copy of your credit report each year from all three of the major credit reporting agencies (TransUnion, Experian, and Equifax). I mention this because your very first move, when you're ready to begin working on improving your credit score after bankruptcy or debt settlement, should be to get a copy of your credit report and study it carefully for errors. (Go to www.ASurvival-GuidetoDebt.com and click on the "Your Credit" link for a quick way to request your credit report.) By using some strategic timing and taking advantage of your right to a free copy from each agency, you can get a current credit report once every four months and pay nothing. It's a good idea to exercise this option regularly, especially when you're beginning the process of credit rehab.

FINANCIAL GPS

You are guaranteed the right to receive a free credit report once each year from each of the three major credit reporting agencies.

If the prospect of contacting these agencies and not knowing what questions to ask seems intimidating, don't worry. Their websites (see the "Survival Tip" below) offer lots of helpful advice for consumers who need to know how to go about requesting and working with their credit reports. They have easy-to-use guides to reading and understanding your credit report. Although the formatting of the report will vary somewhat depending on the bureau from which you receive it, the basic outline and information provided is very similar. Don't neglect this important first step in regaining your clean financial bill of health.

SURVIVAL TIP:
HOW TO CONTACT THE MAJOR CREDIT REPORTING AGENCIES

- Equifax: Equifax.com, 1-800-685-1111
- Experian: Experian.com, 1-888-397-3742
- TransUnion: TransUnion.com, 1-800-888-4213

As you may recall from chapter 4, errors can be found on many, if not most, credit reports. For example, if you've ever been divorced and divided household debts as part of the proceedings, it's fairly common to look on your credit report and still see debts presented as yours that were assigned to your former spouse under the terms of the divorce decree. When you see something like that, you should provide the credit reporting agencies with proof that the debt isn't yours: a copy of your divorce decree stipulating the debt as your former spouse's will probably suffice. Having debt on the report that isn't yours, even if your former spouse has made timely payments on it, is not helpful when you're trying to rebuild your credit rating.

When you get your credit report, first check for the obvious things: correct address, phone contact information, current employment, correct spelling of your name, and correct personal tax identification numbers. This information is typically found at the top of the report.

Next, be sure that the activity on your credit record—usually shown in summary form near the top of the report—sounds familiar. In other words, if you see listings for loans or other activity with lenders or credit card companies whose names you don't recognize, you should immediately take steps to verify that no one has illegally obtained your personal information and used it to get credit under false pretenses. Especially now that you're trying to rebuild your creditworthiness, you can't afford to be victimized by identity theft. Check the status of the listed accounts: Are the accounts shown as "open" really open? Do the amounts associated with the accounts appear accurate? If you see anything out of whack, make a note to do some further inquiry or, possibly, send a dispute letter (more on this later). Go to www.ASurvivalGuidetoDebt.com for more information on credit monitoring, fraud detection, and identity theft.

The "public record" section, as the name indicates, will list any information about your credit history that is a matter of public record: tax liens filed against you, bankruptcies, judgments, foreclosures, collections activity, or other proceedings that have an impact on your credit history. Check this section to make sure that the status of each action is current and correctly reported.

If you filed bankruptcy, you should assure yourself that none of the debts discharged in your case are still shown on the report. Many times, your former creditors will not have taken the trouble to report this fact to the services. The same can be true in debt settlements; make sure that any accounts you have settled are accurately reflected that way on your report.

Certainly, neither an account that was settled for less than the amount due nor one that was discharged in bankruptcy will get you any brownie points with lenders. However, it is important for your future credit rebuilding efforts to make sure they are not shown as accounts that are still open.

You will also see a section giving detailed information for each credit account listed on your report. As with the other parts of the report, review this portion of the report to verify account-opening dates (and closing dates, if applicable), amounts of credit reported, payment history, and other information. You should check the accounts listed on your report to ensure that the status for each account is correct. If you've just emerged from bankruptcy, completed credit counseling, or finished settling your debts, there should probably not be any current delinquencies or collection actions showing on your record. If there are, and if you know the accounts were disposed of, either by settlement or discharge in bankruptcy, you need to provide the credit reporting agencies with appropriate documentation of the final disposition of the accounts.

Your report will also show all inquiries about your credit history by entities who have a legitimate business purpose for requesting the information. Make sure that all of the requesting entities sound familiar. If an unfamiliar company has requested your credit history, it can indicate that someone is trying to use your credit history for a purpose you haven't authorized or requested. This brings up another piece of credit advice: don't apply for credit unless you really need to. Some consumers don't realize that each time someone requests a credit report—whether a prospective lender or the consumers themselves—their credit score takes a small dip. And if a lender pulls your credit report and sees a large number of recent inquiries about your credit or applications for new credit, these circumstances raise questions in the lender's mind about why so many people are so interested in your credit rating, and why you have been making so many applications to borrow money. If you need to apply for credit, that's fine; just don't overdo it, and don't make multiple inquiries about your credit report, other than the three free ones you're entitled to each year.

The "consumer statement" section reflects any communication you have sent to the credit bureau in connection with your credit activity or history. For example, if you had a dispute with a creditor that could not be resolved, you may have sent a letter to the credit bureau explaining your side of the dispute. This information becomes part of your credit record and is available for consideration by prospective lenders or other parties with a legitimate need to know your credit history.

Sending a Dispute Letter. Speaking of communicating with the credit bureaus, remember our discussion of the Fair Credit Reporting Act in chapter 4? You may want to use the sample letter shown there (page 105), or a similar form, to notify the credit bureau of mistakes or inaccuracies on your credit report. You may also recall that the credit bureau has thirty days to respond to your request. Remember that you must document each element of your dispute. If the report shows an account past due that has been settled, include a copy of your settlement agreement. If the report shows a debt as outstanding that was discharged in your bankruptcy, send a copy of the discharge notice. Go to www.ASurvivalGuidetoDebt.com to download a dispute letter template.

2. Make Your Payments on Time

This seems pretty obvious, but according to each of the major credit reporting firms, it is the single largest factor in the computation of your credit score, making up some 35 percent of the total computation. Getting in the habit of making your payments on or before the due date is one of the best things you can do to reestablish a good reputation with lenders. On the flip side, you probably remember all too well what late payments can do to your credit score.

If you are sparing in your use of credit cards, and if you've done an accurate job of setting up your budget and tracking your expenses, you should be in a position to maintain your credit card payments at manageable levels that won't impact your ability to stay current with your other obligations. Making those small payments, and making them on time, will help you begin your credit makeover.

SURVIVAL TIP:
AUTOMATE YOUR PAYMENTS

Consider putting some of your bills on an automatic draft from your bank account. They'll always be paid on time, and you'll have one less check to write. (Just don't forget to deduct the draft from your available balance!)

3. Watch Those Balances!

Many lenders like to see on your unsecured credit accounts balances of no more than 30 percent of your available credit. If you can pay off your credit card balances every month, so much the better. By the way, some people have the mistaken impression that paying off their balances each month is a negative factor for their credit scores because they aren't "managing a credit account" but keeping it zeroed out instead. This is wrong. Your credit issuer looks at your account balance once a month (or every couple of months, in some cases) and reports the balance to the three major credit reporting bureaus. This report doesn't reflect whether the balance was subsequently paid off or carried from month to month. In other words, there is no penalty to your credit score for keeping your credit card accounts at zero. And there is a definite benefit involved in saving the interest charges that would be added to your balance if you didn't pay it off.

The key here is to keep your balances under strict control. Even if you decide to allow a small balance to carry over from month to month (and pay the resulting interest), you should focus on keeping your open balances well below your available credit limit. Remember: using all your available credit—or even most of it—reduces your credit score.

FINANCIAL GPS

Using all your available credit lowers your credit score.

4. Get "Good News" Included on Your Report

A great way to counteract some of the blotches on your credit history is by having it also reflect instances of responsible behavior. Some utility companies, for example, will file "good payment history" notes with the credit bureaus if you request it. You might also talk to your landlord or apartment manager, if you're renting, and ask him or her to send a letter to the credit bureaus to document your prompt payments (assuming you are prompt; if you're not, don't make the request until you've reformed your ways). These brownie points can help when a prospective lender is reviewing your credit report to determine the likelihood that you'll make your payments on time.

A variation on this theme is to try to keep as much bad news as possible off your report. In other words, if you foresee that you're going to be making a late payment, talk to your creditor in advance and try to negotiate with them so that they don't report the late payment to the bureaus.

SURVIVAL TIP:
REBUILD YOUR CREDIT SCORE

- Regularly check your credit report for errors.
- Make payments on time.
- Keep balance low or at zero.
- Try to get favorable information included on report.

TOP FIVE CREDIT CARD MISTAKES

Okay, let's say you've done your homework with your credit report and you're convinced everything on it is accurate. You're ready to apply for that first credit card to begin regaining your good credit reputation. This is an important step for your financial future, so don't blow it by making one of the top five credit card goofs.

1. Failing to Shop for the Best Rate

Even if you've just come out of bankruptcy, you shouldn't jump at the first offer that lands in your mailbox. Take some time to shop around and compare rates. You may not be able to qualify for the rates you were accustomed to before your bankruptcy, but there is still enough competition in the credit industry to guarantee that you can find different, and probably more favorable, rates to choose from if you take some time to check out several different alternatives.

2. Falling for a Low Introductory Rate

Phrases like "0 percent on balance transfers" and "5 percent on purchases for the first year" can certainly get your attention, but beware: often, these low rates are only good for certain types of transactions, or only valid for a certain time period. Be sure to read the fine print on the agreement. It's not unusual for an introductory rate to reset to something in the high double-digit range after the introductory period expires. As the old saying goes, if a rate sounds too good to be true, it probably is.

3. Failing to Read the Contract

Closely related to #2, this error is committed by a surprising number of people. Many of us, assuming that we "know how credit cards work," never bother to understand the details of our credit agreements. Sometimes, the penalty for this ignorance is getting slapped with punitive interest rates or fees for transactions that we thought were "part of the deal." For instance, some of those credit cards that offer such enticing initial rates can charge

Fees can make what you thought was a low-interest card cost almost as much as money borrowed from a loan shark.

you 15 percent, 18 percent, or more on balances resulting from cash advances—even if you've never missed a payment and are well within your credit line.

Sometimes, the "pound of flesh" comes in the form of high cash advance fees or fees for other types of transactions. As a matter of fact, when I was working at a former job for a major consumer finance company (which has since been purchased by a bank whose name you would immediately recognize, it being a major issuer of credit cards), an executive told me that the company made most of its income from interest charges and various account fees. In fact, he said, they were always trying to come up with more things to charge fees for and new ways to apply them.

Does that tell you anything? The fact is that fees can make what you thought was a low-interest card cost almost as much as money borrowed from a loan shark. Read your contract and know what you're agreeing to before you start using the card.

4. Getting too Many Cards

Even though establishing and using credit is important as you begin rebuilding your credit rating, don't get carried away. Having too many credit cards, even if most of them have zero balances, is not usually a positive for your credit score. When lenders review your information, they don't like to see an excessive amount of available credit, because they know what happens when consumers yield to the temptation to use it: they get overextended and begin missing payments. Don't commit this blunder. Instead, limit yourself to one or two cards and keep the balances low or at zero.

5. Making Only Minimum Payments

Most people who find themselves in trouble with their credit cards are the same people who have succumbed to the temptation of making only the minimum required monthly payments on their credit card accounts. If you've just had to file bankruptcy, go through credit counseling, or pursue debt settlement because of too much unsecured debt, you should have learned this lesson by now. Still, year after year this is one of the principal traits that consumers with problem debt have in common. Now that you've turned over a new leaf, get in the habit of paying off your credit card accounts each month or, at the very least, paying a third or more of the balance due. Remember, credit cards should not be used for mere wants or to supplement your cash reserves. They should be for emergencies, as discussed earlier, and only when you have a plan for quick repayment.

SURVIVAL TIP:
FIND CREDIT/DEBIT CARDS WITH REASONABLE FEES AND TERMS.

Visit www.ASurvivalGuidetoDebt.com to review a list of specially selected credit and debit card offers. We've pre-screened these to be certain they have reasonable fees and terms that are more favorable, especially for persons who currently have poor credit ratings.

Without question, there are many other mistakes that people make with credit cards. Paying late, not knowing credit limits, excessive use of cash advances or cash advance checks, overuse—especially for nonessential purchases—and failure to monitor balances and monthly statements are just a few of the ways people get in trouble with credit cards. However, in the list of the top five, I've tried to focus on mistakes that you're most vulnerable to when you're just beginning to reestablish credit.

As mentioned previously, if you're coming out of bankruptcy or some other debt remediation process, you should already have a heightened awareness of the dangers of credit misuse. You know that you have to pay your bills on time; you know that you can't make purchases that aren't in your budget or within your means; you know that if you don't pay off credit card balances, you'll end up sending too much money to the credit card companies, month after month, putting you right back in the vicious cycle you just escaped. Don't do it! Stick to your budget, discipline your spending, communicate financial realities to the others in your household, and keep yourself on track. Focus on the basics and you'll eventually be in control of your finances, rather than having them control you.

FINANCIAL GPS

Top Five Credit Card Mistakes

1. Failing to shop for the best rate
2. Falling for a low introductory rate
3. Failing to read the contract
4. Getting too many cards
5. Making only minimum payments

CREDIT TRAPS TO AVOID

As we conclude this chapter on reestablishing your credit and understanding its proper and responsible use, let me issue a few quick cautions about credit-related scams and traps you should avoid. Most of these credit snares are built around misinformation and the temptation to try using shortcuts. But let me repeat what I said at the beginning of this chapter: you didn't get in trouble overnight, and you won't get out that way either. Rebuilding your credit, like gaining control of your financial future, requires time, patience, and the systematic formation of good habits. Anytime you hear someone promising you solutions to your money or credit problems that are quick, easy, or cheap, you should immediately suspect that they are none of the three.

"Quick" Credit Score Improvement

As discussed in chapter 4 in the section on the Fair Credit Reporting Act (FCRA), you should almost always avoid entities advertising their ability to rapidly improve your credit rating. Usually, they are more interested in collecting a fee from you than they are in making any lasting improvement in your FICO score. As I explained previously, their efforts generally consist of bombarding the reporting agencies with dispute letters on your behalf, many of which may have no basis in fact. Such so-called services are almost never worth the cost in money or time and even more rarely provide the benefits they promise.

Piggybacking

This strategy involves having yourself listed as an "authorized user" of a credit card account established by someone with good credit, supposedly "borrowing" their credit history in order to improve your own. The practice likely originated with parents authorizing credit cards for children's use— somewhat understandable—but has in recent years been commercialized, with certain web-based and other organizations collecting hefty fees for brokering relationships between borrowers with good histories and prospective borrowers with suspect ones.

However, FICO, the organization most lenders and credit bureaus rely on for credit scoring, has announced that it will no longer consider "authorized user" status as relevant to a consumer's credit score. In other words, if your credit score was poor before you "piggybacked" on your rich uncle's MasterCard account, it will still be poor under FICO's new scoring policy. The only way to improve a bad credit score, in other words, is by making timely payments and reducing your debt. This shortcut to a better credit score is probably closed—permanently.

"Clean" Tax Identification Number

Some organizations claim that they can instantly secure a clean credit history for you by obtaining a new tax identification number—sometimes an employer identification number (EIN) rather than the Social Security number issued to each individual. Even though obtaining an EIN may be legal, obtaining it under false pretenses isn't—and could bring about some unwelcome legal consequences. Not only that, but the Social Security Administration is extremely wary about handing out new Social Security numbers, even to people who can demonstrate that their SSNs have been compromised by identity thieves. For these reasons, you should be extremely skeptical of any entity that claims it can get you a "clean" credit record by obtaining a new or different tax identification number—especially if they're asking for payment up front.

Here again, the same principle holds true: there are no shortcuts to a good credit rating.

If you will commit to following the budget you created by using the principles outlined in chapter 9, followed by making careful, strategic use of your available credit and following through on verifying the accuracy of your credit report as discussed in this chapter, you will begin to see steady improvement, not only in your credit scores but also in your general financial health. In all likelihood, you will start to notice that the stress that formerly accompanied bill-paying time each month is starting to decrease because you now have a plan in place that allows you to keep pace with current obligations.

SURVIVAL TIP:
PROTECT YOURSELF
FROM CREDIT SCAMS

For more information on protecting yourself from credit repair scams, see the U.S. Federal Trade Commission article "Credit Repair: How to Help Yourself" at www.ftc. gov/bcp/edu/pubs/consumer/credit/cre13.shtm.

The next step is to establish some good savings habits in order to build up cash reserves for future needs, whether they involve a nice vacation next summer or a worry-free retirement thirty years from now. The next chapter will show you how to get started with this part of your financial makeover.

STEPS IN THE RIGHT DIRECTION

1. Obtain a secured credit card to begin rebuilding your credit score.
2. Commit to making only small, affordable purchases on credit, and pay them off at the end of each billing cycle.
3. Carefully read the contract before signing up for any credit card.
4. Limit yourself to one or two cards.
5. Identify and avoid credit improvement scams.

Chapter 11

COMMIT TO A SAVINGS PLAN

GUIDEPOSTS

In this chapter, you'll learn

- How to develop a practical savings philosophy

- About setting up and maintaining an emergency fund

- How to incorporate your savings plan into your goals

- About the impact of Social Security on your future savings needs

The wisdom of setting aside resources for future needs is as old as Aesop's Fables and the Bible (surprisingly, in fact, the Old and New Testaments contain more advice about money than almost any other single topic). Without question, some sort of disciplined and systematic savings plan should be part of everyone's financial road map. I seriously doubt whether anyone of sound mind and reasonably normal outlook would not agree that everyone should save some portion of income as a hedge against the uncertainties of the future.

If that's true, why does the United States have one of the lowest rates of household savings in the industrialized world, according to data recently released by the Organization for Economic Cooperation and Development (as reported in a story carried on October 17, 2008, by National Public Radio—www.npr.org)? As a matter of fact, in 2005, according to these data, the U.S. savings rate—in consistent decline since 1970—actually fell into the negative range. In other words, Americans consistently spend more than they make. Maybe it's not surprising, then, that so many people are filing for personal bankruptcy, as reported in the introduction to this book.

Interestingly, the current recession may be inspiring more Americans to become savers instead of spenders. With the possibility of losing jobs, falling real estate values, and other dark clouds on the horizon, in recent months the savings rate has begun to rise—and rise sharply—for the first time in many years. That may be the only faintly good result from the currently poor economy.

But just to add a potentially confusing wrinkle, in early 2009, as I write this, the federal government is pulling out all the stops in an effort to convince lenders to—guess what?—*keep loaning money!* That's right: to a nation in the throes of what may turn out to be the worst financial crisis since the Great Depression of the 1930s, one of the messages seems to be that the way back to prosperity is for consumers to take on more debt!

Now, I understand that measures of a national economy's liquidity may involve different practical considerations than those governing what is best for individual households. But in this chapter, we're going to look at ways you can develop a rationale, an approach, and a method for systematically saving money. We'll discuss the whys, whens, and hows of saving, with emphasis on the importance of building in this essential component as part of your plan for regaining control of your finances and your life.

SETTING GOALS, SETTING BOUNDARIES

The first step in establishing your savings plan is to formulate the basic approach to savings that will govern your daily and monthly saving and spending decisions. To begin this process, you need to refer to that foundational financial document we developed in chapter 9: your budget.

Even though you can find tons of advice on how much you need to be saving—from popular and media-savvy personal financial gurus on the Internet and just about every consumer news and financial publication—the ultimate decision has to be governed by the details of your current financial situation and the realities of your available cash flow. Right now, when most of you who are reading this are struggling to get the maximum benefit from the fresh start afforded by bankruptcy, debt settlement, or credit counseling and debt management plans, the focus is probably on more immediate concerns: how to take care of next week, next month, the lump sum payment you have to make next quarter. Long-range concerns like retirement, kids' college, and other similar matters are probably not high on your list of savings needs or priorities at this moment. Some of you should probably not concern yourselves with these matters.

That's fine, and as it should be. At this beginning phase of your financial makeover, your greatest need is to take care of the obligations that impact your life right now, not those that will come into play years from now. Don't allow guilt over "not saving enough" add to the stress you already feel.

However, you also shouldn't simply throw up your hands in despair and assume that "it's impossible for me to save right now." Your savings philosophy should reflect the real world you live in and the resources available to you. Right now, you may not be able to realistically set the goal of saving lots of money for an early retirement or financing a child's education. But perhaps you could meet the more modest goal of paying cash for next summer's vacation at the beach or the kitchen remodel you've been planning. How about accumulating $1,000 or more in a "rainy day" fund, or paying an extra $125 per month on your mortgage to enable you to pay it off early? Set your sights on an objective that makes sense for your situation—right now—and begin taking baby steps toward it. Even small amounts can add up, given time and consistency. Let's take a look at how you can get started.

Goal: Start Small, but Start!

Looking at your budget, can you identify places where you could save on monthly expenses—even a little bit? For example, if you're eating lunch at a fast food place every day at work, taking your lunch instead could save you anywhere from $3.00 to $10.00 per day—$15 to $50 per week! What would happen if you put just halve that amount—$7.50 to $25 per week—into a savings account, even if it earned no interest? (As I write this, rates on simple savings accounts are, in many cases, less than 1 percent per year.) Even at the bottom end of the range, in a year you'd have saved almost $400, and at the top end, you'd have set aside more than $1,000.

Let me share another personal example. A friend of mine—who makes more money and drives a much nicer car than I do—found out that my first house was completely paid off. He asked me how we did it, and I told him that it was really pretty easy: (1) It was a house we could afford; (2) We made automatic payments every month; (3) We kept ourselves poor, always putting any extra money we got toward the mortgage; and (4) We started to see it as a game: "How much can we pay the mortgage down this month?" In a way, it became almost addictive. And before long, we were mortgage free. What a great feeling! My friend didn't seem to understand how such small amounts of money could add up to enough to pay off a house early. Not surprisingly, he still has a mortgage payment.

Take another look at some of the savings ideas mentioned in chapter 2, in the section "Better Defense: Right-Sizing Your Lifestyle." Can you trim monthly entertainment expenses by renting movies or checking them out from your local public library? Can you cut clothing costs by buying from thrift stores and resale shops? All of these small measures can add up to big savings, given consistency and time.

One more personal story: my wife is a monster on eBay—for buying, not selling! We have three young children, and I would say that Mysti buys 75 percent of their clothes on eBay, sometimes paying as little as 5 percent of retail. Heck, I usually can't tell which of my kids' outfits are new and which are from eBay. In fact, they're growing so fast that they wear the clothes for only a few months before it's time to sell them in our annual garage sale. I'm a pretty lucky guy: my wife loves saving money—and she's a sports fan. It doesn't get much better.

The point is that by carefully reviewing your budget and tracking your expenses—sometimes, in very exacting detail—you can probably find $20 to $50 per month that could be repurposed from spending to savings. Avoid self-defeating thoughts about how such small amounts "won't make any difference," and commit yourself to the new habit of putting that money in savings and leaving it there. Remember: these are the basics you must master in order to get from where you were to where you want to go. Believe me, you'll be surprised how fast even small amounts placed in savings will add up if this becomes a regular practice for you. Not only that, but you'll feel a great sense of personal satisfaction when you see those balances start to grow. You might even gain a little more peace of mind—something that was in rare supply when you were drowning in debt.

SURVIVAL TIP:
LEARN TO SAVE REGARDLESS OF THE SIZE OF YOUR BUDGET

For more ideas on how to save money on a tight budget, see the Consumer Literacy Consortium's website, www.66ways.org.

Some consumer savings advisers suggest that simply collecting your loose change and periodically depositing it into your savings account can yield savings deposits of $100 per year or more. Do you have jars of change sitting around in your closet and on the top of your dresser? Take them down to the bank and let them start working for you instead of just taking up space in your house. And, now that you're paying cash, the change jars will fill just that much quicker!

Goal: Pay Yourself First

One thing most financial counselors agree on: you're more likely to save if you put it in your budget, and twice more likely if you make it automatic. Once you've tracked your expenses and compared them with your budget, you should determine the amount that you can allocate to savings and make that deposit first, every month. Before you pay your bills, before you take the kids shopping, before you buy gas for the car, pay yourself. You *cannot* think of this as a "slush" or "fun" fund, though, or you'll be in financial trouble again—and soon. This is a savings payment so that you have an emergency fund to turn to when the worst happens.

There are several ways to accomplish this. Many employers—especially those served by credit unions—offer payroll-deducted payments to savings accounts and other financial instruments. Take advantage of this, and let your money go to savings before your paycheck ever hits your desk. You'll get used to not having the money to spend, and as a result, your savings account will grow.

In fact, some businesses—even very small ones—offer payroll-deducted IRAs as a service to employees. According to the Internal Revenue Service (www.irs.gov), such plans are very simple, require no filings from the employer, and are completely voluntary—the only deposits are made by employees. The annual contribution limit for such plans varies: it's $5,000 in 2009, according to the IRS website. The interest or other earnings on the account accumulate tax free until you begin making withdrawals at retirement, which means that the money builds that much faster for you.

Not only that, but some employers match some percentage of employee deposits into certain types of accounts—usually those for retirement or other long-range purposes. If your employer offers this option, you need to take advantage of it. Once again, such savings tend to grow faster because they are built up on a regular basis (and your employer is putting money in for you). And, just as with the payroll-deducted deposits above, you won't ever see these deposits in your take-home pay, making it much less likely that you'd be tempted to spend the money.

You can also simply write the savings check yourself, before all your other monthly expenditures. Remember: the reason you developed a budget was so you could know, from month to month, how much of your money was going where. If you've done your job properly, and your budget indicates that you could be allocating $20, $50, or $100 per month to savings, then, as the shoe company says, "just do it." Once that money is safely tucked away in your savings account, you're much less likely to spend it on something else—accidentally or otherwise.

If you get paid weekly or biweekly, that means that some months you'll get an "extra" paycheck because of the way the weeks stretch across months. Using the calendar, figure out which months you'll be receiving five checks instead of four, or three instead of two, and commit to putting these checks straight into your savings account.

You can also fund savings with tax refund checks, extra money you make from overtime or outside work, selling stuff you don't need, and probably a dozen other sources. The point is, make that extra money count for something besides extra consumer goods or a few restaurant meals. Once you start to see that savings balance growing, chances are good you'll start enjoying the way it feels to be putting money in the bank instead of always wondering where it went. And it's easier if you'll follow the rule of "paying yourself first."

Boundary: Don't Try to Do What You Can't Do

Especially for the "givers" described in chapter 8, trying to meet the needs of too many other people can derail the best-laid savings plans. Here's a typical scenario: You've managed to sock away your planned savings allocation for several months in a row, and you're starting to see your goal becoming a reality. Then you get a call from a child, a friend, a relative—you fill in the blank—who needs a set of tires, a "loan until payday," help with this month's rent—you fill in the blank. With a sigh, you hand over the money, realizing that you are about to start all over again on the goal that you had so painstakingly set and built into your budget.

I realize I'm walking a fine line here, and believe me, I've been on both sides of the fence: borrowing money from parents and friends for a business deal (that went well, thankfully, enabling me to repay the loans) as well as loaning money to family members and friends, never to see it paid back. Denying help to loved ones and friends when giving it is within our capability is one of the hardest things we can ever do. On the other hand, as I advised the givers in chapter 8, if we don't take care of ourselves, we eventually won't be able to take care of anyone else. In other words, sometimes you have be "selfish" in order to do what's best for yourself and your family. The key is the thought process preceding the decision to give or not give. If you can look at your budget, look at the need, and determine that the delay in meeting your goal is acceptable or even possible to offset by making an adjustment in another area, then you may be able to go ahead and make the gift or loan without worrying about its effect on your financial plan. In fact, you might even want to build in a budget item for a "charity fund." You could put money in this account each month. When the requests come, if the money in your fund is sufficient to meet it, you can hand it over and feel no anxiety or frustration whatsoever because that's what you budgeted it for. If the account is empty or insufficient for the need, you've got a ready-made, nonemotional reason why you must decline.

The point is that you need to be honest with yourself and others about what you can and can't do. Just as it's important for you to communicate clearly and realistically with your family about household money matters, it's also important for you to have appropriate boundaries in financial matters. If you have adult children who have come to depend on you in inappropriate ways, it may be time to have a frank conversation with them about the new realities of your situation. If you have children who are still at home whose tastes are no longer supportable by your budget and financial goals, you may need to help them either discover alternate means of funding their preferences or adjust their expectations to a more workable level for the current circumstances. In other words, maybe it's time for your teenager to get a job!

Goal: Build an Emergency Fund

Another thing that just about every financial planner will tell you is that you need an emergency fund. Even though I completely agree with the advisability of this, I also believe that the level usually advised—six months' salary—may be unrealistic for many people, especially those who have just emerged from bankruptcy or other financial retrenchment. As I mentioned in the discussion of setting a realistic savings philosophy, the steps you plan toward your objective should conform to your present circumstances and funding ability. To slightly overstate the case, it doesn't make much sense to get six months' salary in savings if doing so means you'll get your utilities turned off for nonpayment.

Once again, I advocate starting small and being consistent. Set an immediate goal of getting $500 in your emergency fund. This might not sound like enough to take care of a very big emergency, but it could easily help you avoid the temptation of reaching for a credit card the next time an unexpected expense comes up. It could help you avoid a late payment fee for a utility bill. It could help you avoid having to reinvent your budget every time something unexpected comes up. It could even make several co-pays on doctor's office visits—almost always unplanned, right? Once you get that first $500—or, if you're really focused, $1,000—in your emergency fund, you'll be able to add to it until it's at the level to provide an even greater safety net.

Start small, but start!

Of course, the strategies for saving money on a tight budget, as presented in the section titled "Goal: Start Small, but Start!" apply here as well. Here are a few other ideas for building up your emergency fund.

- When you finish with an installment payment—for furniture, home appliances, or even a car payment—continue making the payment, but to yourself. In most cases, you've already built that "expense" into your monthly budget, so just keep writing the check—but pay it into savings instead.

- Investigate possible savings on car or home insurance. Take the difference—which you're already accustomed to paying—and use it to fund your rainy-day account. The same idea would apply if you could save on your cellular phone plan by switching from cable to satellite (or vice versa), or even by saving on groceries.

- Quit smoking or drinking. Wait! Don't skip over this point! How much healthier—and richer—would you be if you weren't spending on tobacco or alcohol and instead were putting that money in your emergency fund? I have to admit, this is a personal issue with me because my dad died from the long-term effects of smoking and drinking. If you're a regular smoker and/or drinker, take an honest look at your budget and do the math. My prediction is that by saving the money you're currently spending on nicotine and alcohol, you could be well on your way to financial independence in two years, just by taking this one step.

Goal: Plan Major Purchases with Cash, Not Credit

This is a great way to involve the whole family in savings goal setting. Think of where you'd like to spend your next big vacation—a theme park, the seashore, the mountains, or even driving cross-country to see the sights along the way to somewhere you've never been—set a budget for the trip, and start setting aside the money necessary to have the entire trip paid for before you leave. Or, if your family has always wanted a backyard pool, use that as your savings incentive instead. It can be a major home remodel, a new car, or almost anything that the entire family can get excited about and focus on saving for.

This can be a great teaching tool for young children. Do they want the newest video gaming system? Pay them small amounts for doing chores, and set up a "video game account." Track it regularly so they can see how close they're getting to their goal. When you go out to eat, offer them the choice of either getting dessert or putting the same amount of money in the video game account.

The point is that by setting a shared goal and saving money to accomplish it, you've changed the way you think about getting "the fun stuff" from a spending orientation (often using credit) to a savings orientation. Even if circumstances were to force you to use the money you'd saved for some emergency need, you'd still be much farther ahead than if you had to borrow to meet the need. Furthermore, I doubt seriously if anyone ever got into financial trouble because they saved too much money—even if it was for a pool or a new car.

RETIREMENT AND YOUR SAVINGS STRATEGY

Most of us have at least some vague notion of retiring one day: spending more time doing what we want to do instead of doing what we have to do. For folks in their fifties and sixties, the idea of retirement is usually more than vague; it's either a day to eagerly anticipate or one to dread because of the lack of financial resources. And then there are those folks who, by choice or out of necessity, plan on working until they can't physically continue.

Whatever your disposition with regard to retirement, it is certainly something you need to take into account as a part of your overall financial strategy. If your employer offers the option of payroll-deducted contributions to a retirement or pension plan, such as a 401k, IRA, or other tax-advantaged savings plan, you should definitely take advantage of the opportunity. After all, there aren't many chances to allow money to grow on a tax-free basis, but that's exactly what tax-deferred and tax-advantaged retirement plans do. You don't pay taxes on the money you put in, and you don't pay taxes on the accumulations until you begin to draw them out at age 59½ or greater.

But another factor in your retirement—one that I don't see getting enough attention—is Social Security. Although the safety and viability of the Social Security fund is in and out of the news pretty frequently, and politicians like to call press conferences and wring their hands about the "serious problems" with Social Security, it's most likely that you'll be able to collect at least some retirement income from Social Security when you reach the point where you want or need to stop earning your living from nine to five. Now, mind you, I'm not saying that we shouldn't pay attention to the debate over Social Security and hold our legislators accountable for the decisions they make. But I am saying that you can probably count on Social Security providing a somewhat significant portion of income at your retirement.

To get an estimate of what you might expect from Social Security upon your retirement, go to the Social Security Administration website, which features several calculators of varying degrees of accuracy that can help you calculate your future benefits. The website is at www.ssa.gov/planners/calculators.htm.

If you want, you can actually take the time to obtain an estimate based on current law and real-time access to your earnings record. To use the

SSA's "Retirement Estimator," you will need to log in to a secure website using personal information, including your Social Security number. According to the Social Security Administration, the Retirement Estimator does the following:

- Provides an estimate of your retirement benefits comparable to the estimate you receive on your Social Security statement each year
- Lets you create additional "what if" retirement scenarios based on current law

In addition to the Retirement Estimator, the site offers other calculators, including the "Quick Calculator," the "Online Calculator" (which requires you to manually input your earnings history), and the "Detailed Calculator," which, according to the site, "provides the most precise estimates" but must be downloaded and installed on your computer. Unlike the Retirement Estimator, none of the last three tools mentioned is actually linked to your earnings record, but each tool can provide you with good, working estimates of what you can expect Social Security to provide toward your retirement income needs.

For example, using the Quick Calculator, you enter your date of birth, your current year's earnings, and your anticipated retirement date, and the calculator will give you an estimate of your monthly retirement benefit, either in present-value dollars or dollars adjusted for inflation from now until your retirement. Let's do a sample calculation for an individual who is forty years old and earning $35,000 per year.

- Date of birth: January 1, 1969 (forty years before the date I'm writing this)
- Earnings in the current year: $35,000
- Month and year of retirement: January 2036 (sixty-seven is normal retirement age for persons born in 1960 or later)
- Monthly retirement benefit estimate: $1,341

If we assume the person in the example above makes about $2,900 per month ($35,000 ÷ 12), the estimated monthly retirement benefit of $1,341 adds up to about 46 percent of pre-retirement income. If the person opted to work three more years, or until age seventy, the estimated monthly retirement benefit would be $1,671, or just over 57 percent of pre-retirement income.

What this means to you is that you can probably count on Social Security to provide between 45 percent and 60 percent of your pre-retirement income. Though taking a 55 percent or even a 40 percent cut in pay may not sound too appealing, remember that you've got a number of years to work on growing your retirement savings (not including Social Security) to make up the difference. Also consider that most financial advisers say you don't need your full pre-retirement income after retirement; 80 percent of pre-retirement income is a good estimate, according to some sources. There are several reasons for this. Usually, by retirement you aren't supporting children at home any more. Also, your house may be paid for. You may not need two cars anymore. On the other hand, some expenses—medical bills, for example—can be greater in retirement.

The point in all of this is that, especially if you're contributing to an employer-sponsored retirement plan, you probably have more immediate concerns than socking away money for retirement. In fact, if you can get your monthly expenses under sufficient control in the short term, it may be easier for you to make significant headway with your retirement plans in the longer term.

To put it bluntly, by the simple fact of earning wages, you are "saving for retirement" every month. Instead of fretting about retirement, focus on getting your financial boat on an even keel and meeting your simple, short-term goals. Whatever you do, don't budget for retirement savings if you're getting behind on monthly living expenses.

Much of this goes back to the point with which we started this chapter: your savings plan should be a realistic reflection of your current circumstances, resources, and priorities. Don't fret so much over retirement, for example, that you divert critical resources from meeting current needs and objectives.

WHAT ABOUT EDUCATION EXPENSES?

The same principle applies here. Saving to pay for children's or other family members' education is certainly a worthy goal, but it may not be one that fits with your current circumstances. If you're struggling just to stick to your budget, there may not be much left over to contribute to a college fund. In other words, you may need to be a bit selfish in order to do the right thing for yourself and your family.

Once again, though, you may be able to find small amounts to allocate to this purpose. Furthermore, there are more options now than ever for education grants, low-interest loans with generous payback provisions (though you might want to review the information presented in chapters 2, 6, and elsewhere about student loan repayment), and other forms of higher education financing that can help make up for shortfalls in what you're able to save to pay for college. You might even consider having an honest conversation with your child, presenting alternatives such as stretching the amount of time spent obtaining the degree to allow for working a part-time job to help meet education expenses.

The point is that you should set realistic goals and communicate them to the other members of your household. And by now, I hope you realize that this is advice that applies not only to your savings plan but also to just about everything else.

In the last three chapters, we've taken some important steps in establishing the pattern for your financial makeover. We've set up a budget and learned how to use it as the guidance system for your journey to financial health; we've talked about the right ways to begin rebuilding your credit history; and we've discussed ways to find and build savings, even on a tight budget. As we turn to the final chapter of this book, it's time to summarize everything we've learned and also outline a few more ideas to help you stay on track toward a brighter financial future.

STEPS IN THE RIGHT DIRECTION

1. Create a savings plan—no matter how small to begin with—and stick with it.

2. Begin building an emergency fund.

3. Identify a mid-range or short-term financial goal with your family, and commit to saving enough money to meet the goal.

4. Research your retirement savings options and develop a plan of action

Chapter 12

BACKING AWAY
FROM THE EDGE

GUIDEPOSTS

In this chapter, you'll learn

- How to "put it all together" as you assemble your financial plan

- Where to find more helpful resources

- How to stay on course for a more secure future

On January 15, 2009, just after taking off from New York's LaGuardia Airport, a U.S. Airways passenger jet's flight path was crossed by a flock of birds. Two bird strikes rendered the jet's engines useless, and pilot Chesley B. Sullenberger III—"Sully" as he is now known by millions around the world—had to make a grim decision: whether to attempt to get back to LaGuardia and make a dead-stick landing or to try to put the plane down safely somewhere closer. Sully opted to land in the Hudson River.

Witnesses say the veteran pilot made a picture-perfect water landing: the nose slightly lifted so the jet could belly into the water, the wings perfectly parallel to the surface of the river. Every single passenger and crew member got outside onto the wings and was safely transferred to the rescue craft that soon swarmed the site. Sully was the last one off, after making two trips through the aircraft—by this time, filling with ice-cold river water—to make sure everyone else had exited safely.

For his cool head in the midst of a terrifying situation, and for the almost miraculous skill with which he executed the emergency touchdown, Sully was hailed as a hero from New York to California.

In another sense, however, Sully simply did what every pilot is trained to do, whether flying a passenger jet with hundreds of people on board or a solo flight in a single-engine Cessna: he flew the airplane.

Most people who take flying lessons hear this phrase over and over: "Fly the airplane." In other words, whatever may be going wrong, your first task is to maintain correct altitude, keep the wings level, and figure out your flight path to the nearest landing place. When things get dicey or uncertain, focus on the fundamentals and on circumstances you can do something about rather than the ones you can't.

This is a good principle to apply as you begin your fresh financial start. Undoubtedly, somewhere along the way, the unexpected will happen. When it does, fly the airplane. Focus on what you can control, keep on doing the fundamentals, and make any adjustments you can to stay on course. In many ways, that is what this entire book has been about. No matter what stage of the process you're in—deciding how to handle your problem debt, working with a bankruptcy attorney or credit counselor, or establishing a budget to move you toward your financial goals—you should always be flying the airplane.

GETTING A VIEW OF THE FOREST

At this point, maybe it's time to take a few steps back to try to get a panoramic view of where you've been, where you are, and where you want to go. First of all, I sincerely hope that if you are or have been struggling with unmanageable debt, you now can see some light at the end of the tunnel—and be confident that it's not an oncoming train. Once again, the reason I wrote this book was to provide solid, actionable information to people just like you. Whether you've decided to resolve your debt problems on your own, with the help of a credit counselor or debt settlement professional, or even by filing bankruptcy, I hope this book has provided some facts that have added to your confidence in your course of action and your satisfaction at its outcome, if you've proceeded that far. By knowing your rights as a consumer, a homeowner, and a debtor, you have gained a tremendous advantage in the process of formulating a plan for getting out of trouble and reclaiming control of your finances and your life.

If you've read this far, you also now have all the tools and knowledge you need to begin the rebuilding process. From here, it's up to you to stick to your plan and resist the temptation to return to the spending habits that may have contributed to the problems that caused you to pick up this book in the first place. Use your budget to chart your course and monitor how well you're doing; set reasonable goals and communicate them to your family (or, better still, involve your family in setting goals); be smart and strategic about credit use; stick to your savings plan; and strive for consistency in your month-to-month financial management practices. If you can do that, you'll look back on your debt troubles as an important learning experience—one you won't ever have to repeat.

DEALING WITH THE ROOT CAUSES

This might also be a good time to reassess the reasons for your original financial problems in order to form strategies for dealing with any underlying causes that could land you back in trouble. Sometimes, debt trouble is a symptom of some other problem that desperately needs to be addressed.

For example, if unemployment caused you to get behind on your payments, is there anything you can do now to avoid unemployment in the future? Maybe you're in an industry that's struggling because of the current economy. Can you retrain? Can you go back to school to prepare yourself for a career less subject to cyclical economic trends? Or was your unemployment due to excessive absenteeism or some other trait viewed negatively by your employer? Now is the time to be honest with yourself and ask what steps you need to take to make yourself more employable in the future. You may need to communicate to your spouse, partner, or other members of your household your need for their support as you make this transition.

Perhaps you got into debt because of gambling, drug use, excessive drinking, or other addictions. If you don't get help, you are probably doomed to repeat the cycle. Maybe a divorce created the beginnings of your financial meltdown. If so, you may need to consider whether you need to make some fundamental personal changes in order to become healthy—emotionally and financially. Remember the statement from chapter 8, "Wherever you go, there you are"? Changing jobs, moving, or even filing bankruptcy won't alter the behaviors that created your problem. I'm not a psychological counselor by any means, but I do know that if there are underlying causes like those I've just listed, and you don't take the responsibility for addressing them, you probably aren't dealing honestly with the realities of your situation. In the introduction and elsewhere, I said that you alone are responsible for finding solutions to your financial problems. The same is true for any core problems that may be contributing to your vulnerability to financial hardship. The resources are out there, but it's up to you to make the decision to use them.

RESOURCES FOR FINANCIAL EDUCATION

This book is primarily intended as a resource for getting out of debt and beginning your financial rebuilding process; it is by no means the final word on family financial planning. You could fill a good-size library with all the books, CDs, and DVDs available on various aspects of debt, financial management, investment strategies, and other money topics, but you don't have to spend your nest egg to get smarter about personal finance.

In fact, if you're really serious about learning how you and your family can become more financially knowledgeable, you need go no farther than your computer. The U.S. government offers a variety of options for free training and education in the basics of finance and money management. Here are just a few of the web-based resources available:

- www.ASurvivalGuidetoDebt.com. At our website, you can find advice on budgeting, saving, creating financial goals, and almost everything else you need to become a smarter and more disciplined consumer.

- Debt Education and Certification Foundation (DECAF): www. debt-foundation.org. This nonprofit organization provides resources for financial education, as well as approved credit counseling and financial training courses.

- www.MyMoney.gov. This website, maintained by the U.S. Financial Literacy and Education Commission, has some great links, including interactive web-based programs, to help you learn the basics of household financial management. It features free online calculators for figuring mortgage payments, student loans, rent-vs.-buy analysis, and lots more. You'll also find a variety of reports and information about such financial topics as smart borrowing strategies, budgeting, and taxes. There's even a whole section devoted to interactive and informational financial training for kids.

- The Federal Reserve Bank of Dallas sponsors a site called Building Wealth: A Beginner's Guide to Securing Your Future (www.dallas-fed.org/ca/wealth/index.cfm). This site has an interactive curriculum to show you, step-by-step, how to calculate your net worth, create a budget, understand the basic principles of saving and investing, and make better borrowing decisions.

- The Federal Deposit Insurance Corporation (FDIC) developed the "Money Smart" program to offer financial training and information to persons "outside the financial mainstream" (www.fdic.gov/moneysmart). The site offers a section called "computer-based instruction" that allows you to educate yourself at your own pace on the basics of banking, credit, savings, and mortgages.

- The Jump$tart® Coalition is a national organization made up of educational, governmental, industry, and special interest groups "dedicated to improving the financial literacy of kindergarten through college-age youth by providing advocacy, research, standards, and educational resources." Their website (www.jumpstart.org) features a wide array of free and downloadable publications covering many different aspects of personal financial management, both for kids and adults.

Financial education involves a lot more than just learning techniques and principles, however. If you are following your budget and sticking to your savings plan, at some point in the fairly near future you will be in the enviable position of needing to know the best ways of protecting and increasing your savings. As a matter of fact, there's no better incentive for improving your knowledge of money management than actually having some money to manage! Once you've gotten a little experience in month-to-month financial management, you'll probably want to begin educating yourself about ongoing financial trends, the economy, investment, and other money topics in order to equip yourself with the knowledge you need to make good decisions in an always-shifting financial landscape.

One of the best ways you can do this is by keeping yourself aware of the latest financial headlines and how current trends in the economy, banking, and finance can affect you. Here are a few of my favorite websites for keeping up with what's going on in the world of money, investment, and savings.

- CNNMoney.com, the online publication of the Cable News Network, carries the top financial headlines coming out of Washington, New York, Tokyo, and around the world. You can view videos, read news stories, check out the opinions of various analysts, and generally keep on top of what's being done and said by major corporations, policy makers, investors, and other players on the world financial stage.

- Google Finance (www.googlefinance.com), much like the ever-present Google search engine itself, offers free financial news online including the latest information on stock markets, interest rates, and breaking headlines. The site also carries news feeds from some of the largest financial reporting organizations, such as Reuters, *Business Week*, and others.

- Bankrate.com is a great place to get information on savings rates, mortgage and other loan rates, money market accounts, and the latest banking and finance news.

- The *Wall Street Journal* is one of the world's oldest and best-known financial dailies. And now you can read much of the journal's content online by going to www.wsj.com. Although some of the content is reserved for paid subscribers, you can still review the top financial headlines, view video of the day's important events, and read a wide variety of articles and educational pieces.

Just as reliable information is your best ally in the effort to deal with problem debt, educating yourself about how money can work for you will pay dividends in your quest for financial security. These free resources can get you a long way down the road to facing your future with more confidence.

MOVING FORWARD WITH HOPE

As this book draws to a close, I will conclude as I began: with a message of hope. By now, if you have been applying the principles outlined in this book, you have begun dealing (or have successfully dealt) with the debt that is hampering your choices and preoccupying your attention and energy. You have applied the communication skills needed to work with your creditors; you have taken personal responsibility for understanding your rights and obligations as a consumer and a debtor. You have made decisions based on knowledge rather than fear of consequences, and you have taken proactive steps to do what is best for yourself and your family.

I hope that you have already felt the new confidence that comes from going through a difficult situation and emerging successfully on the other side. I sincerely trust that you will take to heart the lessons presented here about budgeting, controlling your spending, exercising careful discernment in your use of credit, and adhering to the steps required to meet the financial goals you have set for yourself and your household.

As you continue to move forward into a brighter future, remember that sticking with the basics—blocking, tackling, and ditch digging—is what separates the successful from those doomed to repeat past mistakes. Don't be tempted to fall back into old patterns of thoughtless, spur-of-the-moment spending. Remember that your budget is your road map to financial success, and follow it.

Remember also a proverb that I often repeat: "If it were easy, everybody would be doing it." As I've tried to make clear, earning your financial freedom depends on making hard choices and forming good habits that don't come naturally to most people. If it doesn't seem at least a little challenging or difficult, you probably aren't doing it right! Over the last few years, through my organization, DECAF, I have seen more than two hundred thousand people in various stages of financial crisis try to get their money troubles sorted out and establish better management habits for their households. Some of these individuals were able to successfully make the transition into stable, financially responsible lifestyles. Others—a year, two years, or five years down the road—found themselves back in the same kind of trouble they had originally come to me for help in escaping.

What makes the difference between those who are able to "kick the debt habit" and those who find themselves repeating the cycle of overspending, problem debt, and financial crisis? One word: *discipline*. The people who get out of trouble and stay out are those who are determined to practice sound financial fundamentals: They stick to their budgets and don't spend more than they earn; they plan ahead and save for major purchases instead of getting them with credit; they plan ahead for future needs and, over time, build the cash reserves needed to deal with the unexpected.

DOUG'S STORY—A NEW BEGINNING

It has now been three years since Doug emerged from bankruptcy. During that time, there have been a number of changes. Carol still hasn't been able to find another job, but she has picked up some temporary and part-time work here and there. Furthermore, since the family budget was adjusted three years ago, during the bankruptcy, to reflect only Doug's income, they have been able to put into savings a significant amount of the money Carol earns. If no major appliances go out and there are no other large, unexpected expenses, in two months they will have achieved one of their mid-range goals: they will have three months of Doug's income in savings. It's the first time the family has ever had an emergency fund that didn't involve using a credit card. That feels pretty good to Doug and Carol.

Not that everything has been rosy: Doug had to have a talk with their oldest child and explain why there wasn't enough cash to purchase her a vehicle by her sixteenth birthday. However, Doug's daughter found an after-school job at a location not too far from their house and has begun saving to make the purchase on her own. Not long ago, she showed Doug a statement from her account that reflected a balance of just over $3,000. She and Doug have begun scanning the classifieds for a reliable used car.

About six months after emerging from bankruptcy, Doug got a secured credit card. The terms of the account required him to make a deposit into an account with the issuing bank; this deposit was equal to the credit line he was granted. By making small purchases and paying them off during the same billing cycle, Doug began rebuilding his credit history. Just two weeks ago, he was notified that he had qualified for an unsecured credit card. He got the card and promptly put it in a dresser drawer; he wasn't certain yet if he was ready for the temptation of carrying even a small amount of unsecured credit around in his pocket. But if he needed it, it was there.

The rental property has turned a small profit each month for the last year, and Doug has forced himself to put that amount back into a savings account to cover repairs and maintenance. Within the next few months he'll have enough in the account to ride out a month or two with no tenants if he has to.

Even though things are still tight, Doug and Carol have decided they enjoy the feeling of knowing, each month, how all the bills are going to be covered. Looking back on their debt troubles and bankruptcy, they can honestly say it has been a good thing, overall. Had they not had to face the prospect of losing cars, their house, and other assets, they would probably never have committed themselves to the disciplined financial approach they now use.

It hasn't exactly been a Hollywood ending, but the future is looking a little brighter every day.

Like Doug, your future can be brighter than your past. By applying the principles set forth in this book, you can achieve freedom from crippling debt and begin building a more secure financial future. I wrote this book for the specific purpose of helping you live a more stress-free, balanced, and enjoyable life; I hope reading it has given you both a positive vision for the future and a road map for reaching it.

I truly believe we live in a time and place of almost unlimited opportunity. I further believe that regardless of the state of the economy, your company, interest rates, or any other external variables, there will always be resources available for those with the determination and discipline to seek them. By reading this book and absorbing the information it contains, you have taken a firm step toward becoming one of those people.

As you move forward with your financial makeover, let me know how it's going: log in to www.ASurvivalGuidetoDebt.com and click on the "contact us" link. Send me an email and fill me in on your successes, your challenges, and your questions.

I hope that by reading this book you have learned the principles that will help you join the group on the plus side of the financial ledger. There really is life after debt; you can lead a balanced, healthy, financially sustainable lifestyle. It takes determination, knowledge, and, above all, discipline—but it is possible. You know how to get started; where you finish is up to you.

STEPS IN THE RIGHT DIRECTION

1. Continue educating yourself about personal financial management using a free online tool or information site.

2. Address any root emotional or behavioral causes that are contributing to your vulnerability to financial difficulty.

3. Stick to your plan, continue meeting your goals, and move forward with hope.

QUICK-REFERENCE GUIDE TO FREE SELF-HELP RESOURCES

For easy reference, I've gathered together in this appendix many of the financial education, planning, and calculation tools referred to throughout *A Survival Guide to Debt*. Remember, you can always log on to **www. ASurvivalGuidetoDebt.com** and get access to budgeting worksheets, online calculators, educational materials, and a wide range of personal financial information and resources.

CREDIT COUNSELING, DEBT MANAGEMENT, AND DEBT SETTLEMENT

- Association of Independent Consumer Credit Counseling Agencies (AICCCA): www.aiccca.org
- Association of Settlement Companies (TASC): www.tascsite.org
- National Foundation for Credit Counseling (NFCC): www.nfcc.org
- U.S. Organizations for Bankruptcy Alternatives (USOBA): www.usoba.org

DEBT AND OTHER FINANCIAL CALCULATORS

- MSN Moneycentral Debt Evaluation Calculator: www.moneycentral.msn.com/personal-finance/calculators/ evaluate_your_debt_calculator/home.aspx—Allows you to determine your debt-to-income ratio based on input you provide; many other calculators for other purposes
- U.S. Financial Literacy and Education Commission: www. MyMoney.gov—More educational resources and several useful online financial calculators
- U.S. Social Security Administration: www.ssa.gov—Especially see the calculators for estimating your future Social Security retirement benefits at www.ssa.gov/planners/calculators.htm

FAIR DEBT COLLECTION PRACTICES ACT (FDCPA)

- Go to www.ftc.gov/bcp/edu/pubs/consumer/credit/cre27.pdf to read the full text of the act

FAIR CREDIT BILLING ACT (FCBA)

- Go to www.ftc.gov/os/statutes/fcb/fcb.pdf to read the full text of the act
- The three major credit reporting agencies:
    1. TransUnion: www.TransUnion.com
    2. Experian: www.Experian.com
    3. Equifax: www.Equifax.com

FAIR CREDIT REPORTING ACT (FCRA)

- Go to www.ftc.gov/os/statutes/031224fcra.pdf to read the full text of the act

FINANCIAL EDUCATION

- Bankrate.com: www.bankrate.com—Focused on banking, savings, mortgage, and credit news, issues, and information
- Consumer Literacy Consortium: www.66ways.org—Tips on ways to save money on everything from groceries to mortgage loans
- Federal Deposit Insurance Corporation (FDIC): www.fdic.gov/moneysmart—A "computer-based instruction" section offers self-paced instruction on the basics of banking, credit, savings, and mortgages
- Google™ Finance: www.googlefinance.com—Financial news, headlines, and informational articles
- Jump$tart® Coalition: www.jumpstart.org—Free publications on personal money management including some designed for kids
- U.S. Federal Reserve Bank of Dallas: www.dallasfed.org—Note especially the online course available at this site, "Building Wealth: A Beginner's Guide to Securing Your Financial Future."
- U.S. Financial Literacy and Education Commission: www.MyMoney.gov—This site contains interactive games and other resources for learning about basic household financial management, budgeting, and other important topics.
- *Wall Street Journal* Online: www.wsj.com—Wide range of financial, market, political, and economic news, along with informational articles and editorials

FORECLOSURE AND LEGAL INFORMATION

- National Association of Attorneys General: www.naag.org—For information on your state's consumer advocacy and your legal rights related to debt settlement, debt management, fair trade practices, etc.
- U.S. Department of Housing and Urban Development: www.hud.gov—Contains information on avoiding foreclosure and the Real Estate Settlement Procedures Act (RESPA)

- U.S. Federal Court System: www.uscourts.gov—For latest information and statistics related to bankruptcy filings and other court-related matters
- U.S. Federal Trade Commission: www.ftc.gov—Wide variety of free online and print publications (available for order) on various consumer finance–related topics including foreclosure and repossession, avoiding credit repair or debt settlement scams, etc.

INCOME TAX QUESTIONS

- Internal Revenue Service: www.irs.gov

STUDENT LOANS

- Student Loan Marketing Association ("Sallie Mae"): www.salliemae.com
- U.S. Department of Education: www.ed.gov

Appendix II

GLOSSARY OF BASIC BANKRUPTCY TERMS

(This partial list of definitions is selected (with slight modifications) from the website of the U.S. Federal Court system, www.uscourts.gov.)

Automatic stay: An injunction that automatically stops lawsuits, foreclosures, garnishments, and all collection activity against the debtor the moment a bankruptcy petition is filed.

Bankruptcy: A legal procedure for dealing with debt problems of individuals and businesses; specifically, a case filed under one of the chapters of Title 11 (Bankruptcy) of the United States Code (referred to in the text as the U.S. Bankruptcy Code).

Bankruptcy estate: All legal or equitable interests of the debtor in property at the time of the bankruptcy filing. The estate includes all property in which the debtor has an interest, even if it is owned or held by another person.

Bankruptcy judge: A judicial officer of the United States district court who is the court official with decision-making power over federal bankruptcy cases.

Bankruptcy petition: The document filed by the debtor (in a voluntary case) or by creditors (in an involuntary case) that opens the bankruptcy case. There are official forms for bankruptcy petitions.

Chapter 7: The chapter of the U.S. Bankruptcy Code providing for "liquidation" (the sale of a debtor's nonexempt property and the distribution of the proceeds to creditors).

Chapter 13: The chapter of the U.S. Bankruptcy Code providing for adjustment of debts of an individual with regular income. Chapter 13 allows a debtor to keep property and pay debts over time, usually three to five years.

Claim: A creditor's assertion of a right to payment from the debtor or the debtor's property.

Confirmation: Bankruptcy judge's approval of a plan of reorganization or liquidation in Chapter 11, or payment plan in Chapter 12 or 13.

Consumer debts: Debts incurred for personal, as opposed to business, needs.

Credit counseling: Generally refers to two events in individual bankruptcy cases: (1) the "individual or group briefing" from a nonprofit budget and credit counseling agency that individual debtors must attend prior to filing under any chapter of the U.S. Bankruptcy Code; and (2) the "instructional course in personal financial management" in Chapters 7 and 13 that an individual debtor must complete before a discharge is entered. There are exceptions to both requirements for certain categories of debtors, exigent circumstances, or if the U.S. trustee or bankruptcy administrator has determined that there are insufficient approved credit counseling agencies available to provide the necessary counseling.

Creditors' meeting, or **341 meeting:** The meeting of creditors required by section 341 of the Bankruptcy Code at which the debtor is questioned under oath by creditors, a trustee, examiner, or the U.S. trustee about his or her financial affairs.

Discharge: A release of a debtor from personal liability for certain dischargeable debts set forth in the Bankruptcy Code. A discharge releases a debtor from personal liability for certain debts known as dischargeable debts and prevents the creditors owed those debts from taking any action against the debtor to collect the debts. The discharge also prohibits creditors from communicating with the debtor regarding the debt including telephone calls, letters, and personal contact.

Exemptions, or **exempt property:** Certain property owned by an individual debtor that the U.S. Bankruptcy Code or applicable state law permits the debtor to keep from unsecured creditors. For example, in some states the debtor may be able to exempt all or a portion of the equity in the debtor's primary residence (homestead exemption), or some or all "tools of the trade" used by the debtor to make a living (e.g., auto tools for an auto mechanic or dental tools for a dentist). The availability and amount of property the debtor may exempt depends on the state the debtor lives in.

Fresh start: The characterization of a debtor's status after bankruptcy (i.e., free of most debts). Giving debtors a fresh start is one purpose of the U.S. Bankruptcy Code.

Liquidation: A sale of a debtor's property with the proceeds to be used for the benefit of creditors.

Motion to lift the automatic stay: A request by a creditor to allow the creditor to take action against the debtor or the debtor's property that would otherwise be prohibited by the automatic stay.

No-asset case: A Chapter 7 case where there are no assets available to satisfy any portion of the creditors' unsecured claims.

Nondischargeable debt: A debt that cannot be eliminated in bankruptcy. Examples include a home mortgage, debts for alimony or child support, certain taxes, debts for most government funded or guaranteed educational loans or benefit overpayments, debts arising from death or personal injury caused by driving while intoxicated or under the influence of drugs, and debts for restitution or a criminal fine included in a sentence on the debtor's conviction of a crime. Some debts, such as debts for money or property obtained by false pretenses and debts for fraud or defalcation while acting in a fiduciary capacity may be declared nondischargeable only if a creditor timely files and prevails in a nondischargeability action.

Plan: A debtor's detailed description of how the debtor proposes to pay creditors' claims over a fixed period of time.

Property of the estate: All legal or equitable interests of the debtor in property as of the commencement of the case.

Reaffirmation agreement: An agreement by a Chapter 7 debtor to continue paying a dischargeable debt (such as an auto loan) after the bankruptcy, usually for the purpose of keeping collateral that would otherwise be subject to repossession.

341 meeting: See Creditors' meeting.

Trustee: The representative of the bankruptcy estate who exercises statutory powers, principally for the benefit of the unsecured creditors, under the general supervision of the court and the direct supervision of the U.S. trustee or bankruptcy administrator. The trustee is a private individual or corporation appointed in all Chapter 7, Chapter 12, and Chapter 13 cases and some Chapter 11 cases. The trustee's responsibilities include reviewing the debtor's petition and schedules and bringing actions against creditors or the debtor to recover property of the bankruptcy estate. In Chapter 7, the trustee liquidates property of the estate and makes distributions to creditors. Trustees in Chapter 12 and 13 have similar duties to a Chapter 7 trustee and the additional responsibilities of overseeing the debtor's plan, receiving payments from debtors, and disbursing plan payments to creditors.

INDEX

ACKNOWLEDGMENTS

Special thanks to my spectacular wife, Mysti, and our joyful kids, Nathan, Rylie, and Regan, for having patience with me throughout this process. Also to my friends Nat, Aaron, and Doug, who make the journey so much fun, and all of the team at DECAF who supported me during this project. To my EO buddies who inspire, challenge, and take me places I would not otherwise go, thank you.

—Mitchell L. Allen

ABOUT THE AUTHOR

 **MITCHELL L. ALLEN** is the founder, president, and chairman of Debt Education and Certification Foundation (www. debt-foundation.org), a leading provider of personal debt management courses. Courses he helped develop have been used in over 200,000 counseling sessions, and he has personally conducted more than 1,000 interviews with individuals in financial crisis.

Mitchell previously worked for Citigroup and The Associates Financial Corporation as senior director of modeling, where he led a team of economists and statisticians in developing statistical models to predict response, risk, and fraud within various private label credit card portfolios.